Communications
in Computer and Information Science   1146

Commenced Publication in 2007
Founding and Former Series Editors:
Phoebe Chen, Alfredo Cuzzocrea, Xiaoyong Du, Orhun Kara, Ting Liu,
Krishna M. Sivalingam, Dominik Ślęzak, Takashi Washio, Xiaokang Yang,
and Junsong Yuan

Editorial Board Members

Simone Diniz Junqueira Barbosa ⓘ
  Pontifical Catholic University of Rio de Janeiro (PUC-Rio),
  Rio de Janeiro, Brazil
Joaquim Filipe ⓘ
  Polytechnic Institute of Setúbal, Setúbal, Portugal
Ashish Ghosh
  Indian Statistical Institute, Kolkata, India
Igor Kotenko ⓘ
  St. Petersburg Institute for Informatics and Automation of the Russian
  Academy of Sciences, St. Petersburg, Russia
Lizhu Zhou
  Tsinghua University, Beijing, China

More information about this series at http://www.springer.com/series/7899

Weixia Xu · Liquan Xiao · Jinwen Li ·
Zhenzhen Zhu (Eds.)

Computer Engineering and Technology

23rd CCF Conference, NCCET 2019
Enshi, China, August 1–2, 2019
Revised Selected Papers

Editors
Weixia Xu
National University of Defense Technology
Changsha, China

Liquan Xiao
National University of Defense Technology
Changsha, China

Jinwen Li
National University of Defense Technology
Changsha, China

Zhenzhen Zhu
National University of Defense Technology
Changsha, China

ISSN 1865-0929 ISSN 1865-0937 (electronic)
Communications in Computer and Information Science
ISBN 978-981-15-1849-2 ISBN 978-981-15-1850-8 (eBook)
https://doi.org/10.1007/978-981-15-1850-8

© Springer Nature Singapore Pte Ltd. 2019
This work is subject to copyright. All rights are reserved by the Publisher, whether the whole or part of the material is concerned, specifically the rights of translation, reprinting, reuse of illustrations, recitation, broadcasting, reproduction on microfilms or in any other physical way, and transmission or information storage and retrieval, electronic adaptation, computer software, or by similar or dissimilar methodology now known or hereafter developed.
The use of general descriptive names, registered names, trademarks, service marks, etc. in this publication does not imply, even in the absence of a specific statement, that such names are exempt from the relevant protective laws and regulations and therefore free for general use.
The publisher, the authors and the editors are safe to assume that the advice and information in this book are believed to be true and accurate at the date of publication. Neither the publisher nor the authors or the editors give a warranty, expressed or implied, with respect to the material contained herein or for any errors or omissions that may have been made. The publisher remains neutral with regard to jurisdictional claims in published maps and institutional affiliations.

This Springer imprint is published by the registered company Springer Nature Singapore Pte Ltd.
The registered company address is: 152 Beach Road, #21-01/04 Gateway East, Singapore 189721, Singapore

Preface

We are pleased to present the proceedings of the 23rd Annual Conference on Computer Engineering and Technology (NCCET 2019). Over its short 20-year history, NCCET has established itself as one of the major national conferences dedicated to the important and emerging challenges in the field of computer engineering and technology. Following the previous successful events, NCCET 2019 provided a forum to bring together researchers and practitioners from academia and industry to discuss cutting-edge research on computer engineering and technology.

We are delighted that the conference continues to attract high-quality submissions from a diverse and national group of researchers. This year, we received 87 submissions, among which 21 papers were accepted. Each paper received 3 or 4 peer reviews from our Technical Program Committee (TPC), which comprised a total of 42 members from academia and industry.

The pages of this volume represent only the end result of an enormous endeavor involving hundreds of people. Almost all of this work is voluntary, with some individuals contributing hundreds of hours of their time. Together, the 42 members of the TPC, the 16 members of the External Review Committee (ERC), and the 13 other individual reviewers – consulted for their expertise – wrote nearly 400 reviews.

Every paper received at least two reviews and many had three or more. With the exception of submissions by the TPC, each paper had at least two reviews from the TPC and at least one review from an outside expert. For the fourth year running, most of the outside reviews were done by the ERC, which was selected in advance, and additional outside reviews beyond the ERC were requested whenever appropriate or necessary. Reviewing was "first read double-blind," meaning that author identities were withheld from reviewers until they submitted a review. Revealing author names only after initial reviews were written, allowed reviewers time to find related and previous material by the same authors, which helped greatly in many cases in understanding the context of the work, and also ensured that the author feedback and discussions at the Program Committee (PC) meeting were frank and direct. We allowed PC members to submit papers to the conference. Submissions co-authored by a TPC member were reviewed exclusively by the ERC and other outside reviewers, and these same reviewers decided whether to accept the PC papers; no PC member reviewed a TPC paper, and no TPC papers were discussed at the TPC meeting.

After reviewing was complete, the PC met at the National University of Defense Technology, Changsha, during June 30–31 to select the program. Separately, the ERC decided on the PC papers in email and phone discussions. In the end, 21 of the 87 submissions (25%) were accepted for the conference.

First of all, we would like to thank all researchers who submitted manuscripts. Without these submissions, it would be impossible to provide such an interesting technical program. We thank all PC members for helping to organize the conference program. We thank all TPC members for their tremendous time and efforts during the paper review and selection process. Efforts of these individuals were crucial in constructing our successful technical program. Last but not least, we would like to thank the organizations and sponsors that supported NCCET 2019. Finally, we thank all the participants of the conference and hope that they had a truly memorable NCCET 2019 in Enshi, China.

August 2019

Weixia Xu
Xiong Tinggang
Zhang Minxuan
Liquan Xiao

Organization

Organizing Committee

General Co-chairs

Xu Weixia — National University of Defense Technology, China
Xiong Tinggang — China Shipbuilding Industry Corporation, China
Zhang Minxuan — National University of Defense Technology, China

Program Chair

Xiao Liquan — National University of Defense Technology, China

Publicity Co-chairs

Zhang Chengyi — National University of Defense Technology, China
Li Jinwen — National University of Defense Technology, China

Local Arrangement Co-chairs

Zhang Yiwei — China Shipbuilding Industry Corporation, China
Li Jinwen — National University of Defense Technology, China

Registration and Finance Co-chairs

Li Yuanshan — National University of Defense Technology, China
Zhang Junying — National University of Defense Technology, China

Program Committee

Han Wei — Xi'an Aviation Institute of Computing Technology, China
Jin Lifeng — Jiangnan Institute of Computing Technology, China
Xiong Tinggang — 709 Institute of China Shipbuilding Industry, China
Zhao Xiaofang — Institute of Computing Technology Chinese Academy of Sciences, China
Yang Yintang — Xidian University, China

Technical Program Committee

Xiao Liquan — National University of Defense Technology, China
Zhao Xiaofang — Institute of Computing Technology Chinese Academy of Sciences, China
Han Wei — Aviation Industry Corporation of China, China
Xiong Tinggang — 709 Institute of China Shipbuilding Industry, China

Yang Yintang	Xidian University, China
Jin Lifeng	Institute of Computing Technology, Jiangnan, China
Dou Qiang	National University of Defense Technology, China
Du Huimin	Xi'an University of Posts and Telecommunications, China
Fan Dongrui	Institute of Computing Technology Chinese Academy of Sciences, China
Fan Xiaoya	Northwestern Polytechnical University, China
Fu Yuzhuo	Shanghai Jiao Tong University, China
Guo Donghui	Xiamen University, China
Guo Wei	Tianjin University, China
Huang Jin	Xidian University, China
Jiang Jiang	Shanghai Jiao Tong University, China
Li Ping	University of Electronic Science and Technology of China, China
Li Yun	Yangzhou University, China
Lin Kaizhi	Inspur, China
Lin Zhenghao	Tongji University, China
Sun Yongjie	National University of Defense Technology, China
Tian Ze	Aviation Industry Corporation of China, China
Wang Yaonan	Hunan University, China
Wang Yiwen	University of Electronic Science and Technology of China, China
Wang Yongwen	National University of Defense Technology, China
Xue Chengqi	Southeast University, China
Yang Xiaojun	Institute of Computing Technology Chinese Academy of Sciences, China
Yu Zongguang	CECT, China
Zeng Yun	Hunan University, China
Zhang Lixin	Institute of Computing Technology Chinese Academy of Sciences, China
Zhang Minxuan	National University of Defense Technology, China
Zhang Shengbin	Northwestern Polytechnical University, China
Zhang Shujie	Huawei, China
Zhao Yuelong	South China University of Technology, China
Zhou Ya	Guilin University of Electronic Technology, China
Jiang Xu	Hong Kong University of Science and Technology, Hong Kong, China
Zhonghai Lu	KTH, Royal Institute of Technology, Sweden
Zheng Wang	Lancaster University, UK
Pengcheng Li	The University of Rochester, USA
Guangda Zhang	The University of Manchester, UK
Xueqing Li	Pennsylvania State University, USA
Yi-Chung Chen	The University of Manchester, UK
Ping Chi	University of California, Santa Barbara, USA

Contents

Confidence Value: A Novel Evaluation Index of Side-Channel Attack

Xiaomin Cai[1], Shijie Kuang[1(✉)], Gao Shen[2], Renfa Li[1],
Shaoqing Li[2], and Xing Hu[2]

[1] College of Computer Science and Electronic Engineering, Hunan University,
Changsha, People's Republic of China
ksj@hnu.edu.cn
[2] College of Computer, National University of Defense Technology,
Changsha, People's Republic of China

Abstract. The side-channel attacks (SCAs) use the correlation between the power leakage information and the key to implement the attack process. The result of SCAs has a certain probability. If guessing an 8-bit key, there is a probability of 1/256 that the key will be guessed coincidentally, resulting in false positive. Therefore, the reliability of result key also needs an index to measure. Thereby, this paper proposes a novel evaluation index based on confidence value (CV). The CV of result key is divided three levels, low false positive, medium false positive and high false positive. CV provides a new reference index for the designers, suppliers and users of cryptographic devices to evaluate the security of devices.

Keywords: Cryptographic device · Side-channel attacks · Confidence value · False positive · FCM clustering

1 Introduction

Cryptographic devices inevitably leak some physical information during working. Physical information includes power consumption, electromagnetic radiation, running time and other side information. SCAs use the correlation between bypass information and key to collect and statistically analyze bypass information to crack the key. SCAs mainly include power consumption attack [1], electromagnetic radiation attack [2] and time attack [3]. In 1996, Paul Kocher [4] proposed a time attack technique, which successfully cracked the key. Since then, non-invasive SCAs technology has launched a research boom in the field of information security [5–7]. In 1999, Kocher [8] proposed the power analysis (PA) attack technology. PA attack became the main attack method in SCAs technology due to its simple operation, wide application range and high success rate. Nowadays, PA technology has successfully cracked many encryption algorithms, such as advanced encryption standard AES [9], data encryption standard DES [10], public key cryptography algorithm RSA [11], and encryption devices such as smart card [12]. PA technology mainly include simple power analysis (SPA) [8], differential power analysis (DPA) [13] and correlation power analysis (CPA) [14].

© Springer Nature Singapore Pte Ltd. 2019
W. Xu et al. (Eds.): NCCET 2019, CCIS 1146, pp. 1–11, 2019.
https://doi.org/10.1007/978-981-15-1850-8_1

Both DPA based on average difference and CPA based on Pearson correlation coefficient are used mathematical statistical analysis method to realize the attack. Mathematical statistical analysis method is inseparable from probability theory, which lead to the accuracy of the attack results has a certain probability significance. Therefore, it is a common concern of designers, suppliers and users to determine the reliability of result key. In order to solve the above problems, this paper starts from the membership matrix of Fuzzy c-means (FCM) clustering algorithm and combines the data fluctuation state to build the CV index. In order to verify the effectiveness of CV, a set of energy trace data are taken as experimental objects respectively. We also explore the influence of energy model, sample size on CV.

The rest organization structure of this paper is as follows: The Sect. 2 introduces the relevant research background, including DPA attack principle, energy model, FCM clustering method. In Sect. 3, the evaluation index of CV is presented. The Sect. 4 explores the influence of energy model and sample size on CV. Our relevant summary and analysis in Sect. 5.

2 Background

2.1 DPA Attacks Based on Average Difference

The DPA [15] based on average difference is that the adversary selects a certain bit signal of cryptographic algorithm process as the target signal (such as the output result of a s-box). According to the value of "0" or "1" of the target signal at the power consumption point D, the power trace of N encryption process is divided into two sets $T_1 = \{T_i[j] | D = 1\}$ and $T_0 = \{T_i[j] | D = 0\}$. Where, $1 \leq i \leq N$, each power consumption trace has M sampling points, j represents the j_{th} sampling point of power trace in trace i, and $1 \leq j \leq M$. $T_i[j]$ is the voltage sampling value corresponding to the j_{th} sampling point. The arithmetic average of sets T_1 and T_0 is calculated and then subtracted, as shown in the following mathematical formula (1) (2)

$$D_1[j] = \sum_{T_i[j] \in T_1} T_i[j] / |T_1| \tag{1}$$

$$D_0[j] = \sum_{T_i[j] \in T_0} T_i[j] / |T_0| \tag{2}$$

|T0| and |T1| are respectively the number of power trace sets T0 and T1, so |T0| + |T1| = N. When the power trace number N is large enough, it is assumed that all intermediate signal values in the power trace except the target signal are randomly distributed, then the average difference of power generated by the inversion of the intermediate signal approaches 0. Then, $\Delta D[j] = D_1[j] - D_0[j]$. If the obtained differential power consumption curve $\Delta D[j]$ shows a pulse peak, the key guesses correct. Conversely, the key guesses incorrectly.

2.2 CPA Attack Based on Pearson Correlation Coefficient

CPA based on Pearson correlation coefficient test method was proposed [16]. Pearson correlation coefficient formula (3) is as follows:

$$C(X,Y) = \{E(X \cdot Y) - E(X) \cdot E(Y)\}/\{Var(X) \cdot Var(Y)\} \tag{3}$$

E(X) is the mathematical expectation of variable *X*, and *Var(X)* is the variance of variable *X*. The larger the value of Pearson coefficient, the greater the correlation between variables *X* and *Y*. The adversary selects the value of multiple internal data as the target signal, such as the hamming weight of all output bits of an intermediate result as the target value. According to *N* random plaintexts and all possible key values, calculate the corresponding target value in all cases, and store it in a $2^m \times N$ matrix $\mathbf{M_p}$, with the value between 0 and m. The collected power curve data is stored in an $N \times j$ matrix $\mathbf{M_t}$. Pearson correlation coefficients are calculated for all "rows" in matrix $\mathbf{M_p}$ and $\mathbf{M_t}$, and $2^m \times j$ correlation coefficient matrix $\mathbf{M_c}$ is obtained. The key value corresponding to the cell "row" with the largest relative value in matrix $\mathbf{M_c}$ is the correct key.

2.3 Energy Model

In DPA attacks, energy models are needed to characterize the correlation between data and energy, mainly including Hamming Distance (HD) model [17] and Hamming Weight (HW) model [18]. The HD model calculates the total amount of transition in a particular operation of the circuit, and maps the energy consumption of the circuit with the amount of transition. The calculation formula of HD model is

$$HD(v_0, v_1) = HW(v_0 \oplus v_1) \tag{4}$$

The HD of state v_0 and state v_1 is the HW of $v_0 \oplus v_1$, $HW(v_0 \oplus v_1)$ is the number of different bit of state v_0 and state v_1. The HW model assumes that the energy consumption is proportional to the number of bits in the value "1", and the formula is

$$E = aHD_{0 \to 1}(v_0 \oplus v_1) + b \tag{5}$$

v_0 is the previous state of a register. v_1 is the later state of the same register; E is the switch of register from v_0 state to v_1 state; The energy consumption of the process $HD_{0 \to 1}(v_0 \oplus v_1)$ is the number of digits flipped by 0 -> 1 during the switch from v_0 to v_1. The a is the proportional coefficient of energy consumption; The b is the energy consumption and noise unrelated to the data processed.

2.4 Membership Function of FCM Clustering

FCM algorithm [19] is a flexible partition clustering algorithm. Membership function describes the probability that an object x belongs to set A, denoted as $u_A(x) \in [0,1]$. When $\mu_A(x) = 1$, object x belongs to set A. When $\mu_A(x) = 0$, object x does not belong to set A. Fuzzy set enables object x to belong to multiple clusters with different membership degrees. Then, membership function of fuzzy set A on $X = \{x\}$ is

$$A = \{(\mu_A(x_i), x_i)|x_i \in X\} \tag{6}$$

3   Confidence Value

Using FCM clustering method, each energy trace is divided into a cluster according to the probability P_{ij} [21]. If the probability of energy trace belonging to cluster C is the maximum, then this energy trace belongs to cluster C. P_{ij} is the probability that the i_{th} energy trace belongs to the j_{th} cluster. For an energy trace s, $\sum_{j=1}^{D} P_{sj} = 1$. $max(P_{sj})$ is the maximum value between $P_{s1}, P_{s2}, P_{s3}..., P_{sD}$. $1 \leq i \leq N, 1 \leq j \leq D$. N is the total number of energy traces, and D is the total number of clusters. Then, the overall membership degree H of the clustering results is

$$H = \frac{\sum_{i=1}^{N} max(P_{ij})}{D} \tag{7}$$

Formula (7) is used to calculate the average value of the maximum probability that each energy trace belongs to one cluster. The basic idea of SCA attack is "divide and conquer", so we use a group of 8 bits to attack the key. There are 9 kinds of HW for 8bit. When HW is 0, 1 and 2, it belongs to cluster 1. When HW is 3, 4 and 5, it belongs to cluster 2. When HW is 6, 7 and 8, it belongs to cluster 3. So the number of clusters is 3, D is equal to 3. Then $H \in [0.33, 1]$. When $H = 0.33$, no differentiated clustering is performed on the samples. When $H = 1$, it each object only belongs to one cluster. It is difficult to obtain $H = 1$ due to the dynamic changing property of encryption algorithm. We used polynomial fitting method to fit the changing morphology of H within the interval [0.33, 1]. Polynomial fitting requires polynomial representation

$$y(x, w) = w_0 + w_1 x + w_2 x^2 + \ldots + w_M x^M = \sum_{j=0}^{M} w_j x^j \tag{8}$$

$Y(x, w)$ is the curve polynomial. M represents the order of the polynomial. The vector $w = (w_0, \ldots, w_M)$. The fitting operation is carried out in combination with the minimization error function

$$E(w) = \frac{1}{2} \sum_{n=1}^{N} \{y(x_n, w) - t_n\}^2 \tag{9}$$

The formula (9) represents the degree of difference between the function $y(x, w)$ and the data set under the given w. The smaller $E(w)$ is, the better the fitting effect is.

A method of analytic mathematics is employed to obtain a unique solution w^* of the error function $E(w)$. $y(x, w^*)$ is utilized to obtain the final fit curve formula

$$y(H) = -316.6H^6 + 1403.8H^5 - 2564.3H^4 + 2470.8H^3 - 1325.6H^2 + 376.2H \\ - 43.3$$

$$(10)$$

SCAs can determine the location of the key by the peak position of mean difference, the maximum Pearson correlation coefficient, the maximum Euclidean distance and so on. The peak fluctuation degree of attack result is another factor needed to construct the CV as the formula

$$\alpha = 1 - \frac{M - subMin}{M - Min} \tag{11}$$

In the following attack process of this article, the Euclidean distance is selected as the basis for determining the key. Therefore, the specific meanings of variables M, $subMin$ and Min in formula (11) will change with the different attack methods chosen by adversary. The clustering center value of each energy trace in this paper represents Euclidean distance. Thereby, α is the data fluctuation coefficient. M is the average of Euclidean distance. $SubMin$ is the sub-small value of Euclidean distance. Min is the minimum value of Euclidean distance. M-$submin$ is the distance between the average and the subminimum, M-Min is the distance between the average and the minimum. The closer the value of $(M$-$subMin)/(M$-$Min)$ is to 0, the closer the volatility α is to 1, the more obvious the peak of the minimum value is, and the easier it is to observe the key. Combining data volatility α and population membership polynomial fitting formula $y(H)$, the CV model is established in formula

$$CV = y(H) \cdot \alpha \tag{12}$$

Because of $y(H) \in (0, 1)$ and $\alpha \in (0,1)$, so $CV \in (0, 1)$. The CV is divided into three levels. Level 1 is that $CV \in (0, 0.33)$, the attack results are at risk of high false positives. Level 2 is that $CV \in (0.33, 0.66)$, the attack results are at risk of medium false positives. Level 3 is that $CV \in (0.66, 1)$, the attack results are at risk of low false positives.

4   Experiment and Interpretation

In order to highlight the evaluation effect of CV index, we construct an energy acquisition platform to obtain the energy trace leaked during the operation of cryptographic chip. The Python language [20] of Anaconda software platform is used to compile the code to analyze and process the energy traces. The object of this experiment is a SoC chip with a special encryption coprocessor. The encryption algorithm is 128-bit AES. In the experiment, the influence of various factors on CV is explored through the control variable method.

4.1   Energy Acquisition Platform

As shown in Fig. 1, the energy acquisition platform mainly consists of SoC chip, computer, acquisition card and upper computer software. SoC chip with two high-speed SMA wires connected to the acquisition card. The workbench software writes the AES algorithm to SoC chip's coprocessor. We open the upper software interface of collecting energy, trigger the SoC chip. The acquisition card begins to work. The sampling frequency is 5G. The sampling depth is 2G. A clock cycle has 250 sampling points. power must be measured by a 0.1 Ω resistor in the VCC line supplying the device under test (DUT). The change in the current of the supply is converted into a voltage signal by resistance. Input 2000 groups of random plaintexts, and the energy acquisition platform starts to work to obtain 2000 groups of energy traces.

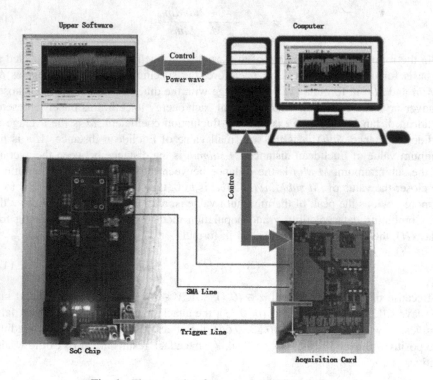

Fig. 1. The scenario of energy acquisition platform

4.2   Influence of Energy Model and Sample Size on CV

After attaining energy traces, we input them into the analysis platform Anaconda. DPA attack is implemented by using FCM clustering method. According to the membership matrix, the CV results can be obtained. The code of this part is shown in Fig. 2. Firstly, the HD model is used for the experiment. The key hypothesis is 198 and the sample size is 2000. The attack results are shown in Fig. 3. In Fig. 3, the horizontal axis is the key assumption. The vertical axis is the Euclidean distance under each key assumption.

```python
if __name__ == '__main__':
    OBJECTIVE = ObjISbox()
    f = open('power188.pkl','rb') # import energy traces date
    power = pickle.load(f)
    f.close()
    power = [power[i] for i in range(len(power))]
    power = array(power)
    num =1000#sample size
    power_1 = power[0:num,6090:6119]
    plain_data = read_plain('datain2000')[0:num]
    clu = FCM(power_1)[0]
    dis = []
    for i in range (256):
        d = mean_onekey(OBJECTIVE,power_1,plain_data,i)
        dis.append(agreed(clu,d))
    plt.plot(dis)
    U = FCM(power_1)[1]              #membership matrix
    J = FCM(power_1)[2]              #target fuction
    CV = CV(dis,U,num)
    print(CV)
    print(dis.index(min(dis)))
```

Fig. 2. The Python code of CV

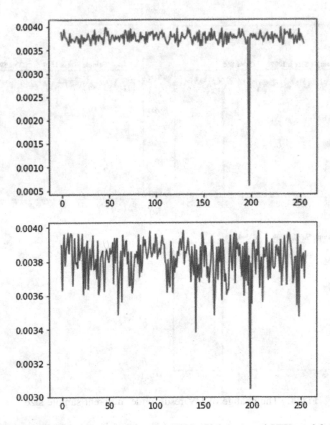

Fig. 3. The attack result diagram under HD model (up) and HW model (down)

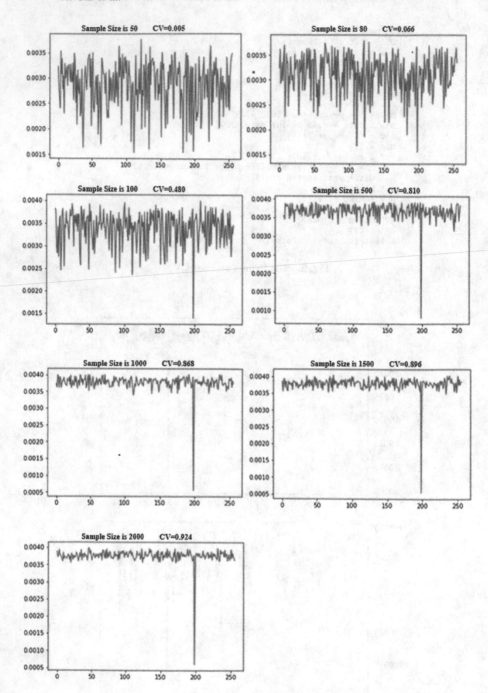

Fig. 4. The change of CV result under different sample size

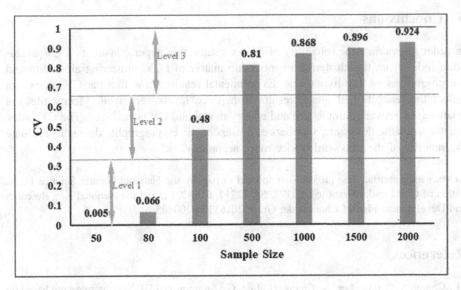

Fig. 5. CV and sample size

As the left figure in Fig. 3, the Euclidean distance of the key hypothesis 198 is obviously the minimum. The spike caused by the data is particularly obvious. CV is 0.924. So, the false positive is Level 3. Then, HW model experiment is selected as the control experiment. The sample size remained unchanged. In the right figure of Fig. 3, we can know that the attack result still has a relatively obvious peak at 198 points. But the CV is only 0.433. The false positive is Level 2. The attack effect is not as good as that of the HW model. For the SoC chip of the attack object, the physical meaning of HD is jump, which has a stronger correlation with energy consumption, while HW represents the transfer of related variables, which has a weak correlation with energy consumption. Therefore, the energy model plays an important role in CV of DPA attack results.

Next, take sample size as variable to explore its influence on CV. Sample size is set as 50, 80, 100, 500, 1000, 1500 and 2000 respectively. The energy model is the HD model. The result is shown in Fig. 4. When the sample size is 50, the attack is failed. As the sample size increases, the CV increases. When the sample size is 80, CV is 0.066 and belongs to Level 1, indicating that the reliability of the results is low, the attack result is at risk of high false positives. When the sample size is 100, CV is 0.48 and belongs to Level 2, indicating that the reliability of the results is general, the attack result is at risk of medium false positives. When the sample size is 2000, CV is 0.924 and belongs to Level 3, indicating that the reliability of the attack result is extremely high, the attack result is at risk of low false positives. Therefore, sufficient sample size is a necessary condition to obtain the correct attack result and ensure low false positives for results. Meanwhile, as shown in Fig. 5, there is a positive correlation between the CV and sample size.

5 Conclusions

In order to evaluate the reliability of SCAs results, this paper constructs a CV evaluation index from the clustering membership matrix of FCM clustering algorithm and the uniqueness of key hypothesis. Experimental results show that the CV index can reflect the reliability of attack results from three levels very well. Meanwhile, the relationship between sample size and energy model and CV is analyzed. The CV index greatly helps the designers, suppliers and users of the cryptographic device to evaluate the security of the password device more accurately.

Acknowledgements. The project is supported in part by the National Natural Science Foundation of China under Grant (61702172, 61672217, 61832018) and the National Key Research and Development Plan of China under Grant 2016YFB0200405.

References

1. Chung, S., Yu, C., Lee, S., Chang, H., Lee, C.: An improved DPA countermeasure based on uniform distribution random power generator for IoT applications. IEEE Trans. Circ. Syst. I Regul. Pap. **64**, 2522–2531 (2017)
2. Gebotys, C.H., White, B.A.: A phase substitution technique for DEMA of embedded cryptographic systems. In: Information Technology, pp. 868–869 (2007)
3. Ding, G., et al.: Electromagnetic emanations of the ICs. In: 2007 4th IEEE International Symposium on Electromagnetic Compatibility Proceeding, pp. 303–305. IEEE Press, Qingdao (2007)
4. Kocher, P.C.: Timing attacks on implementations of Diffie-Hellman, RSA, DSS, and other systems. In: Koblitz, N. (ed.) CRYPTO 1996. LNCS, vol. 1109, pp. 104–113. Springer, Heidelberg (1996). https://doi.org/10.1007/3-540-68697-5_9
5. Gandolfi, K., Mourtel, C., Olivier, F.: Electromagnetic analysis: concrete results. In: Koç, Ç. K., Naccache, D., Paar, C. (eds.) CHES 2001. LNCS, vol. 2162, pp. 251–261. Springer, Heidelberg (2001). https://doi.org/10.1007/3-540-44709-1_21
6. Ors, S., Gurkaynak, F., Oswald, E., Preneel, B.: Power-analysis attack on an ASIC AES implementation. In: Proceedings of ITCC, Las Vegas, pp. 5–7 (2004)
7. Quisquater, J.-J., Samyde, D.: Electro magnetic analysis (EMA): measures and counter-measures for smart cards. In: Attali, I., Jensen, T. (eds.) E-smart 2001. LNCS, vol. 2140, pp. 200–210. Springer, Heidelberg (2001). https://doi.org/10.1007/3-540-45418-7_17
8. Kocher, P., Jaffe, J., Jun, B.: Differential power analysis. In: Wiener, M. (ed.) CRYPTO 1999. LNCS, vol. 1666, pp. 388–397. Springer, Heidelberg (1999). https://doi.org/10.1007/3-540-48405-1_25
9. Oswald, E., Mangard, S., Herbst, C., Tillich, S.: Practical second-order DPA attacks for masked smart card implementations of block ciphers. In: Pointcheval, D. (ed.) CT-RSA 2006. LNCS, vol. 3860, pp. 192–207. Springer, Heidelberg (2006). https://doi.org/10.1007/11605805_13
10. Akkar, M.-L., Giraud, C.: An implementation of DES and AES, secure against some attacks. In: Koç, Ç.K., Naccache, D., Paar, C. (eds.) CHES 2001. LNCS, vol. 2162, pp. 309–318. Springer, Heidelberg (2001). https://doi.org/10.1007/3-540-44709-1_26

11. Fouque, P.-A., Kunz-Jacques, S., Martinet, G., Muller, F., Valette, F.: Power attack on small RSA public exponent. In: Goubin, L., Matsui, M. (eds.) CHES 2006. LNCS, vol. 4249, pp. 339–353. Springer, Heidelberg (2006). https://doi.org/10.1007/11894063_27
12. Messerges, T.S., Dabbish, E.A., Sloan, R.H.: Power analysis attacks of modular exponentiation in smartcards. In: Koç, Ç.K., Paar, C. (eds.) CHES 1999. LNCS, vol. 1717, pp. 144–157. Springer, Heidelberg (1999). https://doi.org/10.1007/3-540-48059-5_14
13. Akkar, M.-L., Bevan, R., Dischamp, P., Moyart, D.: Power analysis, what is now possible.... In: Okamoto, T. (ed.) ASIACRYPT 2000. LNCS, vol. 1976, pp. 489–502. Springer, Heidelberg (2000). https://doi.org/10.1007/3-540-44448-3_38
14. Cao, Y., et al.: On the negative effects of trend noise and its applications in side-channel cryptanalysis. Chin. J. Electron. 23(2), 366–370 (2014)
15. Chari, S., Jutla, C., R., Rao, J., et al: A cautionary note regarding evaluation of AES candidates on smart-cards (1999)
16. Levi, I., Fish, A., Keren, O.: CPA secured data-dependent delay-assignment methodology. IEEE Trans. Very Large-Scale Integr. (VLSI) Syst. 25, 608–620 (2017)
17. Shan, W., Zhang, S., He, Y.: Machine learning based side-channel-attack countermeasure with hamming-distance redistribution and its application on advanced encryption standard. Electron. Lett. 53(14), 926–928 (2017)
18. Moradi, A., Guilley, S., Heuser, A.: Detecting hidden leakages. In: Boureanu, I., Owesarski, P., Vaudenay, S. (eds.) ACNS 2014. LNCS, vol. 8479, pp. 324–342. Springer, Cham (2014). https://doi.org/10.1007/978-3-319-07536-5_20
19. Hamdi, T., Ghith, A., Fayala, F.: Characterization of drape profile using Fuzzy-C-Mean (FCM) method. Fibers Polym. 18, 1401–1407 (2017)
20. McGrath, M.: Python. In: Easy Steps (2014). http://common.books24x7.com/toc.aspx?bookid=74503. Accessed 9 June 2019
21. Shen, G., Zhang, Q., Tang, Y., et al.: Power analysis attack based on FCM clustering algorithm. In: The 14th International Conference on Wireless Communications, Networking and Mobile Computing, WiCOM 2018. EI

Design of High Precision Band-Pass Sigma-Delta ADC in MEMS Gyroscope

Lin Xiao[1(✉)], Jinhui Tan[2], Shaoqing Li[1], and Jihua Chen[1]

[1] College of Computer, National University of Defense Technology,
Changsha, China
1339802819@qq.com
[2] College of Information Science and Engineering, Hunan University,
Changsha, China

Abstract. In order to meet the demands of MEMS gyroscope for high precision and narrow bandwidth of ADC, a band-pass Sigma-Delta ADC with high precision is designed and verified by simulation. The oversampling rate (OSR) and center frequency are obtained through detecting and calculating the data of the gyroscope meter. As a result, The ADC structure of single-loop, six-order, and one-bit quantization is determined, and a suitable resonator is selected. The simulation results of the Simulink model of the ADC circuit show that the signal-to-noise ratio of the ADC can reach 132.2 dB and the effective number of bits can reach 21.70 bits, which satisfies the requirements of high precision and narrow bandwidth of the MEMS gyroscope. Thus, my design can help guide the design of transistor-level circuit for the band-pass Sigma-Delta ADC.

Keywords: MEMS gyroscope · Band-pass Sigma-Delta ADC · High precision · Signal-to-noise ratio

1 Introduction

MEMS gyroscopes for measuring speed and rotation angle are becoming more and more popular in applications such as micro-accessories, inertial navigation, automotive, and electronics [1]. Thanks to high level of integration and stability of digital circuits, the controlling and processing of MEMS gyroscopes are more prone to resort to digital domain [2], thus increasing the demand for ADC. The output signal of the gyroscope's interface circuit has the characteristics of narrow bandwidth and high precision, and is suitable for the Sigma-Delta modulator technology [3]. The band-pass modulator, compared with the low-pass modulator, requires less oversampling and fewer modulator orders under the same effect of noise shaping, thereby reducing power consumption and increasing stability [4]. In this paper, a single-loop six-order band-pass Sigma-Delta ADC is designed. After the simulation done by Matlab Simulink, the signal-to-noise ratio can reach 132.2 dB, and the effective number of bits can reach 21.70 bits, which satisfies the requirements of MEMS gyroscope.

Project Supported by National Natural Science Foundation of China (61832018).

© Springer Nature Singapore Pte Ltd. 2019

W. Xu et al. (Eds.): NCCET 2019, CCIS 1146, pp. 12–21, 2019.
https://doi.org/10.1007/978-981-15-1850-8_2

2 Relevant Technologies

The Sigma-Delta modulator uses oversampling and noise shaping techniques to suppress quantized noise [5]. As shown in Fig. 1, when the sampling frequency f_S is much higher than the signal bandwidth f_B, the quantized noise is equivalent to white noise, which is within $[-f_S/2, f_S/2]$. Only a small part is within the useful signal bandwidth $[-f_B, f_B]$, thus the quantized noise is reduced.

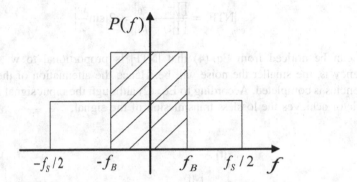

Fig. 1. Noise suppression of oversampling technique

Noise shaping is another technique for noise suppression of Sigma-Delta modulators. Figure 2 is a block diagram of a one-order Sigma-Delta modulator.

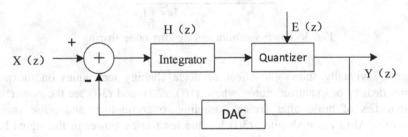

Fig. 2. Block diagram of a one-order low-pass Sigma-Delta modulator

Transfer function of the integrator:

$$H(z) = \frac{z^{-1}}{1 - z^{-1}} \tag{1}$$

The signal transfer function and the noise transfer function of the derivable modulator are respectively:

$$STF(z) = \frac{H(z)}{1 + H(z)} = z^{-1} \qquad (2)$$

$$NTF(z) = \frac{1}{1 + H(z)} = 1 - z^{-1} \qquad (3)$$

The noise amplitude can be calculated from the zero pole:

$$|NTF| = \frac{\prod |z_i - z_0|}{\prod |z_i - p_i|} = 2\left|\sin \frac{w}{2}\right| \qquad (4)$$

It can be noticed from Eq. (4) that |NTF| is proportional to w, the lower the frequency is, the smaller the noise will be. Hence the attenuation of the noise at low frequencies is completed. According to Eq. (2) although the input signal is delayed, the modulator achieves the lossless transmission of the signal.

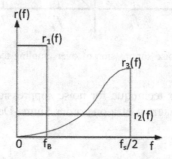

Fig. 3. Power spectrum density after noise shaping

Figure 3 visually shows the effect of noise shaping techniques on the power spectrum density of quantized noise, where r1(f), r2(f), and r3(f) are the power spectrum densities of noise after critical sampling, oversampling, and noise shaping, respectively. After noise shaping, r3(f) has the least noise power in the signal bandwidth f_B.

3   Design and Modeling of Sigma-Delta Modulator

3.1   Design of Modulator

When the gyroscope meter of the input signal has an angular velocity range of ±300 °/s and a measurement accuracy of 0.001 °/s, the input dynamic range will be DR = 20l g (300/0.001) = 109.54 dB. With the sampling frequency $f_S = 480$ kHz, the signal bandwidth $f_B = 400$ Hz, the oversampling rate OSR is 600.

The design of the band-pass modulator uses a low-pass prototyping approach proposed by Constantinides [6]:

$$z^{-1} \rightarrow \frac{-z^{-2} + \cos\left(2\pi\frac{f_0}{f_s}\right)z^{-1}}{1 - \cos\left(2\pi\frac{f_0}{f_s}\right)z^{-1}} \tag{5}$$

It can be known from Eq. (7) that when $\cos\left(2\pi\frac{f_0}{f_s}\right)$ is a rational fraction, the equation can be simplified, which is beneficial to the capacitance setting of the circuit module. As a result, the center frequency is preferably taken as 1/6, 1/4 and 1/3 of the sampling frequency. In this design, the center frequency is set to $f_0 = 1/(6f_s) = 80\,\text{kHz}$.

The relation between signal-to-noise ratio and effective output bits:

$$\text{SNR(dB)} = 6.02 * N + 1.76 \tag{6}$$

It is calculated by Eq. (6) that N is at least 18 bits to satisfy SNR = 110.12 dB > 109.54 dB.

Since the non-linearity of multi-bit quantizer would affect the performance of the modulator and the cascaded modulator is more sensitive to various irrational characteristics of the circuit, a single-loop and one-bit quantizer is used. As followed is the SNR formula of the quantized modulator of single-loop, L-order, low-pass, and one-bit:

$$SNR = 10\log\left[\frac{3}{2} \times \frac{2L+1}{\pi^{2L}} \times OSR^{2L+1}\right] = 1.76 + 10\lg\left(\frac{2L+1}{\pi^{2L}}\right) + (20L+10)\lg(OSR) \tag{7}$$

From the above it is known that the OSR is 600. When L = 2, SNR = 127.77, and when L = 3, SNR = 174.85. Due to non-ideal factors, the signal-to-noise ratio of 127.77 is still too low. Therefore, at least three-order is needed [7]. Based on the prototype of the low-pass modulator, after the conversion to band-pass [8], the modulator is determined to be a six-order band-pass structure.

The lossless discrete integrator type of resonator (LDI) is more suitable for the determination of the feedback factor of the structure, so the LDI structure is selected as the resonator, as shown in Fig. 4, where g is an adjustable factor. LDI type transfer function:

$$H(z)_{LDI} = \frac{Y(z)}{X(z)} = \frac{z^{-1}}{1 - (2+g)z^{-1} + z^{-2}} \tag{8}$$

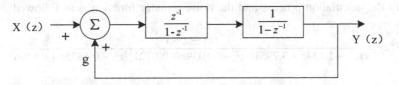

Fig. 4. Block diagram of LDI type of resonator structure

From Eqs. (2) and (3), $SNF = z^{-1}/(1 - z^{-1})$ of the one-order low-pass $\Sigma\Delta$ ADC can be obtained. Meanwhile, through low-pass prototyping method, the signal-to-noise ratio transfer function of the band-pass $\Sigma\Delta$ ADC is:

$$SNF = \frac{-Z^{-2} + COS\left(2\pi\frac{f_0}{f_s}\right)z^{-1}}{1 - 2COS\left(2\pi\frac{f_0}{f_s}\right)z^{-1} + z^{-2}} \qquad (9)$$

From the $H(z)_{LDI}$ and the SNF of the two-order band-pass $\Sigma\Delta$ ADC we can get:

$$\frac{2 + g}{2} = \cos\left(\frac{2\pi f_0}{f_s}\right) \qquad (10)$$

When g is $-1, -2, -3$, the corresponding center frequencies are $1/6\,f_s$, $1/4\,f_s$, $1/3\,f_s$. And the poles of the LDI type are all on the unit circle, so they are stable structures.

3.2   Modeling of Modulator

Common single-loop structures include CIFB (integrator distributed feedback), CIFF (integrator distributed forward-back), CRFB (resonator distributed feedback), and CRFF (resonator distributed forward-back). In terms of the complexity of the feedback form, it is more reasonable to use CRFF [9], because it is more convenient to use force feedback to form a closed-loop detection circuit [10]. Therefore, I select the CRFF structure as the modulator for modeling.

The center frequency of this design is $f_0 = 1/(6f_s)$, so g is -1. The noise transfer function is calculated by the structure as shown in Eq. (11), where A–F is a coefficient composed of a_i, b_i and g_i, as shown below.

$$NTF(z) = \frac{[z^2 - z + 1]^3}{z^6 + Az^5 + Bz^4 + Cz^3 + Dz^2 + Ez + F} \qquad (11)$$

$A = b_1a_1 + b_1a_2 - 3$
$B = -3b_1a_1 - 2b_1a_2 + b_1b_3a_3 + b_1b_3a_4 + 6$
$C = 5b_1a_1 + 3b_1a_2 - 2b_1b_3a_3 - b_1b_3a_4 + b_1b_3b_5a_5 + b_1b_3b_5a_6 - 7$
$D = -5b_1a_1 - 2b_1a_2 + 2b_1b_3a_3 + b_1b_3a_4 - b_1b_3b_5a_5 + 6$
$E = 3b_1a_1 + b_1a_2 - b_1b_3a_3 - 3$
$F = 1 - b_1a_1$

The optimized noise transfer function (synthesize NTF) in Matlab delsig is used to simplify the calculation process and the noise transfer function is as followed:

$$NTF(z) = \frac{(z^2 - z + 1)^3}{(z^2 - 1.154z + 0.7961)(z^2 - 0.8039z + 0.6721)(z^2 - 0.6335z + 0.8306)} \qquad (12)$$

I apply the realizeNTF function in the CRFF structure, and calculate the positive feedback coefficient of the CRFF structure through Matlab, as shown in Table 1:

Table 1. Coefficient of CRFF structure.

i	a_i	g_i	b_i
1	0.5556	−1	1
2	−0.1471	−1	1
3	0.0345	−1	1
4	−0.1949		1
5	−0.0317		1
6	0.0092		1

In order to make each integrator not overloaded, its parameters are optimized, and the optimized structural coefficients are as shown in Table 2:

Table 2. Coefficient of CRFF structure after optimization.

i	a_i	g_i	b_i
1	1.852	−1	0.3
2	−0.4903	−1	1
3	0.2875	−1	0.4
4	−1.624		1
5	−0.6604		0.4
6	0.1917		1

After the application of the coefficients of optimized modulator structure, I obtain the structure model of the six-order, single-loop, and band-pass Sigma-Delta modulator built in Matlab Simulink, as shown in Fig. 5.

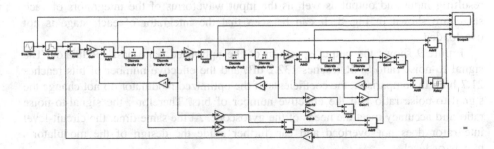

Fig. 5. Modulator structure of six-order, single-loop, and band-pass

4 Simulation and Results

In the simulation, the input signal is a sine wave with an amplitude of 0.1 V and a frequency of 80 KHz. The operational amplifier has a slew rate of 3.802 V/μs, a gain bandwidth of 37 MHz, and a signal bandwidth of 400 Hz.

After running the unoptimized modulator model, the input waveforms of the obtained input and output and the integrators of each stage are displayed in Fig. 6. Since the coefficient b is not optimized, the integrators of each stage are overloaded.

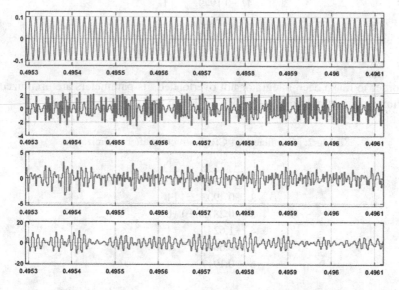

Fig. 6. Waveform of un-optimized band-pass modulator

Figure 7 shows the output spectrum of the modulator. The signal-to-noise ratio SNR reaches 132.1 dB, and the effective number of bits reaches 21.6 bits.

After running the modulator model with the coefficients of optimized CRFF, the resulting input and output as well as the input waveforms of the integrators of each stage are shown in Fig. 8. It can be seen that the integrator of each stage is not overloaded.

Figure 9 shows the output spectrum of the optimized band-pass modulator. The signal-to-noise ratio SNR reaches 132.2 dB, and the effective number of bits reaches 21.7 bits. In comparison, the coefficients of the optimized modulator do not change the signal-to-noise ratio and the effective number of bits. Therefore, the signal-to-noise ratio and accuracy meet the needs of the gyroscope. At the same time, the circuit-level integrator does not overload and can further guide the design of the modulator's transistor-level.

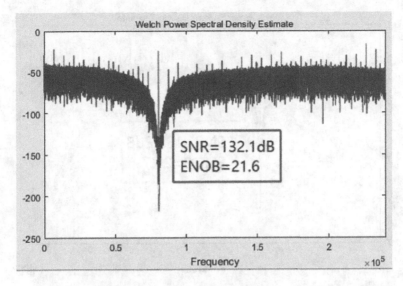

Fig. 7. Spectrum of un-optimized band-pass modulator

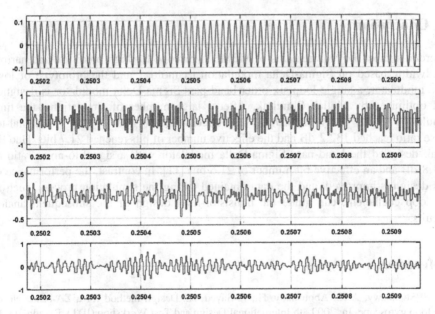

Fig. 8. Waveform of optimized band-pass modulator

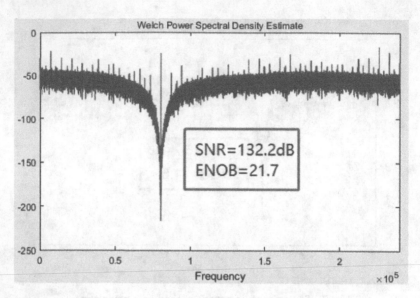

Fig. 9. Output spectrum of optimized band-pass modulator

5 Conclusion

In order to meet the requirements of MEMS gyroscope for high precision and narrow bandwidth, based on Sigma-Delta modulation technology and the prototype of low-pass modulator, a single-loop six-order band-pass Sigma-Delta modulator is designed and optimized by Matlab Simulink. After a large number of simulations, the final simulation results verify the stability and effectiveness of the system. The signal-to-noise ratio reached 132.2 dB and the effective number of bits reached 21.7 bits. Hao Bu et al. designed the band-pass Sigma-Delta modulator with a signal-to-noise ratio of 131.8 dB and an effective bit number of 21.6 bits [11]. In contrast, the performance of this design is improved, and the data obtained during the simulation process, such as the loop coefficient, can guide the transistor-level design of the subsequent analog circuits.

References

1. El-Shennawy, A.K., Aboushady, H., El-Sayed, A.: Design method for a ΣΔ-based closed loop gyroscope. In: 2009 4th International Design and Test Workshop (IDT), Riyadh, pp. 1–4 (2009)
2. Rodjegard, H., et al.: A novel architecture for digital control of MEMS gyros. In: SENSORS, 2004 IEEE, Vienna, vol. 3, pp. 1403–1406 (2004)
3. Ye, W.: Design of micro-mechanical gyro detection modal circuit based on band-pass modulator, p. 10. Harbin Institute of Technology (2018)

4. Cosand, E., Jensen, J.F., Choe, H.C., Fields, C.H.: IF-sampling fourth-order bandpass $\Delta\Sigma$ modulator for digital receiver applications. IEEE J. Solid-State Circ. **39**(10), 1633–1639 (2004)
5. Fraisse, C., Nagari, A.: A $\Sigma\Delta$ sense chain using chopped integrators for ultra-low-noise MEMS system. In: ESSCIRC Conference 2016: 42nd European Solid-State Circuits Conference, Lausanne, pp. 153–156 (2016)
6. Constantinides, A.G.: Spectral transformations for digital filters. Proc. IEE **117**(8), 1585–1590 (1970)
7. Chi, J., Jain, A., Sauerbrey, J., Becker, J., Ortmanns, M.: Interferer induced jitter reduction in bandpass CT $\Sigma\Delta$ modulators for receiver applications. In: 2018 IEEE International Symposium on Circuits and Systems (ISCAS), Florence, pp. 1–4 (2018)
8. Paton, S., Prefasi, E., Dominguez-Suarez, M., Portela-Garcia, M.: A low-IF bandpass $\Sigma\Delta$ ADC for fully-integrated CMOS magnetic resonance imaging receivers. In: 2017 IEEE 60th International Midwest Symposium on Circuits and Systems (MWSCAS), Boston, MA, pp. 1509–1512 (2017)
9. Yamamoto, T., Kasahara, M., Matsuura, T.: A 63 mA 112/94 dB DR IF bandpass $\Delta\Sigma$ modulator with direct feed-forward compensation and double sampling. IEEE J. Solid-State Circ. **43**(8), 1783–1794 (2008)
10. Zhu, Y.: Research on silicon microgyroscope electromechanical combined bandpass Sigma-delta closed-loop detection method, p. 11. Nanjing University of Science and Technology (2017)
11. Hao, B., et al.: Design and simulation verification of band-pass sigma-delta digital modulator. Data Commun. (06), 25–28+51 (2016)

An Efficient Rule Processing Architecture Based on Reconfigurable Hardware

Mengdong Chen(✉), Xiujiang Ren, and Xianghui Xie

State Key Laboratory of Mathematical Engineering and Advanced Computing,
Henghua Science and Technology Park, Wuxi 214125, Jiangsu, China
chen.mengdong@meac-skl.cn

Abstract. In the recovery of security strings in identity authentication mechanism, the combination of dictionary and string transformation rules is an effective method. However, the processing of string transformation rules faces challenges such as performance and energy efficiency. The existing tools and researches are based on software. It's difficult to meet the needs of actual recovery systems. In this paper, an efficient rule processing architecture based on reconfigurable hardware is proposed. The rules are processed using FPGA for the first time. A rule processor is designed and implemented on Xilinx Zynq XC7Z030 chip. The experimental results show that the performance of the rule processor is better than that of Intel i7-6700 CPU in typical cases. The performance power ratio of the rule processor is 1.4–2.1 times higher than that of NVIDIA GeForce GTX 1080 Ti GPU and 70 times higher than that of CPU, which effectively improves the speed and efficiency of rule processing.

Keywords: Identity authentication · Reconfigurable · Character string · Rule · Processor

1 Introduction

In computer and Internet systems, identity authentication is an important information security measure, which is widely used as an effective means to identify and protect personal information [1]. The authentication encryption process requires identity information consisting of a username and a security string. The HASH algorithm is usually used to compute the digest of the security string and the digest is stored together with user credential. When the user authenticates, the authentication system receives the security string input by the user, converts the string into a digest, and compares it with the digest value stored in the system to distinguish the legal user from the illegal user, and complete the authentication process [2].

The recovery of security strings is a reverse process, which tries to find the correct security strings from a large number of possible ones. This reverse process is often used to recover the forgotten security strings [3]. In this process, a large number of strings need to be generated quickly in a short period of time for subsequent HASH algorithm to use. Using existing strings combined with transformation rules is a very fast and effective way to generate strings [4], as shown in Fig. 1. Dictionary file is a collection of known security strings, which has a high hit rate. Rule file is a collection of various

© Springer Nature Singapore Pte Ltd. 2019
W. Xu et al. (Eds.): NCCET 2019, CCIS 1146, pp. 22–33, 2019.
https://doi.org/10.1007/978-981-15-1850-8_3

commonly used transformation rules of security strings. The dictionary can be transformed by rules to generate new strings. On the basis of guaranteeing accuracy, this method enlarges the coverage space of the original strings and ensures a certain search scale, which can improve the success rate of recovery.

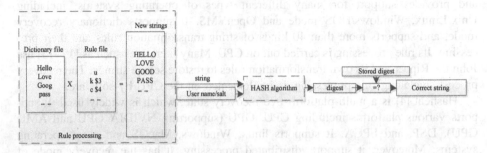

Fig. 1. Process of string recovery based on transform rules

Figure 1 shows the process of rule processing in the dotted frame. Each line in the dictionary file is a security string. Each line in the rule file is a transformation, and a transformation is often a combination of several basic rules. In practice, with a large scale of tasks, the dictionary file may have hundreds of millions of entries, and the rule file may contain hundreds of thousands of transformations. Rule processing requires that all dictionary entries be transformed according to each transformation in the rule file. The number of newly generated strings is the product of dictionary entries and rule entries.

Performance and power cost are important considerations in rule processing. There are dozens of basic transformation rules and complex combinations. The process of transformation is complicated, which is a task that is computationally intensive and requires high processing speed. So far, the known implementation methods are based on CPU and GPU [4–7]. There are many shortcomings in processing speed and system power consumption. Based on the security string recovery system used in practical projects, this paper proposes an efficient rule processing architecture based on reconfigurable hardware. This is the first time that FPGA has been used to speed up rule processing, and a high energy efficiency and reconfigurable rule processor is realized.

2   Related Works

Due to factors such as memory limitations and personal habits, when setting security strings, people usually make a simple transformation of existing strings to generate new ones, such as replacing a specific character, letters uppercase transformation, character inversion, insertion or deletion of characters at a specific location, etc. This transformation is called transformation rule [4, 5]. Several rules are usually grouped together for one transformation to produce one new string.

The use of dictionary combined with rules in security string recovery has attracted more and more attention. Several studies have proved the validity of the rules [8–11]. But their rule processing is implemented on CPU or GPU.

In this field, there are many accumulated string transformation rules. Several security string recovery tools have their own supporting rules, and provide the recovery mode of dictionary combined with rules.

John the Ripper [5] is an open source and free cryptanalysis software. Its main purpose is to recover weak Unix passwords. Now it supports more than 100 algorithms and provides support for many different types of operating systems, including Unix/Linux, Windows/DOS mode and OpenVMS. It supports dictionary recovery mode, and supports more than 40 kinds of string transformation rules and their processing. Its rule processing is carried out on CPU. Many literatures such as [12–14] use John the Ripper and its own transformation rules to restore secure strings. The recovery process, including rule processing, is implemented on the CPU by software.

Hashcat [4] is a multi-platform free recovery suite, which is widely used. It supports various platforms including CPU, GPU (supporting NVIDIA GPU and AMD GPU), DSP, and FPGA. It supports linux, Windows, MacOS and other operating systems. Moreover, it supports distributed processing. It has the recovery mode of dictionary combined with rules too. Its rule processing is mainly carried out on CPU and GPU. Document [15] uses hashcat and its own rules to study. The experiment was carried out on Intel Xeon CPU. Documents [16, 17] use the recovery method of dictionary combined with rules in hashcat, but they are all based on GPU platforms.

Through the above researches, we can find that whether it is academic research, open source software or commercial tools [18, 19], the rule processing is based on software implementation, which is carried out on CPU or GPU platform. The process pays attention to the validity of rules, and does not consider the processing speed and energy consumption of actual systems.

Based on the open source tool hashcat, this paper chooses 41 kinds of basic transformation rules and its own rule files of more than 300,000 entries to study and implements its processor. Table 1 lists several typical transformation rules. Each rule takes a visible character as its mnemonic, and some rules need to carry parameters. The number of parameters varies from 0 to 3. In the table, the string p@ssW0rd is used as input to illustrate the transformation results of the basic rules.

Table 1. Example of typical rules

Mnemonic	Description	Example	Result
l	lowercase all letters	l	p@ssw0rd
r	Reverse the entire word	r	dr0Wss@p
{	Rotates the word left	{	@ssW0rdp
DN	Deletes character at position N	D3	p@sW0rd
iNX	Inserts character X at position N	i4!	p@ss!W0rd
sXY	Replace all instances of X with Y	ss$	p@$$W0rd
*XY	Swaps character at position X with character at position Y	*34	p@sWs0rd

In practice, several single rules are often combined together to form one transformation, such as the case of lD3ss $3, which is combined of three rules, and one new string is generated after all three rules are processed.

3   Description of the Rule Processing Architecture

In order to meet the requirements of secure string recovery, rule processing faces a series of challenges. First of all, there are many types of transformation rules, the processing of individual rules is complicated, and there are complex combinations of rules. Second, the speed requirement of rule processing is high. The number of rule transformations and initial strings that need to be processed for a task is large. In the actual recovery system, the generation speed of new strings needs to meet the requirements of authentication algorithm module, while most of the authentication algorithm modules are pipelined and highly parallelized, which requires high processing speed of rules. Finally, rule processing faces limitations in resources, power consumption, etc., especially in hardware-based recovery systems where restrictions are more stringent.

3.1   Structure of the Hardware Platform

The rule processor in this paper is based on a hybrid heterogeneous computing platform. The core component of the platform is a hybrid core processor, the Xilinx Zynq XC7Z030 [20] chip, which contains two ARM universal embedded computing cores clocked at 1 GHz and a reconfigurable computing core. Two heterogeneous computing resources are tightly coupled through a high-speed interconnect bus. This can support the coordinated execution of general-purpose computing tasks and accelerated tasks. The periphery of the platform integrates 1 GB of low-power DDR memory, 32 GB of flash memory, Gigabit Ethernet interface, high-speed ring network interface, etc. The structure of the hybrid heterogeneous computing platform is shown in Fig. 2.

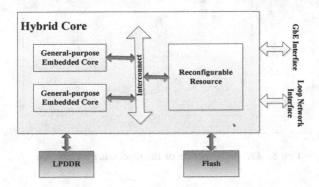

Fig. 2. Structure of the hardware platform

In the hybrid core computing platform of this paper, the main computing power comes from the reconfigurable computing core, namely FPGA, which is suitable for the work with large computation and easy parallelization. The general computing core is suitable for flexible configuration and management. Therefore, in the process of designing the rule processor, the main rule processing function is placed in the FPGA. The general computing core is responsible for configuring and managing the work of the reconfigurable computing core.

3.2 Overall Structure of the Processing Architecture

The rule processing architecture of this paper is divided into 5 modules, as shown in Fig. 3.

REU. The main body of this architecture is 41 rule execute units (REU). REU is responsible for the processing function of rules.

Decoding circuit. Decoding circuit is responsible for decoding transformation rules and scheduling each REU.

Bus interface circuit. Bus interface circuit includes AXI bus interface and is responsible for data interaction with off-chip.

Preprocessing circuit. Preprocessing circuit is responsible for processing consecutive stored rules and dictionary data into rule transformation entries and dictionary entries.

Data interaction network. Data interaction network is responsible for the interaction of data between the REUs and writing the resulting security strings into the result FIFO.

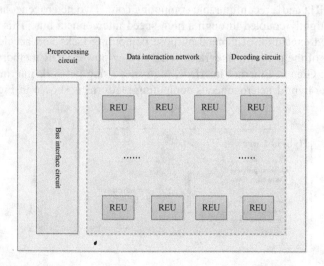

Fig. 3. Overall structure of the processing architecture

The following is a detailed introduction to the key aspects of the rule processing architecture, including the REU, the full pipeline execution structure and the data interaction network.

3.3 Design of the REUs

REU is responsible for implementing the transformation function of each rule. In practical requirements, because the HASH algorithm module is implemented in pipeline, a security string can be verified every clock cycle, which imposes high requirements on the rate of rule execution. In order to maximize the rate of rule execution, the design of a single rule execution process is optimized to be completed in one clock cycle.

For the most part, single rules are combined together for use, in this case, even if the processing of basic rules is completed within 1 clock cycle, multiple cycles are required to complete a complete transformation to generate a new string. At this time, there is only one REU working at each clock cycle, and the utilization of resources is low. Therefore, under the control of the decoding circuit, the whole transformation process should be realized in full pipeline as far as possible.

3.4 Full Pipeline Execution Structure

The decoding circuit is responsible for decoding the rules, deciding which transformation to perform, and scheduling the REUs according to the decoding results. The scheduling can be divided into two ways: full pipeline mode and serial mode.

The rule executing process is to first fix a rule transformation to loop through all the dictionary entries, and then loop through the rule file. Through the statistical analysis of the rule files contained in hashcat, it is found that in up to 85% of the transformation cases, the basic rules used in one transformation are different, which will not cause the conflict of hardware execution units. They are suitable for pipeline treatment. A full pipeline execution structure is designed. The schematic diagram of the execution structure is shown in Fig. 4. The figure is illustrated by the case where three rules are combined into one transformation. At this time, there are three security strings in process in every clock cycle, and a new string is generated every clock cycle. Each time there are multiple REUs working at the same time. For the other few cases, when there are same basic rules in one transformation, the data are processed strictly in serial mode through the effective control of decoding circuit. The next one starts only after the prior string has been completely processed. At this time, generating a new string requires multiple clock cycles.

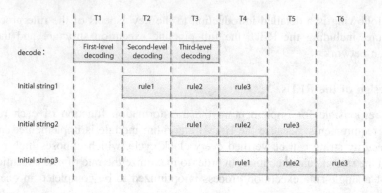

Fig. 4. Schematic diagram of the full pipeline execution structure

3.5   Design of the Data Interaction Network

Because of the complexity of rule combination, there is the possibility of data interaction between any two REUs, so it is necessary to design a fully interconnected data interaction network. In the case of resource constraints, the design of data interaction network aims at low complexity and low resource occupancy. Statistical analysis of rule combination shows that the majority of transformations are combined by less than 4 single rules. Therefore, the hardware rule processor focuses on this case. Based on this, a data interaction network is designed to satisfy the data transfer between any REUs.

By lengthening the time of data interaction to alleviate the complexity of hardware connection, a hierarchical data interaction network based on public registers is designed, as shown in Fig. 5. The REUs are grouped, and the REUs within a group are connected to a public register and then aggregated hierarchically. Data interaction to any REU is achieved through three-layer public registers. The processing results of the REU are stored in the public register, and then the results are collected as input from the public register when the next REU works. The processed results are collected together through the first and second layers, and then dispersed into each REU through the third layer to reduce the complexity of the connection. Each public register is divided into three levels, and the decoding circuit gives the destination label to indicate the level of the basic rule in the combination. Accordingly, the results of each basic rule are stored in the corresponding public registers. The results of the first rule are stored in the first level public register, and the results of the second rule are stored in the second level public register, and so on. Because each level of public registers at any time will only be occupied by one REU, and the interaction time is the same and fixed, it can realize the full interaction between all REUs and ensure the full pipeline execution of rules.

For the case where the same basic rule exists in one transformation, rules are executed serially. The data interaction network can support this effectively by using only part of the common registers under the control of decoding circuit. For the case where the transformation is combined of more than 3 single rules, through the control of the decoding circuit, the processing is also performed in a serial manner, and the network structure is also compatible.

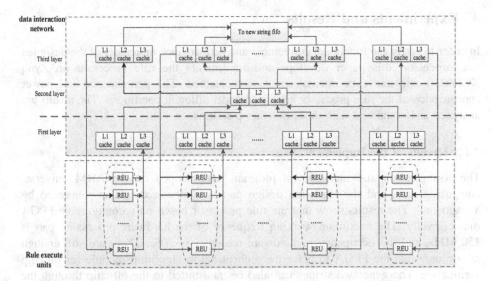

Fig. 5. Hierarchical data interaction network based on public registers

3.6 Data Storage Architecture

The rule processor automatically accesses rules and dictionaries. In order to meet the speed requirements of the high-speed processor for rules and dictionaries, the data storage architecture is divided into three levels.

First level storage: off-chip DDR. The rule and dictionary files are stored in DDR. The CPU in Zynq configures the start address and size information of the rule and dictionary files in DDR to the FPGA logic, and the hardware automatically obtains the rules and dictionary. At the same time, if the new strings generated by the rule processor need to be passed off-chip for use by other applications, they are also automatically transferred to the DDR memory by the rule processor.

Second level storage: On-chip RAM. The rule processor in FPGA pre-fetches the rules and dictionary into the FPGA through the AXI (Advanced eXtensible Interface) bus and caches them in the on-chip RAM. The four high-performance AXI_HP interfaces of the AXI bus can achieve a total bandwidth of 4.8 GB/s when operating at 150 MHz, which can guarantee the speed demand of the rule processor. As processing logic continues to consume data in RAM, the rule processor continuously acquires data from off-chip and guarantees the demand.

Third-level storage: On-chip FIFO. The processing logic acquires dictionary data from the on-chip RAM and performs preprocessing, and then stores the dictionary in the on-chip FIFO buffer for high-speed processing by the core processing logic.

4   Experiments and Results

In order to verify the functional correctness and performance indicators of the designed rule processor, this paper develops and implements the rule processor on Zynq XC7Z030 chip and experimental results are obtained. The performance and power consumption of the rule processor are tested under different conditions. The results are analyzed and compared with those of other platforms.

4.1   Results of the Implementation

The configuration and management program is developed on the ARM universal computing core, and the hardware design part is synthesized and implemented by Vivado tool. The results show that the rule processor based on reconfigurable FPGA runs correctly. The maximum working frequency of the hardware processing part is 150 MHz, and the occupancy of hardware resources is 70%. There are still enough resources inside the FPGA to place the authentication algorithm module for on-chip verification. The generated strings can also be transmitted to the off-chip through the AXI bus for other applications. In a typical case, the processor works in full pipeline, processing 150M transformations and generating 150M new strings per second.

4.2   Comparison with Other Platforms

This paper is the first time to process rules in the way of hardware implementation. The performance and power consumption are compared with the software implementation on Intel CPU and NVIDIA GPU. The same rule file and dictionary file are run on CPU and GPU respectively, and the results are compared with the rule processor in this paper. The comparison is made from two aspects of processing performance and power consumption.

The software implementation uses the latest hashcat 5.1.0, which claims to be the fastest recovery tool in the industry. The results of the software are closely related to its operating platform. For example, the desktop products of NVIDA GPU and those specially used for high performance computing have a huge gap in computing power. This paper chooses the mainstream product platform to test. The CPU platform used is Intel (R) Core (TM) i7-6700 CPU @ 3.40 GHz, 32G memory, and the GPU platform is NVIDIA GeForce GTX 1080 Ti.

The tests are carried out on each platform for the cases that one rule, two rules and three rules are combined into one transformation. The length of strings in dictionary is tested with 8 as an example. The processing performance is counted by how many Mega new strings are generated per second. The results are shown in Table 2.

Table 2. Performance comparison of different platforms when string length is 8 (M/s)

Platform	1 rule	2 rules	3 rules
Rule processor	150	150	150
CPU	220	100	70
GPU	17000	12050	8000

Through analysis, we can find that, because of the fulle pipeline implementation, the combination of rules has no effect on the processing performance of the processor in this paper, but has a greater impact on the CPU and GPU platform. The more rules are combined, the worse the processing performance. The rule processor generates 150M new strings per second in typical cases, which is better than CPU platform and worse than GPU. However, when the rule processor is used to build a large-scale and distributed rule processing system, its computing power will increase significantly.

Experiments have also been conducted for the case where the string length is 12, and the experimental results show that the performance of each platform is basically the same as when the string length is 8. It can be seen that for different string lengths, the processing performance of the three platforms is basically unaffected.

In the actual process, the power consumption of the rule processor and GPU platform is observed in real time. The power consumption of CPU is calculated at 65 W, and the performance power ratio (the number of transformations that can be processed per second per watt) is calculated. The results are shown in Fig. 6. For a typical case where two or three single rules are combined, the performance power ratio of the rule processor in this paper is 1.4 to 2.1 times higher than that of the GPU and 70 times higher than that of the CPU. It can be seen that the rule processor in this paper has advantages in energy efficiency. It runs fast and has low power consumption. It is suitable for constructing large-scale rule processing system.

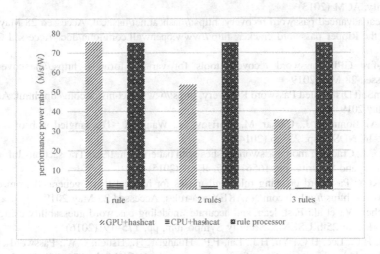

Fig. 6. Performance power ratio of different platforms

5 Conclusion

The processing of string transformation rules is an important part of secure string recovery. Its executing process is complex, and it has high requirements on processing performance and system power consumption. Aiming at these requirements, this paper proposes a rule processing architecture based on reconfigurable hardware for the first time. The architecture effectively utilizes the high parallelism and low power consumption of the FPGA. The experimental results show that, in typical cases, the performance of rule processor on Zynq XC7Z030 FPGA is better than that of Intel i7-6700 CPU. The performance power ratio of the rule processor is 1.4–2.1 times higher than that of NVIDIA GeForce GTX 1080 Ti GPU, and 70 times higher than that of CPU. This architecture effectively improves the speed and efficiency of rule processing. The rule processor designed in this paper has high processing performance, low system cost and low power consumption. It is especially suitable for the subsequent construction of large-scale, distributed and reconfigurable rule processing system, and then provides a basis for the design and implementation of the whole security string recovery system.

References

1. Guo, X., Chen, H., Liu, X., Xu, X., Chen, Z.: The scale-free network of passwords: visualization and estimation of empirical passwords. Comput. Sci. (2015)
2. Wu, Z.Y., Chiang, D.L., Lin, T.C., Chung, Y.F., Chen, T.S.: A reliable dynamic user-remote password authentication scheme over insecure network. In: 2012 26th International Conference on Advanced Information Networking and Applications Workshops, pp. 25–28. IEEE (2012)
3. Mazurek, M.L., et al.: Measuring password guessability for an entire university. In: Proceedings of the 2013 ACM SIGSAC conference on Computer & communications security. ACM (2013)
4. Hashcat advanced password recovery. https://hashcat.net/hashcat. Accessed 28 May 2019
5. John the Ripper password cracker. http://www.openwall.com/john/doc. Accessed 28 May 2019
6. Ultra-fast GPU password recovery tools for various formats. https://passcovery.com. Accessed 28 May 2019
7. ElcomSoft Distributed Password Recovery. https://www.elcomsoft.com/edpr.html. Accessed 28 May 2019
8. Das, A., Bonneau, J., Caesar, M., Borisov, N., Wang, X.: The tangled web of password reuse. In: NDSS, pp. 23–26 (2014)
9. Tatli, E.I.: Cracking more password hashes with patterns. In: IEEE Transactions Information Forensics and Security, pp. 1656–1665. IEEE (2015)
10. NSAKEY: Password cracking rules and masks for hashcat that i generated from cracked passwords. https://github.com/NSAKEY/nsa-rules. Accessed 28 May 2019
11. Melicher, W., et al.: Fast, lean, and accurate: modeling password guessability using neural networks. In: 25th USENIX Security Symposium, pp. 175–191(2016)
12. Chou, H.C., Lee, H.C., Yu, H.J., Lai, F.P., Huang, K.H., Hsueh, C.W.: Password cracking based on learned patterns from disclosed passwords. IJICIC **9**(2), 821–839 (2013)
13. Fahl, S., Harbach, M., Acar, Y., Smith, M.: On the ecological validity of a password study. In: Proceedings of the Ninth Symposium on Usable Privacy and Security, pp. 1–13. ACM (2013)
14. De Carnavalet, X.D.C., Mannan, M.: From very weak to very strong: analyzing password-strength meters. In: NDSS, pp. 23–26 (2014)
15. Huh, J.H., Oh, S., Kim, H., Beznosov, K., Mohan, A., Rajagopalan, S.R.: Surpass: system-initiated user-replaceable passwords. In: Proceedings of the 22nd ACM SIGSAC Conference on Computer and Communications Security, pp. 170–181. ACM (2015)

16. Milo, F., Bernaschi, M., Bisson, M.: A fast, GPU based, dictionary attack to OpenPGP secret keyrings. J. Syst. Softw. **84**(12), 2088–2096 (2011)
17. Xu, L., et al.: Password guessing based on LSTM recurrent neural networks. In: 2017 IEEE International Conference on Computational Science and Engineering (CSE) and IEEE International Conference on Embedded and Ubiquitous Computing (EUC), pp. 785–788. IEEE (2017)
18. Enforce strong passwords across your enterprise. http://www.l0phtcrack.com. Accessed 28 May 2019
19. Cain & Abel. https://cain-abel.en.softonic.com. Accessed 28 May 2019
20. Zynq-7000 All Programmable SoC. https://www.xilinx.com/support/documentation/product-briefs/zynq-7000-product-brief.pdf. Accessed 28 May 2019

Performance Analysis of Existing SIMD Architectures

Chao Cui[1(⊠)], Xian Zhang[2], and Zhicheng Jin[2]

[1] Beijing Institute of Control Engineering, Beijing 100190, China
cuichao0711@163.com
[2] National University of Defense Technology, Changsha 410073, China
944755068@qq.com

Abstract. SIMD (Single Instruction Multiple Data) architectures are widely used in application domains like the wireless communication, video and audio processing, and control engineering. The abundant data parallelism makes the SIMD architecture the proper match in data processing and performance improvement. However, there are also critical inefficiencies in current SIMD architectures. To understand such inefficiency, we carry out a deep investigation in the main components of Long Term Evolution (LTE) protocol, which is an important wireless communication protocol. Performance investigation is taken on a cycle-accurate simulator, featuring the main characteristics of existing SIMD architectures. Based on the investigation, we locate the inefficiencies in two aspects: the data communication operations among different processing units and the support for matrix-style computations. We have also carried out studies with enhanced SIMD architectures in the above two aspects. The overall performance of SIMD architectures can be greatly improved.

Keywords: SIMD · Inefficiency · Communication

1 Introduction

The abundant amount of parallelism, existed in wireless Communication, video & audio processing, computer graphics, and control engineering applications, makes the SIMD (Single Instruction Multiple Data) scheme [1–3] to be the prevailing architectures for data parallel processing. Examples include the processors like Brainwave [1], Imagine [4] and vector processor like VT [6], MAVEN [7]. Signal processors like SODA [8] and AnySP [5] also employ this scheme. The SIMD architecture uses single control flow handling mechanism across multiple SIMD lanes, achieving both high performance and power-efficiency. Moreover, much wider SIMD architectures are expected with the development of both the VLSI technology and data parallel applications, leading to a further improvement of overall performance. Recently, the development of deep neural networks provide perfect match with SIMD architecture, making SIMD architecture a very popular processor design style.

A well know inefficiency point of SIMD architecture is that the efficacy of the overall architecture is reduced greatly when handling divergent control flows [9, 10, 19], as all the SIMD units have to execute in a lock-step manner, while divergent

© Springer Nature Singapore Pte Ltd. 2019
W. Xu et al. (Eds.): NCCET 2019, CCIS 1146, pp. 34–47, 2019.
https://doi.org/10.1007/978-981-15-1850-8_4

control flows break the lock-step execution model. In the normal case upon divergent branch paths SIMD units have to branch into different branch paths, and different paths have to be executed in serial. This has been well studied to improve the overall performance of SIMD architectures. Another inefficient point of SIMD architectures is that the wide SIMD unit cannot be well exploited when processing scalar applications. There are studied try to solve this by conceal the execution of scalar processing in that' the parallel applications.

However, in this paper, we find that that there are still other inefficiencies in existing SIMD architectures, which greatly limit the overall potential of SIMD architectures. These inefficiencies prevent the peak performance of SIMD architectures, leading to both performance loss and a waste of hardware resources. To get valuable insight into these inefficiencies and give architecture designers inspiring implications, we carry out deep analysis of the typical components of wireless communications protocol LTE [11, 12]. These components include the Multiple antennae decoding kernel MIMO (Multiple Input Multiple Output) and FFT (Fast Fourier Transform).

The analysis is carried out on a cycle accurate simulator for SIMD architectures. This simulator features the main characteristics of the state of art SIMD processors [5, 19], including efficient single instruction issuing mechanism, concurrent execution of multiple datapaths, data communication units among datapaths and the multiple-banked memory system. The evaluation locates the inefficiency of SIMD architectures in two aspects: the lack of efficient support in data communication operations, and the time consuming data organization operations for matrix-style computations.

We find that the data communication operation has to be carried out in two cycles in current intra-lane communication unit. In the first cycle, the connection pattern of comm unit is configured, and then data is read from different SIMD lanes and written into destination SIMD lanes in the next cycle. Our paper shows that with better design of the communication unit, where data communication can be done in one cycle, the overall performance of SIMD architectures can be greatly improved. The data reorganization operation is not well considered in SIMD architectures, especially the widely used matrix transposing operations are not well supported, with a dedicated unit for matrix transposing, the overall performance for MIMO like matrix intensive architectures can be further improved.

We have also evaluate optimized SIMD architectures with enhanced communication and data reorganization support, in which the intra-lane communication can be done in one cycle and data reorganization especially the matrix transposition can be done with dedicated register file. The results show that such enhancements can greatly improve the performance of SIMD unit by more than 20%. We conclude that enhancements in intra-lane communication and data reorganization is of great importance to the SIMD architectures.

The analysis results above indicate new directions for the design of SIMD architectures. With the rapid development of both VLSI technology (wider SIMD architecture are being built) and data parallel applications, higher performance of SIMD architectures is expected. At the same time, the power consumption plays a more and more important role [1, 5]. Moreover, it has been proved that the widespread machine learning applications have a perfect match with the SIMD architecture. This puts an urgent demand for efficient SIMD architectures. We believe that the break-through for the above inefficiencies can lead to a better match between SIMD processors and data parallel applications.

The rest of this paper is organized as follows: Sect. 2 gives the application analysis. Section 3 presents the simulation platform and the performance analysis is done in Sect. 4, we also carry out simulations of SIMD architecture enhancement to show the corresponding effect. Section 5 concludes the contributions of this paper.

2   Application Description

This section presents the typical components selected from domains of wireless communications and video processing protocols. These components include the MIMO and FFT kernel, which are widely used in wireless communications like LTE. We want to use these applications kernels to get deep insight about SIMD architecture itself to further guide the design of SIMD processors. The benchmark description is conducted below.

2.1   FFT

A fast Fourier transform (FFT) algorithm [13–16, 20] computes the Discrete Fourier transform (DFT) of an input data array, or the inverse case of DFT. The major function of FFT is to convert data from its original time/space domain to a new representation in the frequency domain. For the inverse case, data is converted from the frequency domain back to its time/space domain. The FFT algorithm can greatly improve the speed of the above transformation by factorizing the DFT/IDFT parameter matrix into a product of sparse factors. The detailed computation procedure is described below.

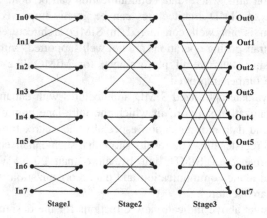

Fig. 1. The computation process of 8-point FFT

The execution process of FFT is composed of two parts: one is the butterfly operations in each processing stage; the other is the data preparation among butterfly stages. Figure 1 illustrates the computation process with an example of 8-point FFT. As shown in the figure, each butterfly operation comprises a complex multiplication and two complex add/sub operations. The communication pattern among processing stages is regular, and the communication step doubled after each processing stage. In each butterfly processing stage, there are abundant data level parallelisms, which can be efficiently accelerated by the SIMD architecture. However, communications among stages can introduce additional operations, which could be an additional burden on the overall performance.

Moreover, with the increase of data size in FFT (e.g., from 8-point FFT to 64, and even 1024 point FFT), the communication among stages becomes much more intense and the amount of stages increases greatly. With the development of FFT application, larger data size is expected, such that it is important to efficiently support the communication operations among different stages to overcome the potential bottleneck.

2.2   MIMO

MIMO (multiple-in, multiple-out) is an algorithm to greatly increase wireless bandwidth and capacity. It achieves this purpose by taking advantage of multiplexing two or more antennas and thus the information can be both sent and received via multiple antennas, which is named as multiple in antennas and multiple out antennas. Normal configurations of such multiple-in and multiple-out antennas including 2*2, 2*4, and 4*4. On conventional radio, one potential concern of employing multiple antennas is that multiplexing would cause interference, but MIMO solves this problem by using the additional pathways to transmit more information at the same time. An recombining procedure is added at the end of signal receiving. With the above scheme, MIMO systems achieve a significant capacity gain over conventional single antenna configurations. Moreover, the reliability of communication is also increased. The benefits of MIMO make it the most promising technique of wireless technologies.

We use the STBC decoding algorithm as the target of our analysis. The main computation pattern is listed below in Eq. (1). H is the channel matrix formed with the channel estimation result. M and N are the number of receiving and transmitting antennas respectively. σ^2 is the predefined parameter, representing the noise power. I_M is the identity unit matrix. MIMO has intensive matrix computations, including the matrix multiplication, transpose and inversion operations. Another characteristic is that, there are abundant data level parallelisms, as each vector $Y_{M \times 1}$ can be calculated independently in corresponding SIMD lanes. Figure 2 shows the formatting process of H matrix and the S vector. Within a typical communication process, there can be up to 14400 such vectors. Thus, great performance gains can be expected when running on the SIMD architecture.

One important feature of STBC MIMO is that it contains intensive matrix computations. The most time consuming part is the matrix multiplication. Although matrix operations contain significant parallelism, which can be potentially exploited by SIMD architectures, it is not straightforward to be accelerated due to the data layout in memory. Take the matrix multiplication as an example, it requires both matrices in row-wise and column-wise layout respectively such that the multiplication can be well parallelized to fully use SIMD units. However, in reality, matrices are always stored in either row-wise or column-wise manner. This requires additional data reorganization operations to get prepared for execution on SIMD architectures.

For MIMO configurations with many more antennas, the data reorganization operation could be even more complex, this could bring additional data reorganization overhead when processing on SIMD architectures.

$$Y_{M \times 1} = H_{M \times N}^{H} \cdot \left(H_{M \times N} \cdot H_{M \times N}^{H} + \sigma^2 I_M \right)^{-1} S_{M \times 1} \tag{1}$$

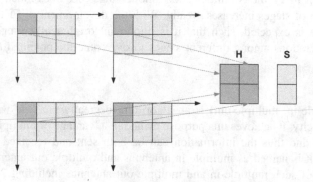

Fig. 2. The illustration of MIMO computation

3   Evaluation Platform

To take a deep investigation on the performance of SIMD architecture, we build a cycle accurate simulator. Figure 3 illustrates the block diagram of the target SIMD architecture that we modeled. The SIMD architecture comprised two units, specially, the scalar unit and the SIMD unit. Scalar unit is capable of control flow handling and scalar application processing, while SIMD unit is oriented for parallel data processing. Note that this is a typical SIMD architecture. DNN processors like Brainwave [1], stream processors like Imagine [4], vector processor like VT [6], MAVEN [7], and digital signal processors like SODA [8] and AnySP [5] employ this architecture as their core SIMD structure. Such structure is somewhat different from word level SIMD design which divide a 64-bit word into multiple smaller sub-word and processing them in parallel, such sub-word level SIMD architecture in always designed as a simple computation unit, and is not suitable for the applications domains that we study in this paper.

The SIMD unit consists of multiple processing elements (PEs), while the scalar unit consists of a scalar control processor. A global scratchpad memory, all connected through a shared bus is also introduced. The global scratchpad memory is used for the SIMD unit and the scalar unit; An AGU is also added for providing the addresses mainly for local memory accesses of SIMD unit; a programmable DMA unit to transfer data between memories and interface with the outside system. The SIMD unit, scalar unit and the AGU pipeline can execute in a VLIW-styled with lock-step manner, controlled with one single program counter (PC). The DMA unit has its own PC, its

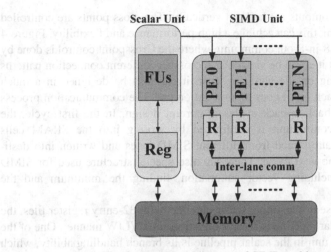

Fig. 3. The block diagram of SIMD architectures

main purpose is to perform memory transfers and data rearrangement. It is also the only unit, which can initiate memory data transfer between the global scratchpad memory and the off-chip memory.

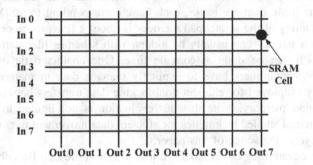

Fig. 4. The structure of comm unit

The SIMD unit consists of a 16-way 32-bit datapath, with 32 PEs working in a lock-step manner. SIMD unit is designed to handle computationally intensive application kernels in wireless communication, video and audio processing domains. Each PE contains a 2 read-port, 1 write-port 16 entry register file, one ALU, one MAC and one Load/Store unit. The MAC unit takes four execution cycles when running at the targeted 500 MHz. Intra-processor data movements are supported through the intra-lane comm unit, (shown in Fig. 3). The comm unit is composed of a SRAM-based swizzle network that adds flexibility while maintaining the performance of a customized crossbar, where the layout is an X-Y style crossbar. The input buses are laid out horizontally and the outputs are laid out vertically. The cross points are controlled with SRAM based pattern, this can achieve a high performance and flexibility. Figure 4 shows an example of an 8-in-8-out comm unit, where the Crosspoint control is done by an SRAM cell. Note that it could be viewed as a crossbar, different connection patterns are supported. Depending on the hardware cost, it can also be designed in a much simple manner, where each input goes to an fixed output. The communication process has to be done in two back-to-back cycles in current design. In the first cycle, the connection pattern of comm unit is configured by writing into the SRAM cells accordingly, and then data is read from different SIMD lanes and written into destination SIMD lanes in the next cycle. There are also special structure used for SIMD reduction operations, including vector summation, finding the minimum and the maximum operations.

Scalar unit is composed of a simple scalar pipeline, with 32-entry register files, the function units in the scalar pipeline is always organized in a VLIW manner. One of the most important function unit in the scalar pipeline is its branch handling ability, which is eliminated in the PEs of SIMD unit due to the SIMD execution style. The scalar unit handles all the control flow related operations and applications that can not be well parallelized. Ideally, we want to use the SIMD unit as much as possible, and employ the scalar unit only necessary.

The memory subsystem contains two parts: the cache for instruction and data which is designed for the SCU; a private local scratchpad memory for the SIMD unit. To increase the memory bandwidth and capacity, the scratchpad memory is always designed with multiple memory banks, each bank corresponding to a SIMD PE. The typical access latency of the scratchpad memory is about a few processor cycles. One thing is that such latency can usually be hidden with schemes like static instruction scheduling, which can be done at compile time. One characteristic of scratchpad memory is that programmers have to explicitly manage data in memory. A DMA engine is usually employed for efficient nonblocking data transfers between the cache and the scratchpad memory. Note that our evaluation is not limited to a particular memory subsystem. Detailed techniques for efficient data movement over this memory subsystem is beyond the scope of this paper.

We set the programming environment similar to that of the Cell Broadband Engine. When programming applications with data level parallelism, programmers need to divide the iterations in a loop structure into sequential stages. In each stage, the data working set size should be fitting within the capacity of the scratchpad memory. The parallel loop iterations are reprogrammed into N SIMD threads, where N is the number of SIMD PEs.

We have developed a detailed cycle-accurate microarchitectural of a typical SIMD processor. The SIMD unit simulation is combined with a cycle-driven memory system simulation that models the multi-banked scratchpad memory. There are 16 SIMD PEs in the SIMD unit, each having a 32-entry register file. The scratchpad memory has 16 banks each corresponding to a SIMD datapath with an accessing latency of four cycles. The SCU has the instruction and data cache, which connects to the main memory. There is also a DMA engine that transfers data between the SCU and SIMD PEs.

4 Performance Analysis

We hand coded the selected application kernels in assembly and optimized the code to full exploit the computation potential of the SIMD architecture. The assemble code serves as the input of the proposed experimental platform. We use the assembly code to fulfill the ability of cycle accurate simulation. To reveal the efficiency of SIMD architecture, we set the scalar unit as the baseline architecture, which can be viewed as a typical CPU processor.

4.1 FFT

Figure 5 shows the performance gains of the SIMD architecture over the baseline architecture when processing FFT. We have implemented four versions of FFT, which are 256-point, 512-point, 1024-point, and 2048 point. Such FFT size covers most of the use cases in the wireless communication domain. As we can see that FFT with different input size achieve high performance gains. However, as the theoretical performance speedup is 16, due to 16 PEs in the SIMD unit. The performance gain of FFT is around 9, which is still less than the theoretical speedup.

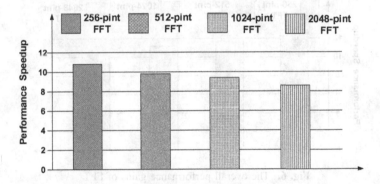

Fig. 5. The overall performance gains

To understand the performance of FFT, we carry out deep analysis of the execution procedure of FFT. We find that the performance is greatly limited by intra-lane communication operations, these operations are caused by the data preparation operations between multiple butterfly stages. The intra-lane communication operations take up about 35% of the overall execution time. The main characteristic of the data preparation is the value between two registers of different SIMD lanes. The value exchange process has to be carried out in two cycles in current intra-lane communication unit. In the first cycle, the connection pattern of comm unit is configured, and then data is read from different SIMD lanes and written into destination SIMD lanes in the next cycle.

Apparently, the intra-lane communication unit is lack of efficient support for data exchange operations. Ideally, such communication operations should be done in one cycle, in which the connection pattern configuration should be done in the back ground, such that data communication can be done in one cycle.

One important trend in Fig. 5 is that with the increase of data size in FFT, the performance gain becomes even smaller. This shows the above limitation of communication unit in SIMD architectures becomes much more serious. In fact, with the development of FFT application, larger data size FFT is expected. Examples include 1 million, and even 2 million point FFTs. For such large size, the limitation of intra-lane communication in SIMD unit could be unaffordable. We conclude that it is important to implement efficient intra-lane communication support in SIMD architectures. Based on the above analysis, we can tell that the SIMD architecture is still inefficient for data exchange among SIMD PEs in terms of intra-lane communication. More efficient communication enhancements should be developed.

To prove our analysis, we modify the simulator with one-cycle intra-lane communication unit, which can exchange values among different SIMD PEs, within one cycle. The philosophy is that the configuration of communication pattern in the comm unit and the data read/write can be done in parallel in the same cycle. So that we can exchange data among SIMD PEs much more efficient.

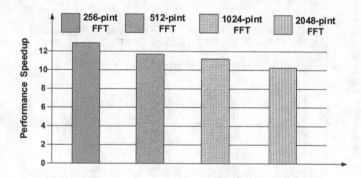

Fig. 6. The overall performance gains of FFT

Figure 6 shows the overall performance gain. As we can see, that FFT with different input size achieve higher performance gains. The average performance gain is about 11. Although this is still under the theoretical speedup, the overall performance is already increased over the baseline SIMD architecture with inefficient intra-lane communication unit design. We believe that better performance can be expected with optimizations at the software level, in which the amount of communication can be replaced by localizing computation as much as possible. We leave such optimizations to our future work.

4.2   MIMO

Figure 7 shows the performance gains of the SIMD architecture over the baseline architecture when processing MIMO. We have implemented MIMO with different antenna configurations including 2*2, 4*2, and 4*4. Note that such configurations are the most commonly used antenna configuration in wireless communication. Theoretically, MIMO contains large amount of matrix operations, which in turn contain a large amount of data level parallelism, which seems to be proper for SIMD architectures. However, as we can see that MIMO with different input size achieves high performance gains, recalling that with 16 PEs in the SIMD unit, the theoretical performance speedup is 16. The performance gain of MIMO is around 11, which is still much less than the theoretical speedup, there exists large space for performance improvement.

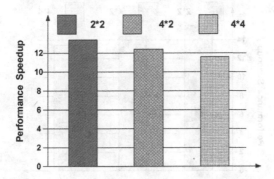

Fig. 7. The overall performance gains of MIMO

To understand the performance of MIMO, we carry out deep analysis of the execution procedure of MIMO. We find the truth is that, the column-wised accesses in matrix operations seriously limit the overall performance. This situation is even worse when both column- and row- wised access is needed. Thus, it is necessary for SIMD architectures to support matrix operation. That is to say, the performance of MIMO when executed on SIMD architectures is greatly limited by data reorganization operations, these operations are caused by the matrix related operations including matrix multiplication and matrix add. The data reorganization operations take up about 27% of the overall execution time. For MIMO kernel, which has intensive matrix computations, including matrix multiplication, transpose and inversion, the performance gain is high. However, the efficiency of SIMD architectures is still limited by the column-wise memory access pattern of the matrix data, which brings additional data alignment operations through intra-lane comm unit and additional memory operations can also be introduced.

The above data alignment operations put a heavy burden on the overall performance, leading to inefficiency in the utilization of hardware resources. It has no computation requirement, only the data layout reorganization. However, existing SIMD architectures handle such data reorganization operations by reading the data out of the scratch pad memory though the data cache, and then write the data back to memory. During the data reorganization process, the SIMD unit is almost idle, wasting a great amount of performance and energy. As we can see from Fig. 7, such data reorganization operations take up much larger execution time with the increase of antenna numbers in MIMO. To gain high capacity and bandwidth in wireless communication,

MIMO tends to be employed in environment with a large number of antennas, this would further reduce the performance of SIMD architectures.

We conclude that it is important to implement efficient data reorganization support in SIMD architectures. Based on the above analysis, we can tell that the SIMD architecture is still inefficient for data reorganizations. More efficient enhancements should be developed.

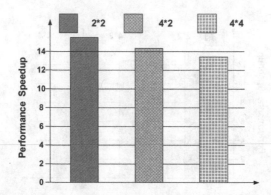

Fig. 8. The overall performance gains of MIMO with optimized data reorganization support

To prove our analysis, we modify the simulator with dedicated data reorganization unit, which can efficiently reorganize data according to the requirement of the applications. The cost of the configuration can be largely concealed in the execution. So that SIMD unit can always processing data without being wasted on data preparation.

Figure 8 shows the overall performance gain of MIMO with optimized data reorganization support. As we can see, that MIMO with different antenna configurations achieve higher performance gains. The average performance gain is about 14. This is only a little under the theoretical speedup, the overall performance is greatly increased over the baseline SIMD architecture with inefficient data reorganization unit design. We believe that better performance can be expected with optimizations like data communication among SIMD PEs. Other optimizations schemes like data reorganization replacement, data localization can further improve the performance when executed on SIMD architectures. We leave such optimizations to our future work.

4.3   Comparison with Existing Schemes

We compare the proposed SIMD architecture, which contains enhanced communication and matrix operations, with existing SIMD architectures [17, 18]. As shown in Fig. 9, the performance results show that with enhancement for communication and matrix operations, the performance gain of SIMD architecture can be greatly improved by 16% on average. This is due to the increasement of the utilization rate in the computation units. The processing bubbles due to the waiting for data preparation are effectively reduced, leading to high efficiency in SIMD unit, and thus achieving high performance gain. Moreover, the communication and matrix operation enhancement interacts positively with each other, providing further performance improvements.

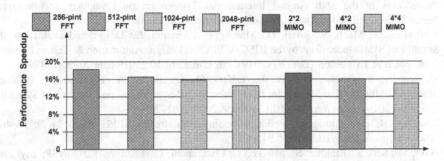

Fig. 9. Speedup over existing SIMD architectures

To conclude, the above analysis indicates that there are still inefficiencies in the intra-lane communication and support for matrix-style processing for existing SIMD architectures. With the increasing of SIMD width, such inefficiency Further studies and deep investigations on the above aspects will greatly improve the efficiency of SIMD architectures. We show that the performance of SIMD architectures can be greatly improved with enhancement on intra-lane communication and data reorganizations.

5 Conclusion

This paper proposes an analysis on the representative data parallel applications with an cycle accurate simulator. From the analysis of representative application kernels including FFT and MIMO, the inefficiencies of existing SIMD architectures are located in the intra-lane communication structure, we find that the data communication operation has to be carried out in two cycles in current intra-lane communication unit. In the first cycle, the connection pattern of comm unit is configured, and then data is read from different SIMD lanes and written into destination SIMD lanes in the next cycle. Besides the communication structure, the matrix-style oriented computation is also not well supported, especially the widely used matrix transposing operations are not well supported. This result advocates further attention and effort in the aspects located above. Our paper shows that with better design of the communication unit, where data communication can be done in one cycle, the overall performance of SIMD architectures can be greatly improved. Moreover, with a dedicated unit for matrix transposing, the overall performance for MIMO like matrix intensive architectures can be further improved.

Acknowledgement. We thank the anonymous reviewers for their valuable work. We greatly improve our work based on the reviews. We also thank Xiaohui Yang and Dongdeng Tang of National University of Defense Technology for their kindly help in building the experimental platform and feedbacks on the performance evaluation.

References

1. Ghandi, M., Heil, S., et, al.: A configurable cloud-scale DNN processor for real-time AI. In: Proceedings of the 36th Annual International Symposium on Computer Architecture, Series ISCA 2018 (2018). https://doi.org/10.1109/isca.2018.00012
2. Tagliavini, G., Mach, S., Rossi, D., Marongiu, A., Benini, L.: Design and evaluation of SmallFloat SIMD extensions to the RISC-V ISA. In: Design, Automation & Test in Europe Conference & Exhibition (DATE) (2019). https://doi.org/10.23919/date.2019.8714897
3. Malkowsky, S., Prabhu, H., Liu, L., Edfors, O., Öwall, V.: A programmable 16-lane SIMD ASIP for massive MIMO. In: IEEE International Symposium on Circuits and Systems (ISCAS) (2019). https://doi.org/10.1109/iscas.2019.8702770
4. Khailany, B., et al.: Imagine: media processing with streams. IEEE Micro **21**(2), 35–46 (2001). https://doi.org/10.1109/40.918001
5. Woh, M., Seo, S., Mahlke, S., Mudge, T., Chakrabarti, C., Flautner, K.: AnySP: anytime anywhere anyway signal processing. In: Proceedings of the 36th Annual International Symposium on Computer Architecture, Series ISCA 2009 (2009). https://doi.org/10.1109/mm.2010.8
6. Krashinsky, B., Batten, C., et al.: The vector-thread architecture. IEEE Micro **24**(6), 84–90 (2004). https://doi.org/10.1109/MM.2004.90
7. Lee, Y., Avizienis, R., et al.: Exploring the tradeoffs between programmability and efficiency in data-parallel accelerators. In: International Symposium on Computer Architecture, pp. 129–140 (2011). https://doi.org/10.1145/2000064.2000080
8. Lin, Y., Lee, H., et al.: SODA: a low-power architecture for software radio. In: Proceedings of the 33rd Annual International Symposium on Computer Architecture, Series ISCA 2006 (2006). https://doi.org/10.1109/isca.2006.37
9. Wang, Y., Chen, S., et al.: A multiple SIMD, multiple data (MSMD) architecture: parallel execution of dynamic and static SIMD fragments. In: IEEE International Symposium on High Performance Computer Architectures (HPCA) (2013). https://doi.org/10.1109/hpca.2013.6522353
10. Wang, Y., Chen, S., et al.: Instruction shuffle: achieving MIMD-like performance on SIMD architectures. IEEE Comput. Archit. Lett. **11**(2), 37–40 (2012). https://doi.org/10.1109/l-ca.2011.34
11. Physical channels and modulation, 3GPP TS 36.211, European, Telecommunications, Standards, Institute (2013)
12. Multiplexing and channel coding, 3GPP TS 36.212, European, Telecommunications, Standards, Institute (2013)
13. Kanders, H., Mellqvist, T., Garrido, M., Palmkvist, K., Gustafsson, O.: A 1 million-point FFT on a single FPGA. IEEE Trans. Circuits Syst. I: Regul. Pap. (2019). https://doi.org/10.1109/tcsi.2019.2918403
14. Incremona, A., De Nicolao, G.: Spectral characterization of the multi-seasonal component of the Italian electric load: a LASSO-FFT approach. IEEE Control Syst. Lett. (2019). https://doi.org/10.1109/lcsys.2019.2922192
15. Buzachis, A., Galletta, A., Celesti, A., Fazio, M., Villari, M.: Development of a smart metering microservice based on Fast Fourier Transform (FFT) for Edge/Internet of Things Environments. In: IEEE 3rd International Conference on Fog and Edge Computing (ICFEC) (2019). https://doi.org/10.1109/cfec.2019.8733148
16. Liu, S., Chen, H., Wan, J., Wang, Y.: Mod (2P-1) shuffle memory-access instructions for FFTs on vector SIMD DSPs. In: IEEE Computer Society Annual Symposium on VLSI (ISVLSI) (2016). https://doi.org/10.1109/isvlsi.2016.71

17. Yang, C., Chen, S., Zhang, J., Lv, Z., Wang, Z.: A novel DSP architecture for scientific computing and deep learning. IEEE Access **7**, 36413–36425 (2019). https://doi.org/10.1109/access.2019.2905302
18. Chen, S., et al.: FT-Matrix: a coordination-aware architecture for signal processing. IEEE Micro **34**(6) (2014). https://doi.org/10.1109/mm.2013.129
19. Wang, Y., Chen, X., Wang, D., Liu, S.: Dynamic per-warp reconvergence stack for efficient control flow handling in GPUs. In: IEEE Computer Society Annual Symposium on VLSI (ISVLSI) (2016). https://doi.org/10.1109/isvlsi.2016.35
20. Dong, W., Rongcai, Z., Qi, W., Yingying, L.: Outer-loop auto-vectorization for SIMD architectures based on Open64 compiler. In: 17th International Conference on Parallel and Distributed Computing Applications and Technologies (PDCAT), pp. 19–23 (2016). https://doi.org/10.1109/pdcat.2016.020

A Coherent and Power-Efficient Optical Memory Access Network for Kilo-Core Processor

Quanyou Feng[✉], Junhui Wang, Hongwei Zhou, and Wenhua Dou

National University of Defense Technology, Changsha 410073, China
fengquanyou@nudt.edu.cn

Abstract. Coherent and power-efficient processor-memory interconnects are of great importance for kilo-core processor design. This paper proposes a hybrid photonic architecture for such interconnection. Specifically, a bandwidth-efficient photonic network which also supports coherence management is used for memory accesses between last-level HBM caches and off-chip HMC memory pools. Simulation results show that the hybrid network achieves up to 11% of system speedup and up to 6 times of energy savings, when compared to conventional electric interconnects.

Keywords: Photonic Noc · HMC · Memory subsystem · Coherence

1 Introduction

For Exascale computing era, many-core processors play an essential role in achieving such performance goals [1]. When the number of cores integrated on many-core chips increases, for example, 1000 cores [2], memory subsystem design, which must sustain the enormous demand for off-chip memory accesses in an energy-efficient manner, has become a critical challenge.

Projected scaling of electrical processor-memory network appears unlikely to meet the enormous demand for off-chip bandwidth within stringent power budget [3]. This work proposes a hybrid optical memory subsystem for kilo-core processor chips. The hybrid system utilizes high-bandwidth HBMs as the on-chip LLC(last-level caches) and high-speed off-chip HMCs as memory pools; circuit-switched photonic transmission is used for processor-memory communication; a special coherence scheme is used to enforce system-wide cache coherence between all LLCs and HMCs. The photonic network meets the enormous bandwidth demand and stringent energy constraints by using high-speed low-power CMOS-compatible silicon photonic devices. Augmented with coherence management, our network becomes a competitive candidate for optical many-core SMP (Symmetrical Multi-Processing) system.

We examine the system feasibility and performances using physically-accurate interconnects simulation environment. Simulation results show that the hybrid network achieves up to 11% of system speedup and up to 6 times of energy savings, compared to conventional electric interconnects.

© Springer Nature Singapore Pte Ltd. 2019
W. Xu et al. (Eds.): NCCET 2019, CCIS 1146, pp. 48–58, 2019.
https://doi.org/10.1007/978-981-15-1850-8_5

The rest of this paper is organized as follows. Section 2 summarizes state of the art of photonic chip-scale networks and presents related backgrounds on HMCs and HBMs. Section 3 details the hybrid memory subsystem architecture. Section 4 presents the simulation results and discussions. Conclusions and future work are included in Sect. 5.

2 Related Works

2.1 On-Chip Photonic Interconnects

On-chip interconnection faces a lot of challenges [13, 14]. Silicon photonic technology [4] paves the way for CMOS-compatible photonic devices, including modulators, detector, waveguides and optical switches, which results in functional optical chip-scale network design. Figure 1 illustrates two basic switching elements for constructing complex optical switches [4]. As the electrical parameters of micro-ring resonators' are adjusted, the photonic path in waveguides can be switched on or off, thus optical messages can go straight through or turn around. With these silicon photonic switches, functional on-chip optical interconnects become feasible [4]. For example, Vantrease [9] and Shacham [8] all proposed different optical memory access schemes, either by on-chip wavelength-division multiplexing or optical switching. Ahmed [16] proposed efficient router architectures for heterogeneous Many-core Hybrid Photonic Network-on-Chip. Kodi [17] combined photonic and wireless technologies to further reduce power consumption for kilo-core NOC design. Meyer [18] presented novel power estimation schemes for the optical NoCs. In these systems, photonic devices, memory devices and logic circuits are stacked together by three dimensional integration (3D-I) [5].

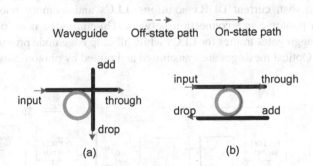

Fig. 1. 1×2 optical switches. (a) Crossing. (b) Parallel.

2.2 HMCs and HBMs

The emerging 3D stacking technology makes large-capacity memory devices feasible, for example, HMCs [7] and HBMs [6]. They all stack up multiple DRAM devices and provide high-bandwidth memory operations by means of multiple independent access channels (see Fig. 2). However, a HMC would work as a separate memory chip while a HBM must be integrated into the user chip package.

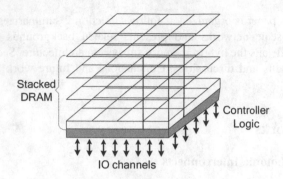

Fig. 2. 3D-stacked memory devices

3 The Coherent Optical Memory Access Interconnects

Scientific applications usually require high bandwidth data channels and stream processing capabilities to facilitate frequent access of continuous memory blocks using DMA. However, high bandwidth accesses consume significant computing power while a functional many-core processor has stringent power budget. Thus, processor-memory interconnects, without doubt, become the key bottleneck in many-core systems. Recent advances in silicon photonics and memory technologies have brought alternative solutions for such challenges.

Figure 3 illustrates our proposed optical memory subsystem for kilo-core processors. Directly integrated on-chip HBMs are used as on-chip last-level caches (LLCs) which provides high-bandwidth low-latency memory access by utilizing the wide parallel buses; Off-chip memory pools built on HMCs deliver an order of magnitude more bandwidth than current DDRx solutions. LLCs and memory pools are interconnected by a photonic interconnection network. On-chip edge node of the optical network (NIC) aggregates traffics for LLCs while off-chip edge node provides access to memory pools. Optical messages are transmitted and routed by photonic switches in the

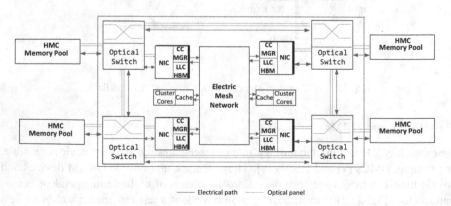

Fig. 3. Chip-scale optical interconnects for memory subsystem of kilo-core processor.

optical plane. In the system, photonic IOs and switches are stacked with the electronic processor plane using 3DI. On the interconnect plane, optical routers and memory interfaces are usually arranged in a simple mesh for ease of chip layout and integration.

In this following section, we first examine the chip-scale photonic interconnects architecture, which is a reliable circuit-switched optical mesh, and then we describe the coherency management scheme for the many-core SMP processor.

3.1 Optical Circuit Switching with Aggregated Traffic

Due the absence of optical logic devices, reliable optical data transmissions are generally managed by an extra electrical control layer. Our hybrid system uses circuit-switching to control optical data delivery (see Fig. 4). In our network, an electric control network is used to provide a mechanism for setting up and tearing down optical end-to-end paths. If an LLC node wants to communicate with off-chip memory, a SETUP message is sent to reserve the optical paths; A BLOCKING message is returned to the LLC if some parts of the path are currently reserved by another circuit; An ACK message is returned if the path successfully makes it to the target memory pool. A TEARDOWN message is sent from the original LLC to release optical paths after data messages are transmitted along the optical paths.

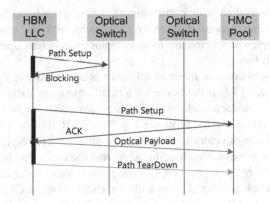

Fig. 4. Optical transmission based on circuit-switching.

Traffic aggregation is used to improve bandwidth utilization and reduce power consumption of photonic links. Photonic links usually consume significant static energy in thermal tuning circuits and optical laser sources, which can be much higher than the static energy cost of electrical links [8]. Hence, networks designed using photonic links need to have high utilization to offset the large static energy overhead. In our photonic mesh, as shown in Fig. 3, the processor-memory interface NIC at source LLC first buffer the memory requests based on certain rules (as described in Sect. 3.2) and then assemble them into large bursts based on the address of destination memory pool. After that, an electrical control packet is created and injected at NIC for path reservation before the optical transmission starts (see Fig. 4). The control packet contains important information for resource reservation, including the message size and destination id, which is used by optical switches to establish optical paths. Upon successful reservation, optical messages are directly transmitted from source NIC to memory pool. Once failure happens, a Blocking packet is transmitted back to the source, which again restarts the reservation procedures. Optical transmission from memory pool to LLC NIC interfaces works similarly.

In our proposed protocol, path reservation provides strong guarantees for reliable communication; Requests assembly improves overall bandwidth utilization. Specialized control unit at optical switches are responsible for processing path-setup requests. It makes its decisions by first processing the electronic control information and then reserves the output ports as well as wavelength channels before the optical messages arrive. Optical switches can be constructed with cascaded switching element based on micro-ring resonator devices [4]. They follow the commands of control units. Off-chip photonic IO signaling is achieved through lateral coupling by through inverse-taper optical mode converters [4]. In the destination memory pool, optical bursts of read requests are first disassembled and then transmitted to corresponding HMC channels; data responses are aggregated into optical messages and sent back to LLCs. Write requests with data are first disassembled and then directly sent to destination HMCs.

3.2 Coherence Control

Hardware support for system-wide cache coherency is of great importance for kilo-core SMP processor. In our proposed memory subsystem, address space sharding and directory-based coherency scheme are used to maintain coherent operations along the deep memory hierarchies.

The whole memory address space of kilo-core processor is evenly divided among all on-chip LLCs. Each LLC is the home for a small amount of memory addresses and processor operations on each address region are guaranteed to be coherent by specialized coherence manager (CCMGR, see Fig. 3). CCMGR adopts a directory-based coherency scheme. Each directory item maintains a sharer list for each cache line block. For example, when a processor reads address 'A', and the cache line block is first stored in corresponding cluster cache, home CCMGR records that cluster cache in its sharer list; when the 'A' block is evicted form a cluster cache, home CCMGR removes that entry in the sharer list. If there exists a copy on another cluster cache, home CCMGR will issue a snoop-and-fetch-data request to that cluster and send the snoop response to the source core when it processes a following read operation on address 'A'. A processor write operation can continue only after CCMGR invalidates all other copies by sending snoop-and-invalidate requests to target cluster caches according to the sharers list (Fig. 5).

For photonic transmission, traffic aggregation can improve bandwidth utilization and reduce power consumption of optical links, but there are some constraints on

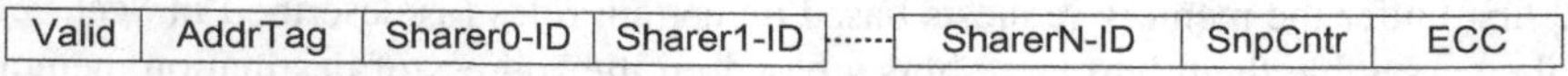

Valid	AddrTag	Sharer0-ID	Sharer1-ID	......	SharerN-ID	SnpCntr	ECC

Fig. 5. Directory contents for an address block.

memory order and coherence in the proposed interconnection system. In each timing slot, burst aggregation must work in the first-in-first-out mode; a memory request should not surpass its preceding requests from the same source LLC. Besides, the assembly process must preserve the ordering requirement of Read-after-Write, Write-after-Write, as well as Write-after-Read [12]; Continuous read or write requests which have RAW, WAW, or WAR dependence should not be packaged into the same burst and must be put into two photonic bursts. Ordering requirement is preserved all along the whole path form LLC down to memory pool; response data for read requests also follow the FIFO order when they are transmitted from off-chip pool to on-chip LLC.

The benefit of CCMGR in our architecture is two-fold. It will reduce off-chip memory accesses by issuing on-chip "snoop-and-fetch-data" requests according to sharers list in the directory. Second, it can provide strong ordering support for memory operations and perform optimal scheduling for off-chip memory traffic. Both will help us improve memory performances of kilo-core systems.

4 Simulation and Results

We study the performance of aforementioned hybrid optical interconnects (HOIS, see Fig. 3) against a baseline 2D concentrated mesh electric network (CMesh). In both systems, a 256-core processor is considered; 8 cores with private L1 cache and a shared L2 cache constitute a cluster; HBMs are used as LLCs; HMCs are used as off-chip memory pools. The processor has a 44-bit physical address space, which is evenly split into 16 regions. 32 clusters caches and 16 LLCs are connected by on-chip electric meshes. The only difference is that a LLC in CMesh is directly connected to an exclusive off-chip HMC memory pool using electrical serial IOs while LLCs in HOIS are connected to off-chip HMCs using photonic circuit-switched interconnects. In our HOIS, 4 memory pools are used (as shown in Fig. 3).

4.1 Simulation Setups

Our study uses the PhoenixSim simulator [10] which is a physical-level accurate simulation platform for optical network research. The HBM LLCs modules, HMC memory pool modules, coherence manager modules and an optical circuit switching module are developed and integrated into the platform. Optical components models are built on a detailed physical-layer library that has been characterized and validated through the physical measurement of fabricated devices. The components include modulators, photo-detectors, waveguides (straight, bending, crossing), filters, and switching elements. The behavior of these devices are characterized and modeled at runtime by attributes such as insertion loss, crosstalk, delay, and power dissipation. The ORION 2.0 power dissipation model [11] is used for electronic router in electrical meshes.

Important parameters used for simulations are summarized in Table 1. The parameters for both networks have been chosen for power-efficient configurations.

Table 1. Optical and electrical parameters.

Configuration	CMesh	HOIS
Cluster cache size	2M	2M
HBM Channels and density	2 × 2 Gb	2 × 2 Gb
HMC memory pool		
# Cubes x #Links per pool	2 × 8	2 × 8
Serial IO	10 Gbps	10 Gbps
Cube bandwidth	320 GBps	320 GBps
Photonic Interconnects		
Data rate	NA	10 Gbps
Resonator witching time	NA	30 ps
Detector energy	NA	50 fJ/bit

4.2 Simulation Results for Synthetic Traces

Synthetic traces help us identify system metrics, such as energy savings and inter-connect delays. The synthetic traces used in the simulations include the uniform and the hotspot. In the uniform traffic pattern, each LLC sends memory requests to all LLCs with the same probability. In the hotspot traffic pattern, one LLC is designated as hotspot, which receives requests from all LLCs in addition to the regular uniform traffic.

Figure 6 shows the metric of energy efficiency: performance gained for every unit of energy spent. As shown in Fig. 6, the traffics with small messages (64 Bytes per cache-line) perform poorly on photonic processor-memory networks. The reason is that the large amount of static energy overhead of photonic devices cannot be compensated by small-size message transmission. So, we enlarge the message size (256 Bytes per cache-line) and perform the simulation again. As a result, the photonic network, HOIS,

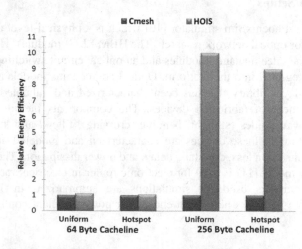

Fig. 6. Simulation results of relative energy efficiency gains.

achieves the most noticeable improvements in energy efficiency (more than 10 times) for uniform traffic. That is because large bulk data movement potentially offsets the static power overhead of photonic links, so the photonic memory access scheme, HOIS, shows higher energy efficiency than the electric CMesh.

Figure 7 shows the results of average transaction latency. Particularly, HOIS shows a moderate amount of latency reduction, i.e., 10.5%–15.9% against CMesh. We find that these performance gains mainly come from the smooth pass-through of optical links for off-chip access in HOIS, while the overhead of electric serial IOs in Cmesh incur larger transaction delays.

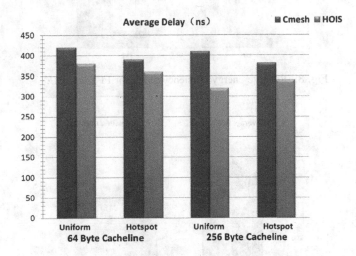

Fig. 7. Simulation results of average delay.

4.3   Simulation Results for Scientific Application Traces

Two applications are considered: fast fourier transform (FFT) and LU factorization (LU). Both come from the SPLASH-2 benchmark [19]. These applications represent typical features of scientific applications. We collect their traces using Graphite simulator [20], which accurately models the memory subsystems (including cache hierarchies with full cache coherence). Memory traces from Graphite are fed into our modules to evaluate the proposed architecture HOIS against CMesh. Default datasets of FFT and LU are scaled appropriately to ensure that statistical values converge to a stable state after long run. Message size in our simulation setup for FFT and LU is 256 bytes per cache line.

Figure 8 shows the simulation results of energy efficiency for FFT and LU traces. Our proposed architecture HOIS achieves noticeable improvements (more than 6 times) against CMesh. Figure 9 shows the results of average transaction latency. Our HOIS shows a latency reduction of 11%–12% against CMesh. Simulation results for real workload traces show almost the same trend as that of synthetic ones. In HOIS, improvements on energy efficiency are contributed mainly by high bandwidth optical

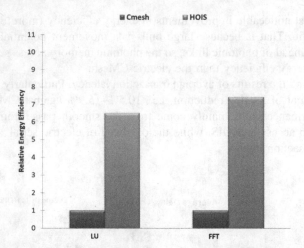

Fig. 8. Relative energy efficiency gains for FFT and LU.

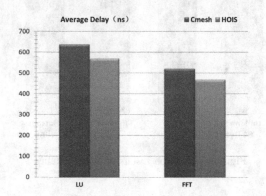

Fig. 9. Results of average delay for FFT and LU.

transmission between HBM LLCs and off-chip HMC memory pools. Performance advances in transaction latency are caused by both optical transmission and reduced off-chip memory accesses due to on-chip filtering of CCMGR.

Our simulation methodology suffers generally from some drawbacks. Only memory traces are studied. A unified environment (including compiler chain, system call support, detailed cache coherence operations) for full system simulation is missing. Many aspects of system runtime have been abstracted away at a higher level. Nevertheless, using the physically-accurate network-level simulation environment, the results still highlight the advantages of our hybrid architecture over conventional electrical schemes in terms of energy savings and communication latencies.

5 Conclusions and Future Work

This paper proposes a hybrid photonic architecture for processor-memory communications. Bandwidth-efficient circuit-switched photonic transmission is used for memory access between HBM last-level caches and off-chip HMC memory pools. Simulations with workload traces show that our network achieves considerable improvements in terms of network latency and power consumption. These performance gains are almost the same as that in our previous study [15]. The main difference is that our previous scheme exploits photonic burst-switching for optical transmission. Other aspects, e.g. detailed cache hierarchies and evaluation of more real workloads are under study.

Acknowledgement. This work is supported by the National Natural Science Foundation of China under Grant 61402502, Grant 61402497 and Grant 61472432, and in part by HGJ under Grant 2018ZX01029-103.

References

1. Schulte, M.J., Ignatowski, M., Loh, G.H., et al.: Achieving exascale capabilities through heterogeneous computing. IEEE Micro **35**(4), 26–36 (2015)
2. Borkar, S.: Thousand core chips a technology perspective. In: Proceedings of 44th ACM/IEEE Design Automation Conference, pp. 746–749 (2007)
3. Sanchez, D., et al.: An analysis of on-chip interconnection networks for large-scale chip multiprocessors. ACM Trans. Archit. Code Optim. **7**(1), 4 (2010)
4. Dong, P., et al.: Silicon photonic devices and integrated circuits. Nanophotonics **3**, 215–228 (2014)
5. Iyer, S.S.: Three-dimensional integration: an industry perspective. MRS Bull. **40**(03), 225–232 (2015)
6. JEDEC Homepage. https://www.jedec.org/. Accessed 21 June 2017
7. HMC Homepage. http://www.hybridmemorycude.org/. Accessed 21 June 2017
8. Shacham, A., Bergman, K., Carloni, L.P.: Photonic networks-on-chip for future generations of chip multiprocessors. IEEE Trans. Comput. **57**(9), 1246–1260 (2008)
9. Vantrease, D., et al.: Corona: system implications of emerging nanophotonic technology. In: Proceedings of 35th International Symposium on Computer Architecture, pp. 153–164 (2008)
10. Chan, J., et al.: PhoenixSim: a simulator for physical-layer analysis of chip-scale photonic interconnection networks. In: Proceedings on Design, Automation & Test in Europe (2010)
11. Kahng, A.B., et al.: ORION 2.0: a fast and accurate NoC power and area model for early-stage design space exploration. In: Proceedings on Design, Automation & Test in Europe (2009)
12. Sorin, D.J., et al.: A Primer on Memory Consistency and Cache Coherence. Synthesis Lectures on Computer Architecture #16. Morgan & Claypool Publishers, San Rafael (2011)
13. Feng, C., Lu, Z., Jantsch, A., Zhang, M., Xing, Z.: Addressing transient and permanent faults in NoC with efficient fault-tolerant deflection router. IEEE Trans. Very Large Scale Integr. (VLSI) Syst. **21**(6), 1053–1066 (2013)
14. Feng, C., Lu, Z., Jantsch, A., Zhang, M., Yang, X.: Support efficient and fault-tolerant multicast in bufferless network-on-chip. IEICE Trans. Inf. Syst. **E95-D**(4), 1052–1061 (2012)

15. Feng, Q., Peng, C., Ren, S., Zhou, H., Deng, R.: A high throughput power-efficient optical memory subsystem for kilo-core processor. In: Xu, W., Xiao, L., Li, J., Zhang, C., Zhu, Z. (eds.) NCCET 2017. CCIS, vol. 600, pp. 52–62. Springer, Singapore (2018). https://doi.org/10.1007/978-981-10-7844-6_6

16. Ahmed, A.B., Meyer, M.C., Okuyama, Y., et al.: Efficient router architecture, design and performance exploration for many-core hybrid photonic network-on-chip (2D-PHENIC). In: International Conference on Information Science and Control Engineering, pp. 202–206 (2015)

17. Kodi, A.K., et al.: Scalable power-efficient kilo-core photonic-wireless NoC architectures. In: International Parallel and Distributed Processing Symposium, pp. 1010–1019 (2018)

18. Meyer, M.C., Okuyama, Y., Abdallah, A.B., et al.: A power estimation method for mesh-based photonic NoC routing algorithms. In: International Symposium on Computing and Networking, pp. 451–453 (2016)

19. Woo, S.C., et al.: The SPLASH-2 programs: characterization and methodological considerations. In: International Symposium on Computer Architecture, vol. 23, no. 2, pp. 24–36 (1995)

20. Miller, J.E., et al.: Graphite: a distributed parallel simulator for multicores. In: 16th IEEE Symposium on High-Performance Computer Architecture, January 2010

CoEM: A Software and Hardware Co-design Event Management System for Middlebox

Jianguo Gou[1(✉)], Wenwen Li[1], Jie Qiu[1,2], Hu Lv[1], and Teng Ma[1]

[1] Jiuquan Satellite Launch Centre in China, Jiuquan 732750, China
792874862@qq.com
[2] Zhejiang University, Hangzhou 310000, China

Abstract. Stateful middleboxes play a very important role in the security and performance of the network. However, they mostly exist as separate devices in network and distributed in different topological nodes. By analyzing the packet processing of these middleboxes, we find that they have many common functions, such as the management of the flow states, the parsing of the packet protocol. The redundant development of these functions not only causes great waste of human and material resources, but also involves relevant expertise, which is extremely error-prone.

To address these issues, we introduce CoEM, a hardware and software co-design event management system for the middlebox. In CoEM, we implement flow classification and flow state management, and we also generate basic events in the protocol parsing process. Basic events generate user-defined events through event generators. Different middleboxes can be implemented by defining these event handling methods. Since multiple middleboxes define event handling methods separately, we set priority to ensure that packets are passed through the right middlebox order. We use the event management system to achieve a stateful firewall. Performance testing shows that the packet processing speed has been improved.

Keywords: Event · Middlebox · Stateful · Network function virtualization

1 Introduction

Middlebox is an intermediate box that acts on the data path of the source and destination hosts, which is different from the standard features contained in the IP router. Middlebox plays an important role in data centers and enterprise networks, primarily for network performance, monitoring, and so on. Common middlebox includes address translation (NAT [1]), load balance [2], firewall, network intrusion detection system (NIDS [3]) and network intrusion prevention systems (NIPS).

However, the middlebox in the market is mostly based on custom ASICs [4], which has fixed function. If new features want to be added to middlebox, a new ASIC has to be re-selected. If there is no ready-made ASIC available in the market, a new ASIC has to be customized. Besides, the development cycle of the ASIC is generally two years. Due to the use of customized ASICs, the scalability of the middlebox is limited. At the same time, since the middleboxes used in the network come from different developers

© Springer Nature Singapore Pte Ltd. 2019
W. Xu et al. (Eds.): NCCET 2019, CCIS 1146, pp. 59–77, 2019.
https://doi.org/10.1007/978-981-15-1850-8_6

and their standards and protocols are different, it is difficult to manage these middleboxes uniformly, which invisibly increases the inconvenience of network maintenance.

With the appearance of NFV [5–10], some software-implemented middlebox has gradually come into vision. The software middlebox runs on a commodity server [11], using protocol-independent languages [12–15], unifying interfaces, service chains to realize different applications [16–21]. It can make up the shortcomings of the hardware middlebox. However, the software middlebox also has its own disadvantages.

Development Redundancy. In the process of software middlebox implementation, each stateful middlebox implementation must repeat the design procedure, such as flow state management [22–24], protocol analysis, etc. However, such functions are almost same in each middlebox, so that the repetitive process costs human and material resources.

Low Performance. Since all the functions are implemented by software, it is not as good as the hardware middlebox in terms of performance and stability, mainly in relatively high software process latency.

Aiming at these problems, it is meaningful to pack some of the general functions of middlebox and provide APIs for upper-layer applications to reduce development difficulties. Since it is hard to develop middlebox based on flow, so we develop a kind of middlebox base on events rather than low-level packet/flow processing. For the reusability of codes, the reuse of event as the basic unit is proposed by analysis of network function. Thus a reusable event management system is provided through a software and hardware collaborative design. We achieve a stateful firewall network function by using the event management system, establish a test environment, and do performance tests on the implemented network functions. The performance tests mainly focus on packet processing latency and throughput. The results show that the use of the event management system can easily realize the network function and improve the processing speed of packets.

2   Related Work

Currently, there are many researches on middleboxes which run on commodity servers. These studies usually use software to implement network functions. In the process of implementing a new middlebox, it is generally necessary to start from packets capturing, packets parsing and packets forwarding. The implementation of these operations is very complicated, and the related operations of each middlebox are basically similar. In order to improve the efficiency of middlebox development and promote code reusability, the related researches can be divided into the following three aspects:

(1) Flow Management Support

In the development of middlebox, flow management [25] is the most basic, and the implementation of flow management is quite complicated. Therefore, some studies have separately extracted the flow management functions and made them into libraries for use in developing middlebox. Libnids [26] is a professional programming interface for network intrusion detection development that uses libpcap [27], so it has the ability to capture packets. At the same time, libnids can recombine TCP flows, so libnids can be used to analyze various protocols based on TCP. Libnids also provides the ability to reorganize IP fragments, as well as port scan detection and anomaly packet inspection. Libnids is a flow-level middlebox library that allows you to build middlebox applications. However, its processing level is below L4, and it is up to the developer to write logic for L4 or above applications.

(2) Modular Middlebox Development

In order to improve the development efficiency of middlebox, a lot of modular middlebox developments have appeared. The network function is divided into different function modules which use unified interfaces for communication. There are three ways to program these function modules. One is to use a single structure mode. The network function is implemented independently on a device or platform. This method is tightly coupled and has poor expansion capability, but the performance is relatively high. The second way is to use the pipeline mode to arrange the function modules according to the pipeline to realize the network function. This mode can realize the sharing of the modules, but it must solve the correlation problems between the modules, such as data correlation and control correlation. For example, James W. Anderson proposed xOMB [28] which is implemented in this mode. It is a flexible, scalable, programmable, open implementation of middlebox running on a commodity server. However, xOMB mainly focuses on the L7 agent, and complete the initialization and termination of the connection through the BSD socket, so it can not complete the development of the middlebox (like NAT and firewall) which is below L7. The third way is to use the service chain to complete the connection between modules by issuing policy configuration. It is easy to change the network functions, but need to handle many problems which appear when you dynamically define function.

(3) Development of the Operating Platform

Bro [29] intrusion detection system has flow management, analysis of flow, it can generate some events and complete the application logic function by defining the processing handlers of these events. However, the granularity of Bro's event is very coarse, it is only good to support intrusion detection related functions. Although Bro provides the support for the redefinition of events, but it is difficult to redefine events through the plugin [30].

Muhammad Jamshed et al. designed mOS [31], a reusable network stack for stateful flow processing in middlebox applications. The API it defines allows developers to focus on core application logic rather than dealing with low-level packet or flow processing. mOS supports modular development of stateful middlebox, greatly reducing the development effort of source code lines. In the Microboxes [32] event management system, the event is hierarchically divided. The event has the inheritance relationship between the parent event and the child event. Unlike the mOS, the event is simply divided into basic events and custom events. Some middleboxes (such as firewall) will match many rules in the implementation of functions, but there is no implementation of the rule-matching-event in mOS and microboxes.

The VFP [33] proposed by Daniel Firestone is a virtual filtering platform for the host SDN in the public cloud environment to filter the port traffic. It mainly acts on the ports of the virtual switch. For each port, there are two processing stages, which is ingress and egress. Each port has multiple layers, and each layer represents a network policy (such as ACL). VFP is implemented based on flow, most of its functions in the layer are functions of the L3–L4 layer.

Through analysis of the current researches, we find that the middlebox development architecture is mostly in the software layer, lack of research on hardware and software coordination architecture; API for middlebox development is either the processing interface below the L4, or the L7 socket interface, L4 to L7 programming interfaces are lacking; Middlebox's packet processing is mainly concentrated in software. For some forwarding-type Middlebox, the processing latency is large. Meanwhile, the research of hardware accelerated packet processing is lacking. Therefore, we mainly conduct in-depth research on event generation, event-based middlebox development model, and hardware accelerated packet processing.

3 Event Management Technology

In order to improve the efficiency of middlebox development, developers divide network functions into multiple functional modules, and organize these functional modules to implement application functions. However, this method requires developers to be familiar with the entire middlebox processing, This puts high demands on developers. At the same time, changes to the functional modules affect all orchestrated network functions, which is not flexible enough. So we do research on middlebox development technology which is based on events.

3.1 Abstraction of the Event

Middlebox is developed based on events, from the developer's view, the input they see is an event, and the application function of the event is implemented by defining the event handler function, which greatly reduces the development difficulty of the developer and reduces the development error rate, because he do not care about complex protocol parsing.

Definition of Event
When we parse a network packet, if it is a TCP SYN request packet, we define that a TCP_ATTEMPT event has occurred. When we receive an http packet, we say that an HTTP event has occurred. Therefore, we define an event which is happened with satisfying one or more conditions.

In general network application system programming, when parsing a packet, it is usually necessary to judge the condition and perform the corresponding action. As shown in Fig. 1, when the event one is satisfied, action one needs to be performed. Similarly, when the event that satisfies condition two occurs, action two is executed immediately. This kind of thing that satisfies a certain condition and needs to perform the corresponding action immediately is called a signal.

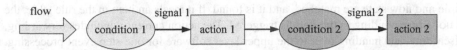

Fig. 1. Schematic diagram of signal processing

Different from the signal, as shown in Fig. 2, when parsing the data flow, it judges whether the condition one is satisfied and recorded, and then it judges whether the condition two is satisfied and recorded. When all the conditions are judged, the result record is taken out, and the corresponding action is done. We call this thing that satisfies a certain condition and the corresponding action is executed asynchronously to be an event.

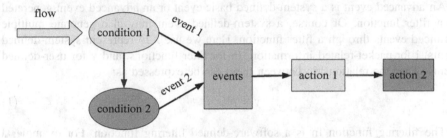

Fig. 2. Schematic diagram of event processing

Basic Event

The basic events are divided into two categories, which are recorded as Class I basic events and Class II basic events. Class I basic events are common events provided by the system itself, such as timeout event, TCP connection establishment event and so on. Some basic events of class I are listed in Table 1. The event id of the basic event of class I is specified as 1 to 100.

Table 1. Class I basic events of event management system.

Event	Description
UNIMAN_ON_PKT_IN	Received a packet
UNIMAN_ON_CONN_START	Connection request, receive a syn packet
UNIMAN_ON_HALF_CONN	Half-connection
UNIMAN_ON_CONN_SETUP	Connection establishment
UNIMAN_ON_TIMEOUT	Connection timed out
UNIMAN_ON_CONN_END	Connection closed

Class II basic events are generated by rule matching. For example, a rule is <SrcIP, DstIP, SrcPort, DstPort, protocol, state, action, eventid>. A packet is analyzed, its 5-

tuple and flow state are matched, and it is found. If it meets an item in the rule table, the action corresponding to the item is triggered. The action currently includes forwarding, discarding, and handing over to the upper layer software for one-step event processing. When submitted to the upper layer software for processing, the event ID is passed to the software to perform corresponding event processing. The event ID of the basic event of Class II is 101–4000.

Advanced Event

Since the basic events defined by the system are mostly L4 events, some Middlebox applications require L7 content analysis or other more granular events, such as events to detect 3 duplicate SYN packets or monitor https requests. System-defined class I basic events are difficult to provide, and the class II basic events we provide are not available, so we need to provide a user-defined event interface to filter basic events to generate advanced events.

An advanced event is a system-defined basic event or an advanced event generated by a filter function. Of course, a system-defined event may also generate multiple advanced events through a filter function. Here we use x to represent system-defined events, i for packet-related information, fn for filter functions, and y for user-defined events. Then the relationship between them can be expressed as:

$$y = fn(x, i) \tag{1}$$

The filtering function fn is a software-defined filtering function. For example, a stateful firewall, its policy is to allow the internal network to access the external network, and to prohibit the external network from accessing the internal network. In this case, it is necessary to generate an internal network to the external network UNIMAN_IN_TO_OUT event and the external event UNIMAN_OUT_TO_IN from the external network to the internal network through the UNIMAN_ON_CONN_START basic event.

3.2   Middlebox Application Development

The development of network functions is accomplished by defining basic events provided by the system and user-defined advanced event handlers. In application development, developers only need to define <event, event-handler> pairs, First define the handler event-handler, then use the registration function API to associate events with event handlers. When the event is generated in the system, it will go to the registered-table to find the event handler corresponding to the event and execute it.

If the firewall is to allow the internal network to access the external network and the external network is prohibited from accessing the internal network, the advanced events UNIMAN_IN_TO_OUT and UNIMAN_OUT_TO_IN need to be generated through the UNIMAN_ON_CONN_START event. As shown in Fig. 3, the developer first needs to write two filter functions, IsInToOut() and IsOutToIn(), which are used to determine whether the TCP connection is from the internal network or the external network. The two filter functions are processed in the UNIMAN_ON_CONN_START event. When the filter function condition of the function is satisfied, a UNIMAN_IN_TO_OUT or

UNIMAN_OUT_TO_IN event is generated, and then the event handler corresponding to the event is executed. If the generated event is UNIMAN_IN_TO_OUT, the PassPacket() function is executed to allow the message to pass. Of course, in the list we have raised, these two events can not happen at the same time. If the UNIMAN_OUT_TO_IN event is changed to the UNIMAN_HTTP_REQUEST event, it can be happened with UNIMAN_IN_TO_OUT event at the same time, respectively, to execute the processing function of two events.

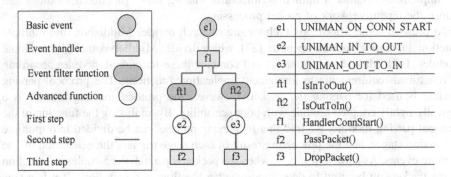

Fig. 3. Event-action diagram

Different network functions have different processing priorities when processing packets, such as firewall and NAT. Packets sent from the intranet to the external network must pass through the firewall first, and then pass through NAT. The response packets of the flow must pass NAT to translate the address, then pass the firewall to filter packets.

For our event-driven network functions, each network function defines an event handler for the event of interest. Different network functions may define their own event handlers for the same event. For example, firewalls, NATs, and load balancers define the UNIMAN_ON_CONN_START event. We assign a different ID to each middlebox. This ID is also used as the priority of the middlebox. The larger the value, the higher the priority, ensuring that a packet passes through the right order of multiple middleboxes.

3.3   Event-Level Reuse

In order to improve the efficiency of network application development, it is an important method to increase code reuse. At present, code reuse is mostly realized by functional components or function modules. By providing users with interfaces, users can arrange components or modules according to their own functional requirements. However, this method reuses the coarser code size, resulting in insufficient flexibility. To change one of the functional modules, other network application functions programmed with the module may have a huge impact, so we consider more fine-grained code sharing, at the same time reduce the repeated execution of the code.

Network Function Analysis

For each Middlebox, their general packet processing has packet capture, packet header parsing, refactoring session state, parsing application layer protocol, and so on. If a flow is processed by multiple Middlebox applications, such as an http flow to pass firewall, load balancing and NAT, each application must perform packet header parsing and session state reconfiguration for the http flow, and these Middlebox applications are implemented under a unified architecture, sharing these functional modules can reduce the repetitive work of packet processing.

At present, some Middlebox architecture research divides Middlebox into multiple functional modules, such as openbox [27], which divides Middlebox into 10 functional modules. Each Middlebox can select and combine these functional modules according to functional requirements to implement application functions. The protocol parsing module is used for parsing the packet. However, the protocol parsing module is a logically tightly coupled module with poor scalability. By analyzing the function of the protocol parsing module, we find that its parsing process can be divided into multiple processing stages, and the processing result of each stage triggers the generation of one or more events. As shown in Fig. 4, when the packet is parsed, the 5-tuples information of the packet can be used to determine whether the flow is a new flow. If it is a new flow, a new_packet event is generated. The packet that generates the event is further parsed to determine whether it is a new UDP flow or a new TCP flow. If it is a new TCP flow, the number of connections is counted. When a certain threshold is exceeded, a dos_attack event is generated. By processing the dos_attack event, such as blocking all subsequent packets of the flow, the dos attack can be prevented.

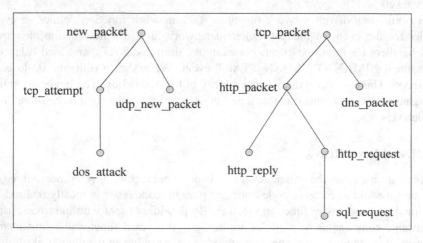

Fig. 4. Packet parsing event topology.

For some complex Middlebox applications, they require not only coarse-grained events such as new_packet event and tcp_attempt event, but also finer-grained events. For example, in NIDS, it needs to perform log analysis on the establishment of http. It also detects whether there is a SQL injection attack in the http packet. In the process of packet parsing, events such as http_packet, http_request, http_reply, and sql_request are generated.

Therefore, we refine the Middlebox packet parsing module into an event management module, and turn the tightly coupled protocol parsing module shared by Middlebox into a shared event management module to reduce the repeated parsing of the packet by sharing more fine-grained events. For example, firewalls, NATs, and load balancers need to process a new network flow, they need to resolve the new_packet event. The firewall finds that a new_packet event is generated, checking the firewall rules to determine whether the flow passes or is blocked. The NAT receives the new_packet event, assigns the translated address and port number, and modifies the header of the message. The load balancer receives the new_packet event and determines the port to which the packet and subsequent packets of the flow are forwarded according to the traffic information of each port.

When we parse the packet of a new flow, the matching field satisfies a certain condition, an event is generated to indicate a process result of parsing the packet. Events can be shared by multiple Middleboxes, so that packets are parsed only once when passing through multiple Middleboxes, it speeds up packet processing.

Reuse of Events

The reuse of events has two meanings: one is that an event is used by multiple Middlebox applications. As shown in Table 2, we list the needs of the 5 Middlebox for 7 events. As for the new_packet event, it is generated when a new flow appears in the network. After receiving the new flow, the firewall should judge whether the flow passes or is blocked according to the rules; if the NAT receives the new flow, it must allocate a new IP address and port number; the load balancer needs to allocate the forwarding path of the new flow. NIDS and NIPS are required to record the network activity of the new flow. For application layer events such as sql_attack events, firewalls, NATs, and load balancers are not required, but both NIDS and NIPS are required to detect sql attacks.

Table 2. Analysis of event types in middlebox.

Application	every_packet	new_packet	tcp_attempt	tcp_timeout	http_new_packet	sql_attack	soft_attack
Firewall	×	√	√	√	√	×	×
NAT	×	√	×	√	×	×	×
Load balancer	×	√	×	×	×	×	×
NIDS	√	√	√	√	√	√	√
NIPS	√	√	√	√	√	√	√

Another meaning is that another event is generated by filtering conditions from one event, thus avoiding an event to resolve the judgment from the beginning. As shown in Fig. 4, when we determine the http_reply and http_request events, we start with the http_packet event, so there is no need to re-determine whether the packet is a http protocol packet.

Since the filter function of an event can be a small logic function, we use event reuse to be more granular and more flexible than component reuse.

Event Processing Dependency

Using the event and event handler function to implement Middlebox, there is a packet that may correspond to multiple events. For example, the parsing of a packet triggers the TCP_PACKET event and the SEQ_ERROR event, and we know that when the seq number of a packet is out of bounds, we think of it as an illegal packet and do not process the TCP_PACKET event. Therefore, we added priority to the event. When a packet triggers multiple events, it is processed according to the priority.

For a processing packet, it can determine whether the packet passes after all the events have been processed. However, when an event is processed to determine that the packet is discarded, the packet can be discarded without further processing. Therefore, in the implementation, a packet passing/discarding flag is designed, and each time an event is executed, the flag bit modification and operation are executed. The packet is forwarded only when all events have been executed and the last flag is 1.

4 Design and Implementation of CoEM System

In this section, we will elaborate on the structure of the CoEM system and the implementation techniques of the hardware and software. The network packet forwarding activities are converted into event activities through the CoEM system, so users can implement middlebox application by defining these event activities without starting from the packet parsing.

4.1 Design of CoEM System

The CoEM system is shown in Fig. 5 and is divided into two major parts, the software part and the hardware part. The hardware part implements the class I basic event generator and arranges it into the hardware programming platform, the other four modules of the hardware part are provided by the programming platform. Packets are parsed by the class I event generator. For example, the TCP protocol is parsed to determine the state of the packet flow corresponding to packets. When the class I event generator resolves the protocol, the state of the flow is tracked and converted to meet the development of stateful network applications.

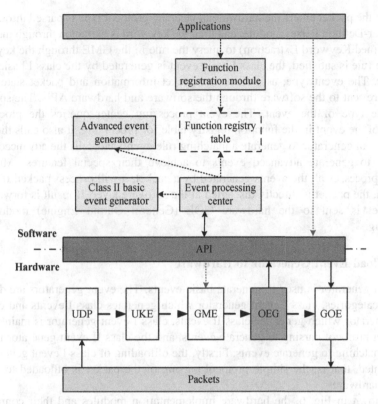

Fig. 5. The architecture of event management system

The software part mainly consists of four modules: function registration module, advanced event generator and class II basic event generator and event processing center. The function registration module registers a user-defined event handler to the event-handler table so that the event parsing module can query the event handler based on the event type. The advanced event generator generates high-level events through user-defined event filtering functions based on basic events uploaded by hardware or generated high-level events. The class II event generator generates the corresponding event mainly through the configured rule information, such as an event that satisfies a 5-tuples message. The event processing center module parses the event type according to the information uploaded by the hardware, queries the event-handler table according to the event type, and calls the processing function execution module to complete the event processing.

Users register the application-related event handler through the event handler registration interface provided by the function registration module, and send certain configuration information to the hardware through the interface provided by the hardware platform, such as the matching rule in the GME (General Matching Engine) module.

When the packet enters the hardware device, the protocol type is parsed through the UDP (User-Defined Parse) module, and then the keyword is extracted through the UKE (User-defined Keyword Extraction) to query the rule in the GME through the keyword. When the rule is satisfied, the class I basic event is generated by the class I basic event generator. The event type, as well as the packet information and packet state information, are sent to the software through the software and hardware APIs. The software parses the type of the event. The event processing center queries the processing function of the event in the function registry table for processing, it also calls the class II basic event generator to generate a matching rule event, and calls the advanced event generator to generate advanced events to achieve their special features. After the software processes all the events generated by a packet, it will process packet. If action is discard, the packet is directly discarded at the software layer. If result is forwarding, the packet is sent to the hardware GOE (General Output Engine) module for forwarding.

4.2   Offload Event Generator to Hardware

The event generator is used to generate basic events. The event generators are divided into two categories, class I event generator which generates class I events and class II event generator which generates class II events. class I event generator is mainly used for packet protocol parsing to generate events, and the class II event generator is used for rule matching to generate events. Firstly, the offloading of class I event generator is implemented, that is, the simple protocol parsing of the packet is offloaded to implement in hardware.

As shown in Fig. 6, the hardware implementation modules and their connection relationships are presented in the process diagram. The function of UDP module is to analyze the packet protocol according to the user-specific processing requirements, and estimate whether the packet satisfies the user-defined attribute classification, thereby generating a packet feature vector (PFV) for subsequent control packet processing. The user-defined keyword extraction module obtains the keywords of the packet according to the feature vector of the packet, so as to perform subsequent keyword matching. The general table lookup engine performs a table lookup based on the keywords generated by the user-defined keyword extraction module, and then obtains information that controls the packet processing action and the output action. The General Output Engine (GOE) implements shaping of packet outputs based on token buckets, such as limiting traffic to specific CPU software UAs or protocol stacks, limiting traffic destined for specific ports to specific ports, and so on. The above four modules can be reused as function modules on the existing development platform. The main work we do in the hardware is to develop class I Event Generator (OEG), which mainly parses the packet, transforms the state information of the flow and uses events to describe the current state of the network. For example, if we receive a SYN packet, a UNIMAN_ON_CONN_START event will be generated.

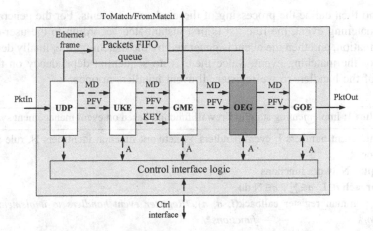

Fig. 6. The processing diagram of event generator in hardware

4.3 Software Section of Event Management System

The software part of the event management system is mainly responsible for parsing the basic events of class I generated by the hardware. Considering that the packet processing has a sequential relationship, we currently implement single thread packet processing. In the later implementation, we may consider using multi-core to generate multi-thread to process packets of different flows. Different flows are mapped to different cores for processing, and related packets of the same flow are mapped to the same core for processing. This avoids frequent state switching and ensures sequential processing of packets related to the same flow.

At the same time, the software part also needs to implement the strategy delivery, such as what kind of flow the above layer software cares about, what kind of events are concerned. These are all issued through policies to enable the related functions.

Since a packet may generate multiple events, we upload events in the form of a bitmap. For example, an 8-bit bitmap value is 00100001, which means that the packet generates two events. Event with id 1 represent the UNIMAN_ON_PKT_IN event and event with 6 indicate the UNIMAN_ON_CONN_END event has happened. Then we separately call the handler of these two events to execute.

The software part of the event management system needs to enhance the user's rich programming interface, so that users can easily implement their application functions through these programming interfaces. In the implementation process, we consider registering user-defined event handlers into the event management system using function registration.

4.4 Implementation of Firewall Function

The stateful firewall implementation based on the event management system is shown in Fig. 7. First we determine which basic events are needed, define the handlers for these basic events, then determine which advanced events are needed, define the filter functions, call these filter functions in the relevant event handlers, generate advanced events, and then define the processing of these advanced events. For the generation of the rule matching event, the rule list is first instantiated according to the user-defined rule information, and then the event is generated by the matching rule, finally define the handler for the matching event. Since there is no sequential dependency on the registration of the handler, so we register all event handlers at once.

Algorithm 1: Implementing stateful firewall function based on event management system

Input: event numbers I, event handlers $\sum$, network function identifiers N, rule information R.

Output: Network functions.

1   **foreach** $i \in$ I, $\sigma \in \sum$, $n \in$ N **do**
2   uniman_register_callback(i, σ, n);/*Register event handlers to implement network   functions*/
3   **foreach** $r \in$ R **do**
4   add_rule(r); /*Add network function rules, instantiate rule list*/
5   receive_packet_handle();/*Receive packets to process*/

Fig. 7. Implementation of stateful firewall function

Figure 8 shows the processing of packets in the stateful firewall. First, the packet which has been parsed by the hardware is captured, and the state information of the current packet corresponding flow (line 2) is obtained; the event type is generated by the loop analysis, which is processed in turn (lines 3–4); The current packet information instantiates a rule object, system searches the rule table through the object. If a hit rule is found, it will return the matching event id, and processes the rule matching event (lines 5–7); finally, it determines the packet to forward or discard (line 8).

Algorithm 2: packet processing in the stateful firewall

Input: Input packets $\sum$, status S corresponding to the packet or flow, event E generated by the hardware.

Output: Output packets $\sum'$.

1   **foreach** $\sigma \in \sum$ **do**
2   s = uniman_get_currentFlowState();/*get the status of the current packet corresponding to the flow, s is the state of the flow*/
3   **foreach** $e \in$ E **do**
4   event_handle(e,σ,s);/*handle event e*/
5   r = Rule(σ,s);/*instantiate a rule object based on the current packet*/
6   i = match_rule(r) ;/*Match the rule table and return the event id of the hit rule*/
7   event_handle(i,σ,s);/*handle events with event id i*/
8   process_packet(σ); /*After all events have been processed, the packet is processed.*/

Fig. 8. Stateful firewall packet processing

5 Evaluation

For middlebox, it is critical to meet the application needs of high-traffic networks. In performance test, we mainly tested latency and throughput.

5.1 Latency Test

In the latency test, we send packets of different byte lengths to test the processing latency in the stateful firewall. The packets of each byte length are sent 100,000 times, and the average value of the latency is calculated. The latency of processing the same packets was tested in a firewall based on the Bro system and iptable which is a common stateful firewall. The operating environments of Bro-based stateful firewall and iptables stateful firewall are the same as the CoEM environment. The computer is the Lenovo Y470. Its CPU is Intel(R) Core(TM) i5-2450M CPU@2.50 GHz, the memory is 4G, the network adapter is Broadcom NetLink(TM) Gigabit Ethernet, and the operating system is Ubuntu 16.04.

(1) **Latency Comparison between Stateful Firewall Based on CoEM and Stateful Firewall Based on Bro Event Management System.** Both firewalls are implemented based on an event management system. The implementation of firewall function is accomplished by defining event handlers. The latency comparison is shown in Fig. 9(a). We can see that latency achieved by CoEM is significantly lower than firewall based on the Bro event management system, because we implement complex TCP protocol parsing and state transition in the hardware, which improves the processing speed of the packet.

(2) **Latency Comparison between Stateful Firewall Based on CoEM and Iptables Stateful Firewall.** The stateful firewall based on CoEM implements the firewall function by defining event handlers. The iptables stateful firewall is also a stateful firewall, but its protocol parsing and the upper-layer application are coupled together, and there is no abstraction of events. The latency comparison is shown in Fig. 9(b), we can see that the latency of state firewall based on CoEM is significantly lower than the iptables stateful firewall. This shows that the definition of the event does not lead to more packet processing latency.

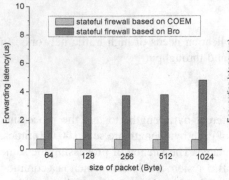 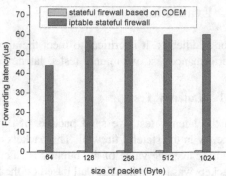

(a)Latency comparison between stateful firewall based on CoEM and stateful firewall based on Bro event management system.

(b)Latency comparison between stateful firewall based on CoEM and iptables stateful firewall.

Fig. 9. Latency test of stateful firewall

5.2 Throughput Test

The throughput of network function is an important indicator of device evaluation. In throughput test, we tested the maximum throughput of CoEM-based stateful firewall for packets of different byte lengths, as well as the throughput of firewall based on Bro system and iptable stateful firewall.

(1) **Throughput Comparison of Stateful Firewall Based on CoEM and Stateful Firewall Based on Bro Event Management System.** Both firewalls are implemented based on event management system. The implementation of firewall functions is accomplished by defining event handlers. The throughput comparison is shown in Fig. 10(a). We can see that the throughput of the stateful firewall implemented by CoEM is significantly higher than that of the stateful firewall based on the Bro event management system, because we implement complex TCP protocol parsing and state transition in the hardware, which improves the processing speed of the packet. Correspondingly, the throughput is improved. At the same time, some of the packets are forwarded directly through the hardware and are not sent to the software for processing, which is also a reason for improving throughput.

(2) **Throughput Comparison between Stateful Firewall Based on CoEM and Iptables Stateful Firewall.** The stateful firewall based on CoEM implements the firewall function by defining event handlers. The iptable stateful firewall is a common stateful firewall. Its protocol parsing and the upper-layer application are coupled together, and there is no abstraction of events. The throughout comparison is shown in Fig. 10(b), We can see that the throughput of the stateful firewall implemented by CoEM is similar to that of the iptable stateful firewall. This is because the iptable firewall uses multiple thread processing packets, while the current implementation of the CoEM-based stateful firewall is still single thread.

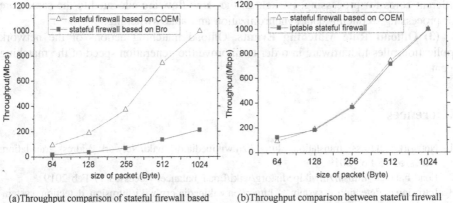

(a)Throughput comparison of stateful firewall based on CoEM and stateful firewall based on Bro event management system.

(b)Throughput comparison between stateful firewall based on CoEM and iptables stateful firewall.

Fig. 10. Throughput test of stateful firewall

6   Conclusion and Future Work

In this paper, we study the related development models of middlebox, design and implement an event management system for network middlebox, which is used to deal with practical problems such as complexity, repeated implementation and low performance. The system parses the packet activities in the network into different event activities, so developers can develop middlebox from events rather than packets. It can reduce time and effort to parse packets for developers, and simplify application development. At the same time, because the system uses event-level reuse, the reuse of functional modules is smaller and the code reuse rate is higher, which can reduce repetitive development work. Since some functions can be accelerated by hardware, we mainly offload the parsing of packets to hardware, which improves the performance of the network application. A stateful firewall is implemented based on CoEM event management system. Test results show that the CoEM event management system effectively simplifies development of middlebox and improves the performance of middlebox.

The event management system provides a good interface for the innovative development of middlebox applications, and developers can efficiently develop high-performance middlebox. However, we just implement fewer class I basic events, more events need to be implemented through user customization. Packet parsing is currently only by single thread with low performance. Future work will be carried out in the following aspects:

(1) **Provide More Class I Basic Events.** We will analyze a variety of middlebox functions, and offload more events which they share to hardware. It can reduce user-defined work, accelerate the generation of events and improve system performance.

(2) **Adopt Multi-core and Multi-threading.** The performance of single thread is limited. We consider using multi-core and multi-thread to distribute different flows to

different cores for processing. Packets of the same flow are allocated to the same core for processing, reducing data synchronization and state switching.

(3) Offload Rule Matching Events. Offload matching actions of the network application rules to hardware in order to improve the generation speed of the matching event.

References

1. Network address translation. https://zh.wikipedia.org/wiki/Network_address_translation. Accessed 15 Feb 2019
2. Load balance. https://zh.wikipedia.org/wiki/Load_balance. Accessed 17 Feb 2019
3. Intrusion detection system. https://en.wikipedia.org/wiki/Intrusion_detection_system. Accessed 22 Feb 2019
4. Application-specific integrated circuit. https://en.wikipedia.org/wiki/Application-specific_integrated_circuit. Accessed 24 Feb 2019
5. Network Function Virtualization(NFV); Architectural Framework. https://www.etsi.org/deliver/etsi_gs/NFV/001_099/002/01.02.01_60/gs_NFV002v010201p.pdf. Accessed 26 Feb 2019
6. Network Functions Virtualisation (NFV); Infrastructure Overview. https://www.etsi.org/deliver/etsi_gs/NFV-INF/001_099/001/01.01.01_60/gs_NFV-INF001v010101p.pdf. Accessed 26 Feb 2019
7. Network Functions Virtualisation (NFV); Virtual Network Functions Architecture. https://www.etsi.org/deliver/etsi_gs/NFV-SWA/001_099/001/01.01.01_60/gs_NFV-SWA001v010101p.pdf. Accessed 26 Feb 2019
8. Han, B., Gopalakrishnan, V., Ji, L.: Network function virtualization: challenges and opportunities for innovations. IEEE Commun. Mag. **53**(2), 90–97 (2015)
9. Mijumbi, R., Serrat, J., Gorricho, J.L.: Network function virtualization: state-of-the-art and research challenges. IEEE Commun. Surv. Tutor. **18**(1), 236–262 (2017)
10. Yi, B., Wang, X., Li, K.: A comprehensive survey of network function virtualization. Comput. Netw. **133**, 212–262 (2018)
11. Martins, J., Ahmed, M., Raiciu, C.: ClickOS and the art of network function virtualization. In: Networked Systems Design and Implementation, pp. 459–473 (2014)
12. Sivaraman, A., Kim, C., Krishnamoorthy, R.: DC.p4: programming the forwarding plane of a data-center switch. In: ACM Special Interest Group on Data Communication, p. 2 (2015)
13. Hancock, D., Der Merwe, J.E.: HyPer4: using P4 to virtualize the programmable data plane. In: Conference on Emerging Network Experiment and Technology, pp. 35–49 (2016)
14. Bosshart, P., Daly, D., Gibb, G.: P4: programming protocol-independent packet processors. In: ACM Special Interest Group on Data Communication, vol. 44, no. 3, pp. 87–95 (2014)
15. The P 4 Language Consortium. The P4 Language Specification. https://p4lang.github.io/p4-spec/p4-14/v1.0.4/tex/p4.pdf. Accessed 5 Mar 2019
16. Zave, P., Ferreira, R.A., Zou, X.K.: Dynamic service chaining with Dysco. In: ACM Special Interest Group on Data Communication, pp. 57–70 (2017)
17. Palkar, S., Lan, C., Han, S.: E2: a framework for NFV applications. In: Symposium on Operating Systems Principles, pp. 121–136 (2015)
18. Katsikas, G.P., Barbette, T., Kostic, D.: Metron: NFV service chains at the true speed of the underlying hardware. In: Networked Systems Design and Implementation, pp. 171–186 (2018)

19. Zhang, W., Liu, G., Zhang, W.: OpenNetVM: a platform for high performance network service chains. In: Workshop on Hot Topics in Middleboxes and Network Function Virtualization, pp. 26–31 (2016)
20. Gemberjacobson, A., Viswanathan, R., Prakash, C.: OpenNF: enabling innovation in network function control. In: ACM Special Interest Group on Data Communication, vol. 44, no. 4, pp. 163–174 (2015)
21. Katsikas, G.P., Enguehard, M., Kuźniar, M: SNF: synthesizing high performance NFV service chains. PeerJ, 1–30 (2016)
22. Bianchi, G., Bonola, M., Capone, A.: OpenState: programming platform-independent stateful openflow applications inside the switch. In: ACM Special Interest Group on Data Communication, vol. 44, no. 2, pp. 44–51 (2014)
23. Kablan, M., Alsudais, A., Keller, E., Le, F.: Stateless network functions: breaking the tight coupling of state and processing. In: 14th USENIX Symposium on Networked Systems Design and Implementation, pp. 97–111 (2017)
24. Zhu, S., Bi, J., Sun, C.: SDPA: enhancing stateful forwarding for software-defined networking. In: International Conference on Network Protocols, pp. 323–333 (2015)
25. Bezahaf, M., Alim, A., Mathy, L.: FlowOS: a flow-based platform for middleboxes. In: Workshop on Hot Topics in Middleboxes and Network Function Virtualization, pp. 19–24 (2013)
26. Libnids. http://libnids.sourceforge.net/. Accessed 12 Mar 2019
27. Libpcap. https://github.com/the-tcpdump-group/libpcap. Accessed 12 Mar 2019
28. Anderson, J.W., Braud, R., Kapoor, R.: xOMB: extensible open middleboxes with commodity servers. In: Architectures for Networking and Communications Systems, pp. 49–60 (2012)
29. Paxson, V.: Bro: a system for detecting network intruders in real-time. Comput. Netw. 31 (23), 2435–2463 (1999)
30. The Bro Project. Writing Bro Plugins. https://www.bro.org/sphinx-git/devel/plugins.html. Accessed 12 Feb 2019
31. Jamshed, M.A., Moon, Y., Kim, D.: mOS: a reusable networking stack for flow monitoring middleboxes. In: Networked Systems Design and Implementation, pp. 113–129 (2017)
32. Liu, G., Ren, Y., Yurchenko, M.: Microboxes: high performance NFV with customizable, asynchronous TCP stacks and dynamic subscriptions. In: Conference of the ACM Special Interest Group on Data Communication, pp. 504–517 (2018)
33. Firestone, D.: VFP: a virtual switch platform for host SDN in the public cloud. In: Networked Systems Design and Implementation, pp. 315–328 (2017)

A Battery SOC Prediction Method Based on GA-CNN Network and Its Implementation on FPGA

Wenzhen Guo[✉] and Jinwen Li

College of Computer Science and Technology,
National University of Defense Technology, Changsha, China
guowenzhen17@nudt.edu.cn, lijinwen@sina.com

Abstract. Battery SOC is affected by many uncertain factors, so it is difficult to predict the exact value. In view of this situation, a convolution neural network prediction method optimized by genetic algorithm is proposed. Taking voltage_measured, current_measured, temperature_measured, current_load and voltage_load as input vectors of the neural network, genetic algorithm is used to generate the initial weights of neural network, and the GA-CNN battery SOC prediction model is constructed. The software and hardware GA-CNN neural network is realized by C language and FPGA programming respectively. The software implementation verifies the correctness of the algorithm, and the hardware implementation achieves the effect of real-time monitoring. The experiment results of C language show that the battery SOC prediction results based on GA-CNN neural network are more accurate. The hardware simulation results are consistent with the software results.

Keywords: Convolution neural network · GA algorithm · SOC estimation · FPGA

1 Introduction

The power battery has the characteristics of limited measurable parameters, coupled characteristic, instant decay, strong time-varying, nonlinear, etc. Its mathematical modeling is a multi-domain and multi-disciplinary problem. The SOC of the battery refers to the charged state of the li-ion battery, which is equivalent to the fuel gauge of the fuel vehicle. It is the ratio of the capacity that can be actually provided in the current state to the capacity that should be provided after full charge. As one of the important determinants of energy management, SOC plays an important role in optimizing vehicle energy management, improving power battery capacity and energy utilization, preventing overcharging and overdischarging, ensuring safety and longevity of power batteries during use.

The estimation of battery SOC is influenced by many factors, including discharge current, temperature, battery cycle life and self-discharge. At present, the common battery SOC estimation method [1] mainly includes characterization-based method [2], ampere-time integration method [3], model-based method [4, 5] and internal resistance

© Springer Nature Singapore Pte Ltd. 2019
W. Xu et al. (Eds.): NCCET 2019, CCIS 1146, pp. 78–90, 2019.
https://doi.org/10.1007/978-981-15-1850-8_7

measurement method [6]. But these methods also have their own limitations. On one hand, it is susceptible to uncertain factors. For example, the characterization-based method is susceptible to temperature, working condition, aging degree and other factors. The results of ampere-time integration method are greatly affected by the exact value of the initial SOC of the battery. Model-based method is greatly affected by noise, and the internal resistance measurement method is greatly affected by the working conditions of the battery. On the other hand, it has a strong dependence on the accuracy of measuring instruments or models [7]. The characterization-based method requires precise measuring instruments. The ampere-time integration method has a high requirement on the accuracy of current sensors, and the model-based estimation method has a strong dependence on the accuracy of models.

In addition, there is a data-driven method, which refers to establishing and training a direct mapping relationship model between battery current, voltage, temperature and battery SOC based on a large amount of offline data. This method hardly needs to consider the details of internal chemical reactions of power cells, and the estimation accuracy is high.

At present, the commonly used method of neural network to predict the battery SOC is mainly based on the BP neural network and RBF neural network, such as ZHAO Gang's SOC estimation of lithium battery for electric vehicle based on PSO-BP neural network [8], Kong Xiangchuang's Co-estimation of Lithium Battery SOC Based on BP-EKF Algorithm [9], Feng Zhimin's SOC Prediction for Electric Vehicle Battery Based on AFSA-RBF Neural Network [10], Zhao Xuan's Multiply Parameters State-of-charge Estimation of Battery for Pure Electric Bus Based on GGAP-RBF Neural Network [11].

However, the most serious problem of RBF is the inability to explain its reasoning process and reasoning basis. In addition, the central point of the hidden layer basis function is selected together in the input point sample set, which is difficult to reflect the true input-output relationship of the system. There are also non-convex optimization problems, gradient disappearance problems and over-fitting problems in BP neural network process.

To solve the above problems, this paper proposes to establish a training model using the GA-CNN algorithm. Improve the data processing method, use the training data of three different test processes of the same battery as input, calculate three different SOC results through the convolution neural network, and obtain the final SOC result by averaging method, which reduces the error caused by data test errors. Compared with traditional BP neural network, the complex network structure and large-scale settable parameters of CNN give it strong fault tolerance and robustness. Another important feature of CNN is the weight distribution of the training network. The weight of layer close to the input is small, and the weight of layer near the output is large. It avoids the problem of too fast gradient loss in the back propagation process of BP neural network.

However, the traditional convolution neural network is trained by the steepest descent algorithm [12]. The learning performance of the steepest descent algorithm is greatly influenced by the choice of the initial weight of the neural network. If the initial weight selection is not good, the training process is easy to fall into the local optimum. Considering that genetic algorithm has the ability of searching global and local optimal solutions efficiently, this paper proposes a battery SOC prediction model based on convolution neural network optimized by genetic algorithm [13].

2   Principle and Structure of GA-CNN

2.1   Basic Principles of Convolution Neural Networks

Convolution neural network is a kind of feedforward neural network with deep structure and convolution calculation. It is composed of neurons with learnable weights and bias constants. The mathematical model abstracted from each neural network unit is as follows [14], also known as a perceptron, which receives multiple inputs (x1, x2, x3…) to produce an output. The process is similar to how nerve endings perceive stimuli from various external environments and then generate electrical signals that can be transmitted to nerve cells. The purpose of CNN is to extract features from a certain model, and then classify, identify, predict or make decisions based on features (Fig. 1).

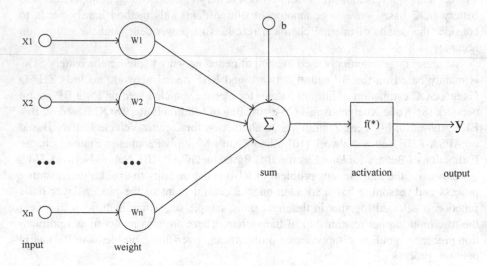

Fig. 1. Neuron model

The CNN training process:

1. Generate initial weights of neural networks by GA algorithms;
2. The input data is propagated forward through the convolution layer, the pooling layer and the full connection layer to get the output value;
3. Calculate the error between the output value and the target value of the network;
4. When the error is greater than expected value, the error is sent back to the network, and the error of full connection layer, pooling layer and convolution layer are obtained in turn. When the error is equal to or less than expected value, the training is completed;
5. Update the weights according to the calculated errors. Then go to the second step (Fig. 2).

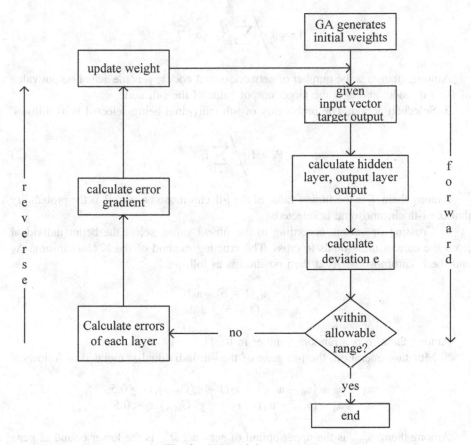

Fig. 2. CNN training process

2.2 Genetic Algorithm

Genetic algorithm is a parallel stochastic search optimization method which simulates the genetic mechanism of nature and the theory of biological evolution. By selecting, crossing and Mutation mechanisms, a group of candidate individuals are retained in each iteration, and this process is repeated. After several generations of evolution, the fitness reaches an approximate optimal state [15].

General steps of genetic algorithm [16]:

1. Initialize the population. The initial weights of CNN convolution layer and full connection layer are generated randomly by decimal coding as the initial population. Determine population number, maximum iteration number, chromosome length, range, expected output error and other parameters.

2. Calculate fitness values. Based on the initial weight, the predicted output value is calculated using a convolution neural network, and the reciprocal of the sum of squared errors between the predicted output value and the target output value is taken as the individual fitness value.

$$f_i = 1 \bigg/ \sum_{i=1}^{n} (y_i - a_i)^2. \tag{1}$$

Among them, n is the number of network output nodes, y_i is the actual output value of the i-th node, and a_i is the target output value of the i-th node.

3. Selection action. The probability of i-th individual being selected is as follows.

$$P_i = f_i \bigg/ \sum_{i=1}^{n} f_i. \tag{2}$$

Among them, f_i is the fitness value of the i-th chromosome, and P_i is the probability that the i-th chromosome is selected.

4. Crossing operation, according to the fitness value, select the better individual from the current individuals to cross. The crossing method of the K chromosome A_k and the L chromosome A_l at the j position is as follows.

$$a_{kj} = a_{kj}(1-b) + a_{lj}b.$$
$$a_{lj} = a_{lj}(1-b) + a_{kj}b. \tag{3}$$

Among them, b is a random number in [0, 1].

5. Mutation operation, the j-th gene of the i-th individual is mutated as follows.

$$a_{ij} = a_{ij} + (a_{ij} - a_{max}) \times r_2(1 - g/G_{max}), r_2 \geq 0.5.$$
$$a_{ij} = a_{ij} + (a_{min} - a_{ij}) \times r_2(1 - g/G_{max}), r_2 < 0.5. \tag{4}$$

Among them, a_{max} is the upper bound of gene a_{ij}, a_{min} is the lower bound of gene a_{ij}, r_2 is the random number in [0,1], g is the current iteration number, and G_{max} is the maximum evolution number.

6. Repeat steps 2, 3, 4, and 5 until the network optimized by the genetic algorithm achieves the required accuracy (Fig. 3).

2.3 Neural Network Structure

The basic operation units of convolution neural network include convolution operation, pooling operation and full connection operation [17].

The function of convolution layer is to extract features from input data, which is to perform inner product operation on the sub-matrix of a block according to a number of certain weights (i.e., convolution kernel), and its output is the extracted feature. The formula is described as follows:

$$y = f \left(\sum_{i=1}^{n} w_i x_i + b \right). \tag{5}$$

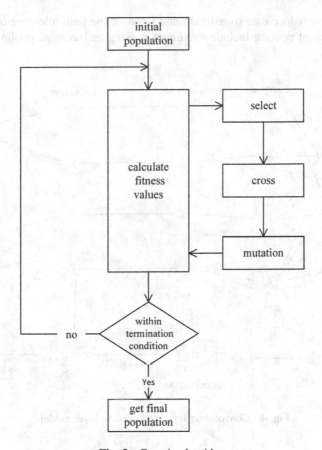

Fig. 3. Genetic algorithm

The size of the convolution core is generally smaller than the size of the input matrix, so the features extracted by the convolution will pay more attention to the local, and each neuron only needs to perceive the local, so each layer generally needs multiple convolution kernels to convolute the input matrix, and then the global information can be obtained by combining the local information at a higher level. The higher the number of layers, the more global the extracted features are.

The excitation layer maps the output of convolution layer in a non-linear way. The output of neural network without excitation function is a linear equation, which approximates the curve with complex linear combination. After the non-linear excitation function is added, the neural network may learn to segment the plane with smooth curve instead of using complex linear combination to approximate the smooth curve. Common excitation functions include Sigmoid function, tanh function, Relu function and ELU (Exponential Linear Units) function [18].

The pooling layer is sandwiched in the middle of continuous convolution layer, which means sampling or aggregating a piece of data to compress the amount of data and parameters, reduce data over-fitting and improve the fault tolerance of the model. Common types of pooling include maximum pooling and average pooling (Fig. 4).

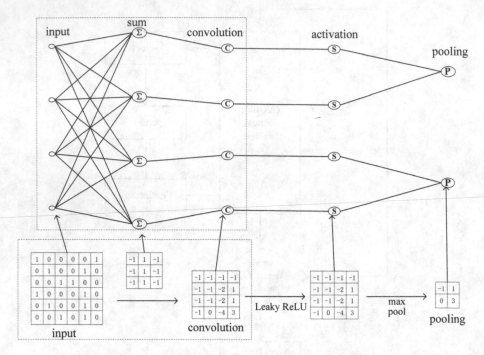

Fig. 4. Convolution layer and pooling layer model

After the convolution and pooling operations of several layers, the obtained characteristic matrix is expanded row by row, connected into vectors, and input into the full connection network. The full connection layer can integrate the local information with category discrimination in the convolution layer or the pooling layer. Usually, the full connection layer is at the tail of the convolution neural network.

The network architecture of GA-CNN is combined layer by layer. The behavior between layers is determined by the corresponding weight w and offset value b. The training data is used to learn w and b in the network structure, so as to generate correct prediction data [19].

3   Realization of SOC Prediction for Battery by GA-CNN

The specific steps of this experiment are divided into three steps: pre-processing offline data, model establishment and training, model testing.

3.1 Pre-processing of Offline Data

The pre-processing of offline data is to arrange the data into the data format that meets the input and output requirements of the established model, including data cleaning, normalization, data partitioning and so on. Data partitioning refers to dividing normalized data into training set and testing set according to a certain proportion.

This article downloaded the test data set from the NASA website [20]. The website address is as follows: https://ti.arc.nasa.gov/tech/dash/pcoe/prognostic-data-repository/. The input data is voltage_measured, current_measured, temperature_measured, current_load, voltage_load. Three groups of 10*30 matrices with different output are selected respectively. The input vectors are arranged into 30*30 matrices according to the arrangement of upper, middle and lower. The output data is the battery capacity of the three groups of experimental data discharged to 2.7 V respectively.

3.2 Establishment and Training of the Model

According to the amount of training, the structure of the model is preliminarily determined, and then the model is built by training set.

In this paper, considering that the battery feature richness is not high, and it needs to be implemented by FPGA, the network structure should be as simple as possible, so this paper adopts a 5-layer processing model. After the pre-processing data, the input is

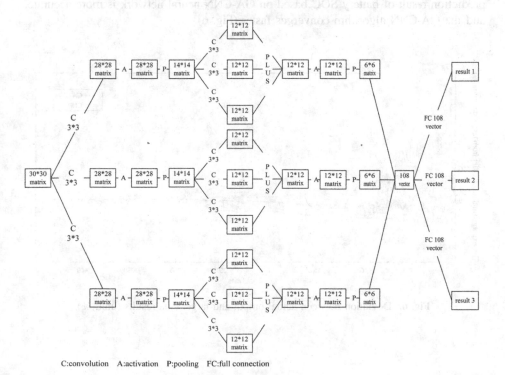

C:convolution   A:activation   P:pooling   FC:full connection

Fig. 5. Training model

a matrix of 30*30, and initial weights is generated by GA algorithm. The first layer is the convolution layer C1, which uses 3*3 convolution mask to slip convolution to get the primary characteristics of the matrix. The second layer is pooling layer S2, which is used to downsample the local characteristic matrix obtained from layer C1, using 2*2 average pooling mask to achieve 1/4 downsampling of the characteristic data. The third layer is the convolution layer C3, using the 3*3 convolution mask to further extract the features of the characteristic matrix obtained by pooling to obtain the advanced features of the matrix. The fourth layer is the pooling layer S4, which further uses the 2*2 average pooling mask to downsample the high-level features of the C3 matrix. The fifth layer is the full connection layer F5, which finally obtains the recognition result of length 3 through the sum of the full connection weights on the S4 feature vectors (Fig. 5).

After the positive dissemination, calculate the error between the result and target value, and then the error of each layer is returned one by one. Treat the error matrix as the convolution kernel, convolve the input feature map, and obtain the deviation matrix of the weight. Then add the weights to the original convolution kernel to get the updated convolution kernel.

In this paper, the maximum training step is set to 2000 steps, and the target accuracy is set to 0.00001. In the training process with traditional CNN structure, the error reached 0.000857% after 750 steps of training, and in the training process with GA-CNN neural network, the error reached 0.000986% after 441 steps of training. The prediction result of battery SOC based on GA-CNN neural network is more accurate, and the GA-CNN algorithm converges faster (Fig. 6).

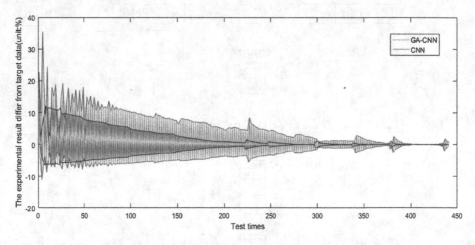

Fig. 6. Deviation between actual output and target data results (unit: %)

3.3 Model Testing

The test set is adopted to test the model and judge whether the accuracy meets the requirements. If it meets the requirements, the training is completed; otherwise, return to the first step to redesign.

Based on the trained network, the test samples are input, and the test results show that the prediction error is within the range of 3%. The network has good tracking ability, can accurately predict SOC value, and meet the design control requirements.

4 Implementation of GA-CNN Network on FPGA

Field-Programmable Gate Array, which is based on the design idea of semi-custom gate array, has the characteristics of ASIC [21]. Compared with DSP, it is not affected by the number of operation units. It also has a greater degree of parallelism, which can be used to repeatedly allocate computing resources. Multiple modules can be independently calculated at the same time on FPGA [22].

4.1 The FPGA Module of GA-CNN

Corresponding to the software algorithm, the GA-CNN circuit implemented by FPGA includes several main modules.

GA-CNN: Top-level module that controls timing logic of the whole system (execution order).

GA module: generate initial weights of neural networks.

cnnForFPGA: convolution neural network module.

cnnffL series modules: in these modules, the input data is propagated forward through convolution layer, pooling layer and full connection layer to get output value.

cnnbpL series modules: in these modules, calculate the error between output value and target value of the network, return the error to the network, and the error of full connection layer, pooling layer and convolution layer is obtained successively.

cnngradL series modules: in these modules, update weights according to the obtained deviation.

dataRead: read data from the specified file.

dataWrite: write the calculation result to a specified file.

dataJudge: judge whether the deviation between the output value and the target value is within the allowable range (Fig. 7).

4.2 Analysis of Simulation Results of FPGA Experiment

After the program is written, the simulation results of hardware and software are consistent through behavior level simulation. Since the hardware cannot handle decimals, all data are converted to integers for calculation. The output value is 2^{20} times the theoretical value. The total width of the output data is 28 bits, including 1 symbol bit, 7

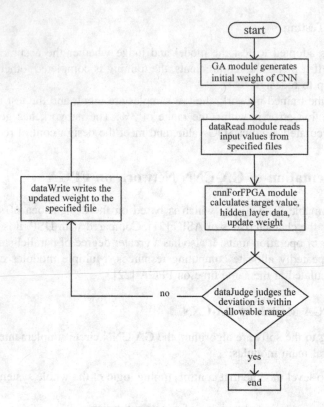

Fig. 7. FPGA structure model

integer bit and 20 decimal bit [23]. There is a slight deviation between some values and theoretical values because fixed-point simulation algorithm is used in hardware simulation and floating-point simulation is used in software simulation, and the truncation of data bits at fixed-point produces deviations.

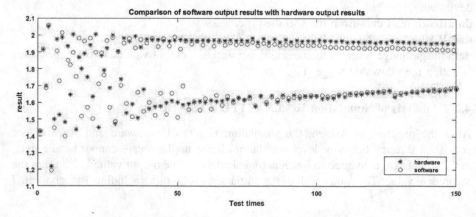

Fig. 8. Comparison of software output and hardware output

The development board used in this paper is xcvu13p-fsga2577-1-e. The result of synthesis operation is as follows, 11724 units of DSP, 446532 units of CLB Registers, 2799360 units of LUTs are used, the total used area is 9848436, and the working frequency of the actual hardware logic is 100 MHz (Fig. 8).

5 Conclusion

Aiming at the weakness of traditional BP and RBF neural network method, this paper designs a GA-CNN structure for battery SOC prediction, with the battery data set for the training of the network model and parameter adjustment, and achieves the effect of real-time monitoring by hardware programming. Finally, the simulation results verify the correctness of hardware implementation. At the same time, due to making full use of the speed of hardware, the implementation of battery SOC prediction based on FPGA is very suitable for practical application.

References

1. Zhao, Q., Wenzl, H., Bohn C.: Li-ion polymer battery SOC estimation using Bayesian Filtering. In: Proceedings of the 31st Chinese Control Conference, July 2012
2. Xiong, R.: Core Algorithm of Battery Management System for EVs, pp. 84–85(2018)
3. Li, Z., Lu, L., Ouyang, M.: Comparison of methods for improving SOC estimation accuracy through an ampere_hour integeration approach. J. Tsinghua Univ. (Sci. Tech.) 50(8) (2010)
4. Fan, X.: Research on equivalent circuit modeling and state of charge estimation of lithium-ion battery. Southwest University of Science and Technology Master Degree, June 2017
5. Hong, Z., Xu, L., Min, W.: Adaptive Kalman filter based state of charge estimation algorithm for lithium-ion battery. Chin. Phys. B 24(9), 098801 (2015)
6. Qiao X., Chi, W., Chen, W.: Battery Management System Development in Electronic, pp. 181–184 (2018)
7. Li, Y., Sun, Z., Wang, J.: Design for battery management system hardware-in-loop test platform. In: The Ninth International Conference on Electronic Measurement & Instruments, ICEMI 2009 (2009)
8. Zhao, G., Zhu, F., Dou, R.: SOC estimation of lithium battery for electric vehicle based on PSO-BP neural network, September 2018
9. Kong, X., Zhao, W., Wang, C.: Co-estimation of lithium battery SOC based on BP-EKF algorithm. Autom. Eng. 1.39(6) (2017)
10. Feng, Z., Tian, L.: SOC prediction for electric vehicle battery based on AFSA-RBF neural network. J. Chongqing Technol. Bus. Univ. (Nat. Sci. Ed.) 33(5) (2016)
11. Zhao, X., Ma, J., Liu, R., Wang, G.: Multiply parameters state-of-charge estimation of battery for pure electric bus based on GGAP-RBF neural network. China J. Highway Transp. 28(4) (2015)
12. Wang, B., Wang, Y.: Some properties relating to stochastic gradient descent methods, J. Math. (PRC) 31(6) (2011)
13. Feng, N., Wang, Z., Pang, Y.: BP neural networks based on genetic algorithms and its application in prediction of battery capacity. China Acad. J. Electron. Publish. House 35(12) (2011)

14. Umuroglu, Y., et al.: FINN: A Framework for Fast, Scalable Binarized Neural Network Inference, December 2016
15. Huang, H., Wu, L., Li, S.: The BP neural network based on GA optimization in the application of the stock index forecasting. J. Yunnan Univ. **39**(3), 350–355 (2017)
16. Wang, L., Qiao, L., Wei, L.: Optimal convolutional neural networks learning method combined with genetic algorithm. Comput. Eng. Des. **38**(7) (2017)
17. Ye, M.: Research on gesture recognition based on CNN. Wireless Internet Technology, October 2017
18. Muthuramalingam, A., Himavathi, S., Srinivasan, E.: Neural network implementation using FPGA: issues and application. Int. J. Inf. Technol. **4**(2), 86–92 (2008)
19. Hli, X., Li, C., Tian, L., Zhang, Y.: Research on optimization of parallel training for convolution neural network. Comput. Technol. Dev. **28**(8) (2018)
20. Huang, J.: Research and simulation of power battery classification and screening algorithm. South China University of Technology, June 2017
21. Zhao, R., Niu, X., Wu, Y., Luk, W., Liu, Q.: Optimizing CNN-based object detection algorithms on embedded FPGA platforms. In: Wong, S., Beck, A.C., Bertels, K., Carro, L. (eds.) ARC 2017. LNCS, vol. 10216, pp. 255–267. Springer, Cham (2017). https://doi.org/10.1007/978-3-319-56258-2_22
22. Wang, K., Sheng, M., Han, R., Li, B., Liu, C., Shen, R.: Implementation and optimization of convolutional neural networks on FPGA. Lab. Sci. **21**(4) (2018)
23. Lu, L., Zheng, S., Xiao, Q., Chen, D., Liang, Y.: Accelerating convolutional neural networks on FPGAs. Scientia Sinica Inf. **49**(3), 277–294 (2019)

The Implementation of a Configurable MBIST Controller for Multi-core SoC

Chunmei Hu[1](✉), Xiaoxuan Li[2], Zhigang Fu[1], Qianqian Tang[1], and Rong Zhao[1]

[1] School of Computer, National University of Defense Technology, Deya Street 109, Changsha 410073, P.R. China
chmhu001@163.com
[2] Xidian University, Taibai Street 2, Xian 710071, P.R. China

Abstract. Aiming at the problem of memory test power caused by the increasing proportion of embedded memory in multi-core SoC, this paper analyzes the existing issue and proposes a configurable MBIST controller to reduce test power consumption. This paper adopts MBIST configuration scan-chain to organize test groups and adopts a configurable PLL scan-chain to drive memories to its working frequency. Clock optimization method is also adopted to reduce test power. The method proposed has the advantages of low test power, flexible test configuration and less hardware added. The method can also diagnose the site of failing memories. The actual testing of the multi-core SoC on ATE V93000 shows that the proposed method effectively reduces power consumption, and meets the requirement of memory test.

Keywords: MBIST · Group test · Scan chain · Test power consumption · ATE test

1 Introduction

With the increasing system complexity of integrated circuit, especially the development of system-on-chip (SoC), integrated circuit testing faces more and more challenges [1]. Moreover, the scale of function modules on SoCs is also growing, especially the memory size. Many SoCs have shown that embedded memory will account for two-thirds of the chip area. The test power consumption problem of the memory built-in self-test (MBIST), which is widely used for embedded memory test, become more and more concerned [2].

The power consumption during memory testing is usually bigger than during normal memory accessing. On the one hand, the pseudo-random test vectors generated by the linear feedback shift register (LFSR) have low correlation with each other [3], which increases the flipping activity of the nodes in the circuit during the self-test [4]. On the other hand, in low-power chips, only a small number of circuit modules generally work, while testing requires that as many nodes as possible flip, which also leads to an increase in test power consumption [5]. The large test power consumption will inevitably increase the temperature of the chip. As the temperature increases, the failure rate of the system will rise, resulting in a decrease in the yield of the chip.

© Springer Nature Singapore Pte Ltd. 2019
W. Xu et al. (Eds.): NCCET 2019, CCIS 1146, pp. 91–100, 2019.
https://doi.org/10.1007/978-981-15-1850-8_8

In order to solve the problem of MBIST test power consumption, many scholars have made various improvements and attempts from different directions. Low-power BIST technology can be classified as microscopically improving MBIST structure and macroscopic test control [6]. The starting point of microscopic is to reduce the flipping activity of the test vector. For example, to introduce a simulated annealing algorithm in the process of generating test vectors to optimize and remove redundant test vectors [7]. The starting point of macro is to reduce power consumption by scheduling hierarchical testing. One method is to control the power switch according to the needs of each module, and turn off the non-operating power supply [8]. Another method is to propose a binary algorithm for the allocation and scheduling of test resources [9]. Some scholars also start MBIST through JTAG, enabling parallel and single testing [10].

Although many methods have been proposed, there are some shortcomings. Decreasing the flipping activity of vectors through cutting test vector and improving the correlation between the test vectors can not solve the problem fundamentally. As the macro method is concerned, the current scheduling schemes are not flexible enough, and it also adds additional logic which affects performance. This paper aims at a configurable MBIST controller and proposes a test group method based on scan chain. At the same time, clock configuration optimization is also used to further reduce test power consumption.

2   Multi-core SoC Structure

The design of this paper based on a high-performance SoC chip which integrates 8 cores. The core operates at 1 GHz, contains a three-level storage system with 4.5 MB storage capacity, and has more than five clock domains associated with memories. The types of memory include both single-port and dual-port, both RAM-based and REGISTER-based. In addition, there are a large number of peripherals on the chip, including low-speed memory access interface, high-speed serial rapid IO(SRIO) etc.

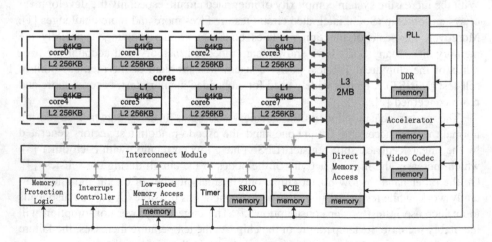

Fig. 1. The distribution structure of the memory in the SoC

The function of these peripheral components also depends on various type of memories. The memories in multi-core SoC are distributed as shown in Fig. 1.

As shown in Fig. 1, each core has a L1 cache with 64K and a L2 cache with 256K. The volume of L3 cache is 2 MB which is shared by 8 cores. The on-chip peripherals also contain a lot of RAMs to assist in realizing the various functions. For Such a complicated memory structure, if the traditional parallel memory test is executed, the nodes in memory will flip simultaneously and rapidly, resulting in an increasing in test power consumption and increasing of on-chip temperature. Excessive test power consumption can cause damage to the SoC during testing and also affect the reliability of SoC. The configurable group test and clock configuration optimization are proposed in this paper As shown in the following two chapters to reduce the power consumption of memory test.

3 Configurable Group Test

In the traditional MBIST design, the parallel test method is used to start all memories on chip at the same time. The maximum power consumption of the test is the sum of the power consumption of each memory. It will be very large, causing the chip temperature to rise and extremely burn out the circuit. Another effective method of educing power consumption is cutting down the frequency of test. The disadvantage is that testing time and testing cost will increase [11]. And what's more, as the process size decreases, to ensure the quality of product, it is more and more necessary to test every memory at its actually working frequency during product testing. Cutting down the frequency will reduce the test coverage of SoC memory, which leave a hidden trouble for SoC quality.

In this paper, a configurable group test based on scan-chains is proposed. The configurable group test method has two scan-chains. One is MBIST configuration scan-chain which is responsible for dividing into groups. The other is PLL scan-chain which is responsible for multiplying PLL clock.

The structure diagram of the two scan-chains is shown in Fig. 2. MBIST controlling scan-chain gives the MBIST enable signals (mbist_en) in current group which is arranged by tester. The location information of the memory in current group is configed in mbist_scan_in. As the SI signal shifts to the right SDFF along with mbist_clk, the mbist_en signal in current group is placed in the accurate Q port. Through this way, tester can group one or more memories to be under test. Through MBIST controlling scan-chain, all memories on SoC can be grouped flexibly not only at design phase but also at product test phase. The SoC in this paper has 52 memory enable signals, so MBIST controlling scan-chain has 52 filp-flops and serial shift-in phase has 52 cycles. The order of 52 filp-flops is shown in Fig. 3.

The product test of memory is required to be performed at its normal working frequency, and PLL is needed to multiply input reference clock during test. In this paper, We use PLL scan-chain to configure the frequency of PLL and the configuration method is also serial shift-in similar to MBIST controlling scan-chain. Comparing with the method of system's PLL starting, the method of scan chain is much simpler and scan save a lot of system running time. Comparing with the method of fixing limited

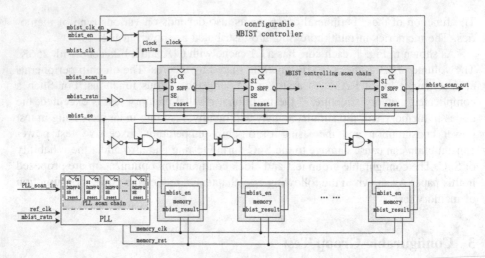

Fig. 2. The structure diagram of the two scan-chains

mbist_scan_in →	Core0 L1P	Core0 L1D	Core0 L2	...	...	Core1 L1P	Core1 L1D	Core1 L2	...	...	
	Core2 L1P	Core2 L1D	Core2 L2	...	...	Core3 L1P	Core3 L1D	Core3 L2	...	...	
	Core4 L1P	Core4 L1D	Core4 L2	...	...	Core5 L1P	Core5 L1D	Core5 L2	...	...	
	Core6 L1P	Core6 L1D	Core6 L2	...	...	Core7 L1P	Core7 L1D	Core7 L2	...	...	
	L3	M1553B	SRIO	PCIE	...	...	...	...	...	...	
	...	...	mbist_scan_out →								

Fig. 3. The order of 52 filp-flops in MBIST controlling scan-chain

numbers of test frequency point on design phase, the method of scan chain is more optional. PLL scan-chain connects the critical register bit about dividing and multiplying factors. In addition, this method can also provide direct bypass clock testing during wafer test.

Another advantage of the two scan-chains is that the objective test memories and working frequency can be adjust in ATE environment without regenerating test pattern. Because the meaning of every bit in scan-chains is fixed and the shift-in is subsequently, we can modify the pattern in Smartest software tool to change the objective test memories or working frequency.

The memory test of each group is time-sharing. In order to balance the test power of each group, we recommend to group memories according to their size and the physical location of memory in the place and route, so thermal hot spot can be distributed and overheat can be avoided effectively. A example of grouping about the SoC in this paper is shown in the following table.

Table 1. Approximate grouping of full-chip MBIST tests

Groups	Modules
Group 1	L3
Group 2	core0, core4
Group 3	core1, core5
Group 4	core2, core6
Group 5	core3, core7
Group 6	Direct Memory Access, Accelerator
Group 7	DDR, Low-speed memory access interface
Group 8	Video codec
Group 9	SRIO, PCIE

In the above table, the memories of the chip are divided into 9 groups according their size and physical location. For example, L3 is the biggest memory on chip, so it is tested separately. Core0 is on the upper-left hand on GDSII and Core4 is on the bottom-right hand. This combination is beneficial for dispersing hot spots. 9 groups are tested one by one to complete all memories test.

This method not only reduces the maximum power consumption, but also diagnoses the locations of fail memory. Excepting for shifting in the site of memory to be tested, MBIST controlling scan-chain also provides the means to diagnose the site of failing memories. As showed in Fig. 2, every test result of 52 memories is connected to the D port of respective flipflop. When the MBIST test is completed, we can use the scan chain control method which includes a capture cycle and 52 shift-out cycles, and the result of 52 memories can be shifted out on the Q port of the last flip-flop. If the memories in current group pass test, the waveform of shift out is the same as shift in. If the waveform of shift out is different from shift in, it can be diagnosed according the sequence of scan chain. This is beneficial for the classification and downgrading of the SoC.

4 Clock Optimization to Reduce Power

The clock frequencies required by each memory on multi-core SoC are different. There are high frequency of 1 GHz which required by L1 program cache and low frequency of 125 MHz which required by low speed storage access interface. The SoC in this paper has five clock domains in memory test mode. As we have partitioned memory test to many groups, it is necessary to turn off the clock which is nothing to do with current group in order to reduce power consumption. Clock gating is used in this paper at key nodes to control the module clocks of each group in this design.

Figure 4 is the clock and reset control of group1. The clock of MBIST controller is gated by clock gating1. The clock of memory is gated by clock gating2. The logic expression of right-output of control0 is "group1_mbist_en | !(group1_mbist_en|-group2_mbist_en|group3_mbist_en|group4_mbist_en|group5_mbist_en|group6_mbist_en|group7_mbist_en|group8_mbist_en|group9_mbist_en)". The select port of MUX is (group1_mbist_en|group2_mbist_en|group3_mbist_en|group4_mbist_en|group5_mbist_en|group6_mbist_en|group7_mbist_en|group8_mbist_en|group9_mbist_en). When group1_mbist_en is effective, the clk of MBIST controller is active. The clk of memory is also active. The rstn of function logic is set to 1'b0 and function logic is kept to static. When group1_mbist_en is ineffective and group2_mbist_en is effective, the clk of MBIST controller and memory in group1 is inactive. The rstn of function logic in gorup1 is set to 1'b0 and the circuit in gorup1 is kept to static. When none group*_mbist_en is effective, the clock of all MBIST controller is inactive and the clock of all memory is active. The function logic is out of reset. This method can ensure that the active group works normally and the inactive groups keep in low power state.

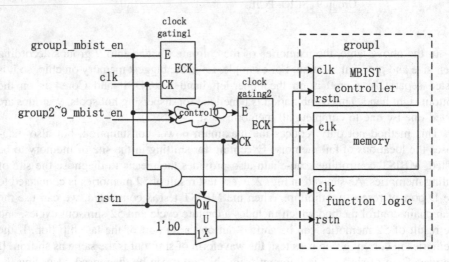

Fig. 4. The clock gating design of group

5   Experimental Results and Analysis

According to the above chapters, this paper implements a configurable grouping test and does clock optimization in the multi-core SoC. At the same time, this paper uses the strategy of intra-group parallel, inter-group serial, serial between clock domains, and inter-module serial to further reduce power consumption.

As expected, the multi-core SoC has taped out successfully. Many ATE(Automatic Testing Machine) tests about memories have been executed successfully. The ATE platform which we use is ADVANTEST V93000 as shown in Fig. 5. The V93000 is a SOC chip test platform and can tests a wide range of devices, from low cost IoT to high

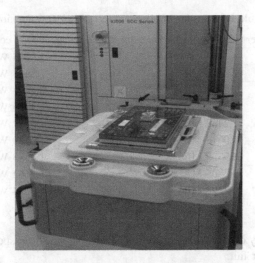

Fig. 5. Physical drawing of ADVANTEST V93000

end product, such as advanced automotive devices or highly integrated multicore processors [12]. The software SmarTest executes all the controlling function about V93000.

We used configuration scan-chain to setup test status from group1 to group9 as shown in Table 1. SmarTest software applies appropriate voltage through MSDPS power board card, and tests the average current of each group using PMU(parameter measurement unit). Through the real-time display of test results and data on the Ulreport interface on SmarTest, this paper obtains the current value of the voltage domain in which the memory is located. Then, through W = V * I, the power consumption of all groups are calculated, as shown in the following table.

As can be seen from the data in Table 2, the maximum power consumption of MBIST is just 1.7044 W for group 1 in which the three-level storage (L3) is located. The power of group1–group4 has little difference because they all have two cores with same GDSII. If the traditional parallel method is used, the resulting power consumption will be close to the 13.33152 W of the power consumption of all the groups. This value is obviously too large for the embedded SoC chip. By consulting the specification of the chip, the maximum power consumption requirement of the SoC is 10 W. The method of this paper significantly reduces the maximum power consumption of the MBIST test. The result of every group test is about 17% of the rated maximum power consumption, and meets the test requirements. What's more, the power consumption of each group obtained by this method is relatively uniform, so that the reduced power consumption is most effective.

For further research, we have done memories test of 1200 chips on room temperature. The result shows about 2.5% chips are failed on memories. We have diagnosed the failing site of the 30 chips using the MBIST controlling scan-chain as described in chapter III. The failing sites of 16 chips are concentrated on L3 which is the biggest memory on chip and its frequency of work is up to 500 MHz. It shows Large areas and fragmented memories are more prone to production failures. On the

Table 2. Statistics of all group test power consumption

Group number	Capacity of the memory in the design	Power consumption
Group 1	2 MB	1.7044 W
Group 2	1.2468 MB	1.5624 W
Group 3	1.2468 MB	1.6476 W
Group 4	1.2468 MB	1.4755 W
Group 5	1.2468 MB	1.5392 W
Group 6	1.0078 MB	1.6280 W
Group 7	0.9389 MB	1.3683 W
Group 8	0.8306 MB	1.3664 W
Group 9	0.8293 MB	1.0234 W

contrary, the memory of low speed peripheral device such as low-speed memory access interface hardly ever fail.

Because the memory test group can config flexible through MBIST controlling scan-chain at ATE environment without regenerating test pattern, we do the research about the relationship between test power and the number of cores. We start from core1, and then add one core each time and record the power. The result is shown in Fig. 6. With the increase in the number of cores, that is, the increase in the size of the test memories, the power consumption is also increasing. The test power consumption is proportional to the size of the test memories.

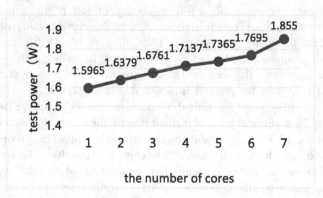

Fig. 6. The relationship between test power and the number of cores

Because the frequency of chip can config flexible through PLL scan-chain at ATE environment without regenerating test pattern, we also do the research about the relationship between test power and the frequency. We add the frequency from 500 MHz to 1.48 GHz. The test power is shown in Fig. 7. When the frequency is 1.48 GHz, the test power is about three times as in 500 MHz which is about one-third of 1.48 GHz.

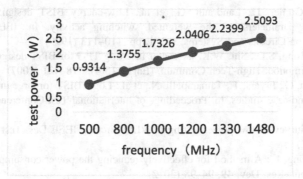

Fig. 7. The relationship between test power and the frequency

6 Conclusion

This paper proposes a method of configurable grouping test and clock power optimization for multi-core SoC memory test. The final product test is divided into 9 groups through MBIST configuration scan-chain and PLL is working using PLL scan chain to achieve high frequency the same as in function mode. The methods of clock power optimization, intra-group parallel, inter-group serial are performed to further reduce test power. The paper does a lot of tests on ATE V93000, including balancing power of each group, researching on the relationship between test power and the number of cores, researching on the relationship between test power and the frequency. The result of the measurement shows that the maximum power consumption of the test method is significantly reduced, and the power consumption of each group is roughly equal. The result also shows the method proposed in this paper can be used conveniently in ATE environment, and it can effectively reduce the amount of work that tester regenerates test patterns.

References

1. Li, J., Li, R., Yang, J., et al.: Low-power built-in self-test based on partial scan. Solid State Electron. Res. Prog. **25**(1), 72–76 (2005)
2. Song, H., Shi, Y.: VLSI testability design technology for low-power BIST. Electron. Device **25**(1), 101–104 (2002)
3. Qiu, H., Wang, C.: Pseudo-random test vector generation method based on built-in self-test. J. Huaiyin Teach. Coll.: Nat. Sci. Ed. **5**(3), 212–215 (2006)
4. Zorian, Y.: A distributed BIST control scheme for complex VLSI devices. In: Proceedings of VLSI Test Symposium, pp. 4–9 (1993)
5. Girard, P.: Survey of low-power testing of VLSI circuits. Des. Test Comput. (IEEE) **19**(3), 80–90 (2002)
6. Sun, H.: Research and Implementation of IP Core Low Power Test. National University of Defense Technology (2014)

7. Girard, P., Guiller, L., Landrault, G., et al.: Low-energy BIST design: impact of the LFSR TPG parameters on the weighted switching activity. In: IEEE International Symposium on Circuits and Systems, vol. 1, pp. 110–113 (1999)

8. Tan, E.M., Song, S.D., Shi, W.K.: A vector inserting TPG for BIST design with low peak power consumption. High-Tech Commun. (Engl.) **13**(4), 418–421 (2007)

9. Hetherington, G., Fryars, T., Tamarapalli, N., et al.: Logic BIST for large industrial designs: real issues and case studies. In: Proceedings of International Test Conference, pp. 358–367 (1999)

10. Girard, P.: Survey of low-power testing of VLSI circuits. IEEE Des. Test Comput. **19**(3), 82–92 (2002)

11. Yuan, Q., Fang, L.: A method for effectively reducing the power consumption of memory BIST. Comput. Res. Dev. **49**, 94–98 (2012)

12. Chen, F.: ATE-based FPGA test. Fudan University (2011)

Structure Design of a Fully Enclosed Airborne Reinforcement Computer

Jiang Feng Huang(✉)

The Computer Department, Jiangsu Automation Research Institute,
Lianyungang, China
huangjiangfeng@jari.cn

Abstract. The Structure design method of a fully enclosed airborne reinforcement computer is discussed and the design scheme is introduced. The chassis structure, thermal design, electromagnetic compatibility and anti-vibration design of the case are emphatically introduced, and corresponding technical solutions and main structural diagrams are given for key technical problems. The fully enclosed computer mentioned in this paper has been applied in engineering and has well anti harsh environmental performance.

Keywords: Structure design · Airborne reinforcement computer · Thermal design · EMC design · Anti harsh environment

1 Introduction

In recent years, the "anti-harsh environment" reinforcement computers with high reliability are being used more and more widely. The "anti-harsh environment" means long-term work and storage under harsh conditions such as a wider range of ambient temperature and humidity, strong mechanical vibration and shock. In addition, the anti-harsh environment reinforcement computer also needs to have the characteristics of salt spray prevention, mold resistance, moisture resistance, low pressure resistance, etc., and the power supply allows for large voltage fluctuations, strong anti-electromagnetic interference, anti-electromagnetic leakage and anti-nuclear radiation capacity.

In many methods for improving the reliability of a computer system, the physical reinforcement measures usually adopted are to comprehensively reinforce the computer or to perform secondary auxiliary reinforcement on some commercial computers, which mainly depends on the specific use environment of the computer. The environmental condition of the airborne reinforcement computer is determined by the installation location of the computer on the aircraft and the environment of the aircraft. The aircraft itself has harsh environments (such as narrow space, weight limitation, high-intensity vibration and impact) and complex external environments such as tropical or cold regions, high-salt spray sea surface or strong magnetic field areas that it may fly over. Therefore, the airborne reinforcement computer must be fully reinforced to ensure that the chassis and the internal components have good stiffness and strength, and can provide a good environment for the operation of internal components (modules) from the harsh environment.

© Springer Nature Singapore Pte Ltd. 2019
W. Xu et al. (Eds.): NCCET 2019, CCIS 1146, pp. 101–111, 2019.
https://doi.org/10.1007/978-981-15-1850-8_9

In addition, with the continuous improvement of electronic equipment miniaturization, integration and functional performance, the use of high heat flux, high-power components, strengthening the internal heat dissipation of computers, electromagnetic compatibility and other issues need to be considered in structural design.

In this paper, a structural design method of a fully enclosed airborne reinforcement computer against harsh environment is introduced in combination with engineering practice, which is mainly described from the aspects of chassis structure, thermal design, electromagnetic compatibility, anti-vibration and anti-shock and three-proof design.

2   Structural Design of Chassis

In order to facilitate the installation and connection in the aircraft, the size of 1ATR is adopted in the onboard reinforced computer box (ATR is a specification issued by the Aeronautical Radio Incorporation in 1956). The box part (the frame) of the chassis is brazed by the left and right heat exchange slots, the fin, the side plate and the front and rear baffles, and the dimension precision and the tolerance of the shape and position are high. The inner surface of the heat transfer slot plate is a guide slot structure, which can guide the module to slide up and down in the guide groove, and can form a high strength connection through the guide slot and the wedge locking device on the

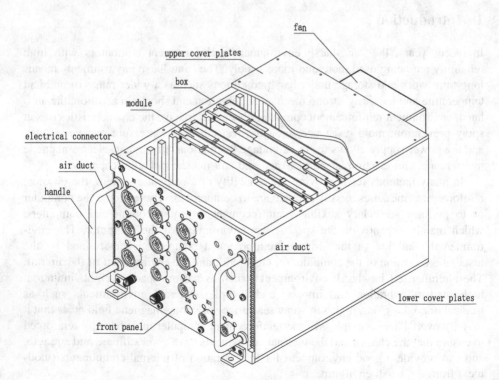

Fig. 1. Structural sketch of 1ATR reinforced computer

module. And the outer surface is composed of an independent and closed cooling duct with the heat dissipation fin and side plate. The fan is located at the rear end of the frame and connected with the cooling air duct. The front panel is located at the front end of the frame, with an electrical connector on it, which is responsible for the input and output of the external signal. The full seal cavity consists of the upper and lower cover plates that located at the upper and lower sides of the frame, together with the front panel and the frame, which realizes the complete physical isolation from external environment and the protection of the internal module which is not affected by the factors such as damp heat and electromagnetic interference. The structure of the chassis is shown in Fig. 1.

3 Thermal Design

Thermal design is an important guarantee for strengthening the long-term stability of the reinforced computer. As the temperature increases, the failure rate of electronic components increases rapidly. If the chassis cannot be effectively dissipated in time, it will directly affect the performance of the ruggedized computer [1].

There are two main reasons for the increase of computer temperature. First,the packaging density of microelectronic devices is increasing with the development of science and technology, resulting in the rapid increase of the power density (heat flux) value of chips. Second, the increase of device function leads to the increase of the density of internal components and the concentration of heat.

For the reinforced computer, the ultimate goal of the thermal design is to find a low heat resistance heat transfer channel between the source and the sink to ensure the rapid transmission of heat inside the chassis [2]. Therefore, the whole channel heat dissipation, module cooling, material selection and fan selection are studied in order to meet the reliability requirements.

3.1 Heat Dissipation Design of the Whole Machine

First, the frame of the chassis is formed by vacuum brazing. The welding filler metal is fused in the high temperature state and filled the gap between the joints by the action of capillary, so that the contact thermal resistance between adjacent parts is greatly reduced, and the whole machine's transfer and heat conduction can be effectively improved. Since the reinforced computer adopts a fully sealed structure design, the heat generated by the components on the printed circuit board in the chassis cannot be directly exchanged with the outside air. It can only be transmitted to the left and right heat transfer slots through the heat conduction cold plate and gather on the heat fins in the air duct. Under the action of forced air suction from the axial fan at the rear of the chassis, the cold air sucked from the air ducts on both sides of the front panel of the chassis is heat exchanged with the heat radiating fins, and is taken out of the chassis by the fan to achieve the heat dissipation effect [3].

Second, make the location of the module a reasonable layout. Because the heat of each module is different, the position of the module is very easy to cause the uneven heat distribution in the cavity. The long-term work may lead to the rapid increase of the local temperature inside the chassis. The modules of the power supply are put in the back end of the chassis close to the fan side, and the heat transfer board is fitted with the rear panel of the chassis to reduce the influence on the temperature of the internal environment of the chassis [4]. The main board or thermal sensitive devices and other important modules are placed at the front end of the cabinet or away from the large calorific module. On the one hand, it can make the cold air entering the air duct in the front panel and heat exchange earlier. On the other hand, it can also reduce the influence of power and other modules' heat emission on the motherboard [5]. The internal structure and cooling path of the chassis are shown in Fig. 2.

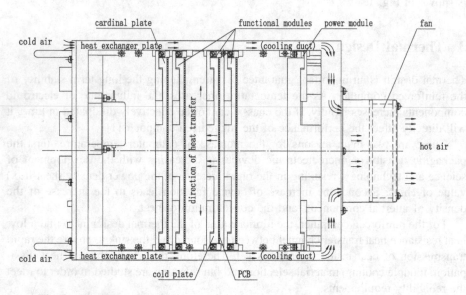

Fig. 2. Internal structure form of chassis and schematic diagram of cooling path

3.2   Heat Dissipation Design of Module

Electronic components are the main source of heat when reinforced computers are working normally. In order to reduce the heat generation of the whole machine, it is necessary to select the appropriate components and the optimized design work of the PCB printed board. The components should first meet the design parameters, power, frequency and other characteristics and leave a certain allowance compared with the design value. At the same time, the selection is optimized with reference to the non-temperature sensitivity, structure, precision, material and aging precision of components [6]. Industrial grades and above which have good high temperature resistance are preferred. The optimum design of PCB printed circuit boards can make the components layout neat and arranged in rows as far as possible, and is conducive to the adoption of heat dissipation measures in the structure.

For most PCB using DIP integrated block, it is almost impossible to transfer heat through the lead because the lead line of the DIP element is thin and hard. The method of assembling pure copper heat conduction cold plate under the DIP element can be used to dissipate heat, as shown in Fig. 3. And it is verified by calculating the shell temperature rise of PCB components with the formula (1).

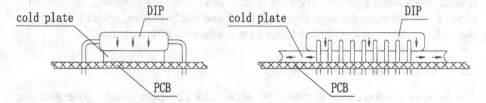

Fig. 3. Diagram of cooling path for DIP components

$$\Delta t = \frac{\varphi_1}{8kA}\left(l^2 - 4x^2\right) \tag{1}$$

Where φ_1—Unit length heat flow (W/m);

A—Cross section area of heat conduction strip (m²);

k—Thermal conductivity of heat conduction strip (W/(m·°C));

l—Length of printed board (m);

x—Calculating the distance from a point to the center on a thermal conductor (m).

For surface mounted high-power integrated circuits, cold plate is usually used to achieve heat dissipation on the chip. Metal materials with large thermal conductivity are chosen as coldplate, such as copper or aluminum alloy. The outer side of the cold plate is smooth and flat, and the inner side has a corresponding height of convex platform at the location where the chips need to be cooled. The primary heat exchange between the chips and the cold plate is realized by the close bonding of the chips with high-quality thermal conductive pads [7].

The cooling way of the cold plate is divided into two ways: The outer side of the cold plate is directly attached to the inner wall of the cabinet to achieve heat dissipation (such as the power module in Fig. 2). Or heat can be transferred to the two ends of the module near the wedge locking device through the cold plate itself, and then the cold plate can be closely fitted with the guide groove of the chassis wall to realize the conduction and heat dissipation between the cold plate and the chassis frame, as shown

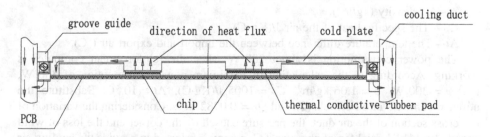

Fig. 4. Diagram of cooling path for high power integrated circuits

in Fig. 4. The wedge locking device facilitates the module to insert into the chassis smoothly, so that the module is firmly fastened to the guide rail slot of the box to resist impact and vibration. On the other hand, the module inserted into the chassis generates reverse mechanical pressure when the wedge locking device is locked, increases the contact area between the cold plate and the frame guide groove, reduces the contact thermal resistance, and promotes better heat conduction of the module.

3.3   Material Selection

The airborne reinforcement computer is characterized by light weight, good strength, easy processing, good conductivity and good thermal conductivity. Aluminum alloy should be selected as the main material. Especially, the frame part of chassis should be Vacuum Brazed, and 3A21 aluminum manganese series anti rust aluminum or 6061 wrought aluminum should be selected. As a result of good corrosion resistance, pressure processing and welding performance, 3A21 anti-rust aluminum has long been the material of choice for domestic airborne reinforcement computer boxes due to its good corrosion resistance, pressure processing and welding performance. 6061 aluminum alloy can also be strengthened by heat treatment to improve its strength. Therefore, on the basis of meeting the same mechanical index, the case with 6061 aluminum alloy as the main material is easier to realize thin wall structure and has better environmental adaptability. In addition to the frame part, the rest of the chassis is usually made of 2A12 aluminum alloy. The mechanical properties of 2A12 aluminum alloy are better than those of 3A21, but the weld ability is poor, so they are often used as support for panels, cover plates or internal structural parts.

3.4   Fan Selection

There are many factors to be considered in the selection of the fan, but the main parameters are the air volume and wind pressure. The cold air entering the cabinet passes through the air duct and absorbs the heat on the fin, which will cause the air to heat up. According to the equation of heat balance,The ventilation amount for the whole machine is:

$$Q_f = \frac{\varphi}{\rho C_P \Delta t} \tag{2}$$

Where φ—Total loss power of electronic equipment (W)

ρ—Air density (kg/m^3)

C_P—The specific heat of the air J/(Kg•C)

Δt—The temperature difference between the import and export air (°C).

The power consumption is about 280 W when the reinforcement computer is working. According to the calculation of maximum power consumption of 300 W, i.e. $\varphi = 300$ W, $\rho = 1.06$ kg/m^3, $C_P = 1005$ J/(Kg·C), $\Delta t = 10$ °C. Substitute the above parameters into Formula (2), and $Q_f = 0.0282$ m^3/s. Considering the variation of the cross section of the air duct, the pressure caused by the corner and the loss of wind speed, the 4414H axial fan of ebm-papst Company is selected to provide the cooling air for the chassis. The main parameters of the fan are: voltage 24VDC, power 8.6 W, and air volume 240 m³/h.

4 EMC Design

The airborne reinforcement computer will be subjected to various electromagnetic interference in various environments in the life period, such as the rest of the equipment/components, the radio station outside the aircraft, the radar and even the enemy's electromagnetic attack weapons. Aiming at the complex electromagnetic environment in which equipment is used; the following standards are put forward for its electromagnetic compatibility

CE 102: Power line conduction emission 10 kHz–10 MHz;
CS 101: Power line conduction sensitivity 25 Hz–50 kHz;
CS 114: Transmission sensitivity of cable beam injection 10 kHz–400 MHz;
RE 102: Emitter emission from electric field 10 kHz–18 GHz;
RS 103: Field radiation sensitivity 10 kHz–40 GHz;

When the reinforcement computer is on, the energy of electromagnetic interference is generally transmitted in two ways: conductive coupling and radioactivecoupling. Therefore, the two most important items in the above EMC standards are the conduction emission CE 102 and the radiation emission RE 102. When designing, different methods are adopted for the suppression of conductive coupling and radioactive coupling. The former is suppressed by filtering, the main measure is to use signal interference filter and power interference filter, and the latter is controlled by electromagnetic shielding, which is mainly based on reasonable structure design and optimized wiring [8, 9].

4.1 Shielding of Removable Panel of Reinforcement Cabinet

The main factor affecting shielding integrity is the joints on shielding. The ideal shielding method is solid shielding, that is to say, shield is a completely closed metal shell with continuous and uniform electric structure. But in fact, this kind of shield does not exist. Vacuum brazing is used in the frame of the chassis to realize the permanent joint between the parts, but the connection between the detachable face/cover plate and the frame can only be fastened by screw, and there will always be a gap at the joint. Due to the influence of the screw spacing, the smoothness of the matching surface and the war page of the sheet material, the contact surface inevitably produces a gap, which reduces the shielding effectiveness of the chassis [10].

The solution is as follows: Firstly, the conductive oxidation process is carried out on all the surfaces of all metal structures, so that they have good conductive effect; secondly, we can reduce the gap length or increase the slot depth from the following three aspects: The first is to increase the number of screws and shorten the distance of the screw (the length of the gap); the second is to improve the machining precision of the components, such as the roughness of the joint surface of the aluminum alloy parts is lower than Ra1.6 μm, and the conductive rubber strip is pressed in the concave seal groove to reduce the length of the gap; the third is to increase the gap depth properly by bunting at the joint or a step structure.

The common shielding structure of the chassis joints is shown in Fig. 5. The shielding effectiveness shown in Fig. 5b is better due to the proper increase of the depth of the leakage of the shield.

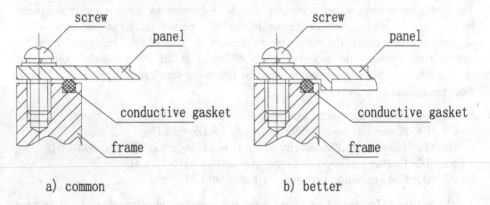

a) common   b) better

Fig. 5. Diagram of electromagnetic shielding structure for two common box joints.

4.2 Shielding at the Head, Hole, etc.

The front panel of the reinforced computer is equipped with a power switch, indicator head and other devices. The installation parts of these switches or devices need to open a corresponding hole in the panel, and there will be a certain gap at the joint of the panel. In order to prevent electromagnetic leakage in the gap, conductive padding is usually added to the joint surface of switch or device and front panel, and shielding measures are added near the hole, such as covering all components with metal shielding cover. One of the commonly used electromagnetic shielding measures for power switches is shown in Fig. 6.

4.3 Shielding of Cable and Connector

It is also an extremely dangerous electromagnetic energy leak window to reinforce the electrical connector and connection cable on the reinforced computer, which seriously affects the level of the electromagnetic emission of the whole machine. In order to suppress leakage, on the one hand, the shielded cable and its corresponding connector should be used, and the cable shielding layer and the connector are connected completely around the cable to make a good connection between the connector shell and the shielded layer of the connected cable; on the other hand, to reduce the electromagnetic leakage at the gap, the connectors between the connector and the panel are all lined with conductive gaskets. For the shielding performance of the high-frequency coaxial connector, the threaded connection is better than the bayonet type. For the occasion with high shielding requirement, thread type connector is preferred.

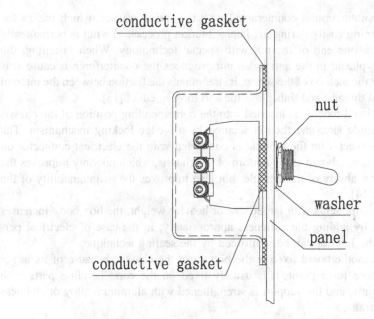

Fig. 6. Diagram of electromagnetic shielding for power switch

5 Anti Vibration and Impact Resistance Design

Generally speaking, the vibration frequency range of aviation environment ranges is from 10 to 2000 Hz, and the acceleration range is about 15 to 20 g. As the airborne reinforcement computer is generally rigidly and directly installed, it does not carry the shock absorber itself. So it is necessary to pay special attention to the anti vibration and impact resistance design of the chassis itself, the chassis and module, the modules and components, and the rest of the components. The specific measures are as follows:

(1) Choose the reasonable structure form and improve the rigidity of chassis structure. The main force-receiving member of the chassis frame has been welded into a whole, which greatly improves the vibration and impact resistance of the whole machine. Besides, under the condition of reducing the wall thickness of the non stress surface, the stiffen of the shell and support can be improved by setting up the ribs or ribs [11, 12].

(2) Fasteners and connectors must take reliable anti loosening measures - mainly including the use of spring washer anti loosening, thread glue curing, anti loosening nut interspersed and other anti loosing measures to ensure the reliability of the fastener installation. The spring washer is suitable for all kinds of disc screw. The medium and low strength thread glue is suitable for the locking and sealing of the M2 - M12 sunk head thread, and the looser nut is used when some rubber products are fastened. During the fastening process of rubber products, because of their own elasticity, the rubber products are subjected to the axial compression of the screw during the screw tightening process, which will produce greater reaction force, and

the part counteraction is counteracted with the spring washer, which makes the screw loosening easily during the later vibration process. The nut is permanently embedded in one end of the nut with special technology. When fastening, the engineering plastic in the anti loose nut produces the counterforce because it is extruded by the method of the screw. It strengthens the friction between the internal and external threads, and thus plays the anti loosing effect [13].

(3) Every functional module is inserted into the corresponding position of the chassis along the guide slot, and then is secured by a wedge locking mechanism. The electrical connector on the module is connected with the electrical connector on the printed motherboard at the bottom of the chassis, which not only improves the anti vibration ability of the module, but also improves the maintainability of the equipment [14].

(4) For some components with larger size or heavier weight, the box body increases its stiffness by adding the stiffeners appropriately; in the case of electrical performance, the interior can be reinforced by the sealing technique.

(5) For printed motherboard fixed at the bottom of the chassis, because of its larger area and more force point, it is usually fixed on the corresponding parts with multiple points, and the support is strengthened with aluminum alloy or stainless steel fixed frame.

(6) For some large quality components such as transistors and power supplies, in addition to the direction of installation, the strengthening measures should be taken in accordance with the type of pipe and welding, welding methods, etc. (mechanical press plate, adhesive fixed, local sealing and fixing, etc.).

(7) In addition, the inside of the chassis should avoid direct electrical connection with wires and cables; if it is unavoidable, measures should be taken at the corresponding parts for reinforcement, such as adding a wire bracket along the direction of the wire and effectively strapping.

6 Other Protective Measures

In the life period, the airborne reinforcement computer will experience various harsh external environments, such as the rainforest, the ocean or the desert, and so on, so it is necessary to take protective measures [15]. The reinforced computer is covered with aluminum alloy material and the exterior surface is coated with anti humid, salt sprayresistant and fungal resistant acrylic paint. All the open surfaces of the box are sealed by three ethylene propylene rubber waterproof seal, which reduces the corrosive harm to the surface of the components, such as dust and water vapor in the air The nonbearing structural parts such as cold plate are anodized with aluminum alloy, and 304 stainless steel materials are used in the force structural parts such as screw and handle, and the surface of the printed board is sprayed with three proof lacquers to improve the stability and reliability of the whole machine, and meet the requirements of "three proofing" (moisture proof, saltspray prevention and fungalproof).

7   Conclusions

In order to verify whether the performance indicators have achieved the desired results, the vibration test, low temperature work test, high temperature work test and electromagnetic compatibility test have been carried out successively after the design, processing and debugging of the reinforced computer.

The test results show that the computer has passed all the test validation successfully and verified that the design scheme of the chassis is reasonable and effective, and it has the condition of long-term stable and reliable operation.

The airborne reinforcement computer based on the design idea of this paper has compact structure, high space utilization rate. And the performance of heat dissipation, electromagnetic compatibility, anti-vibration and three proofing can meet the requirements of the indicators. At the same time, a series of environmental test data, which is finally passed by the computer, also provides a more powerful basis for further improvement design.

References

1. Zhang, Yu.: Experimental study on thermal design of sealed electronic enclosure. Electro-Mech. Eng. **31**, 5–8 (2015)
2. Zhao, T., Zhang, J., Lin, P.: Optimization of low-noise airflow field of laptop's thermal system. Noise Vib. Control **34**, 47–51 (2014)
3. Huang, F., Chen, Y.-J.: Thermal design for the processor in a certain type of electronic equipment. Mech. Res. Appl. **29**, 139–141 (2016)
4. Sha, C., You, Y., Hu, C., et al.: A thermal design for high density storage servers. Computer Engineering & Science. **37**, 2228–2231 (2015)
5. Zhao, B.: Comparative study on heat dissipation performance of liquid cooling and air cooling technology of airborne chassis. Mech. Res. Appl. **28**, 10–11 (2015)
6. People's Republic of China National Military Standard: Reliability Prediction Handbook for Electronic Equipment. Military Standard Publishing and Issuing Department, Beijing (2006)
7. Liu, J.: Study on cooling structure of sealed case of a radar. Electro-Mech. Eng. **28**, 36–38 (2012)
8. Tian, J., Wei, J., Zhao, B.: Electromagnetic compatibility design of the printed circuit board of airborne electronic equipment. Electron. Des. Eng. **22**, 137–140 (2014)
9. Liu, Y.: Design of communication equipment cabinet with electromagnetic compatibility. J. Hebei Acad. Sci. **33**, 35–38 (2016)
10. Yang, L., Zhao, G., Dong, W., et al.: Sealed design of avionic device. Mech. Eng. **5**, 214–215 (2014)
11. Yuan, L., Huang, J.: The structure and defense design of a portable reinforcement machine. Mod. Manuf. Eng. **7**, 123–125 (2012)
12. Li, K., Yang, L., Pang, W., et al.: Structural design and dynamics simulation for anti-adverse circumstance cabinet. Mach. Des. Manuf. **9**, 35–37 (2012)
13. Shi, R., Li, P., Shi, G.: Mechanical analysis of some rocket-borne reinforced computer based on ANSYS. J. Shanghai Univ. Eng. Sci. **29**, 342–346 (2015)
14. Luo, X.: Experimental study on acoustic noise of the forced air cooling reggedized computer. Dev. Innov. Mach. Electr. Prod. **29**, 10–11 (2016)
15. Xian, F., Liu, J., Yi, Y., et al.: Protection and coating technology of PCBA in electronic assembly field. Electron. Process Technol. **36**, 278–280 (2015)

Design Discussion and Performance Research of the Third-Level Cache in a Multi-socket, Multi-core Microchip

Nan Li[✉], Rangyu Deng, Ying Zhang, and Hongwei Zhou

College of Computer Science, National University of Defense Technology,
Changsha, Hunan, China
hello_linan@163.com

Abstract. L3cache is an essential part of microchips, which is integrated into most of the microchips such as Intel and AMD chips. FeiTeng serial microchips is an independent research and designed microchip. Our research is based on a 64-cores multi-socket FeiTeng chip. To increase the performance of this chip, L3cache is designed for this chip. This paper first discusses the design of L3-cache. Then two crucial evaluation indexes, the latency and bandwidth, are researched. From the simulation, it can be found that when opening L3cache, the latency can reduce 10% at most compared with the latency when closing L3cahce. Moreover, when opening L3cache, the bandwidth can increase twice under the circumstance of accessing a small amount of data. Considering the analysis, it can be concluded that for a multi-socket, multi-core system, L3cache can largely improve the systemic performance.

Keywords: Third-level cache · Computer architecture · Microchip design · Performance analysis of Microchip

1 Introduction

A special ultra-high-speed memory usually is needed to increase the speed of processing within a microchip by making data available to a processor at a rapid rate. Such a high-speed memory is known as a cache and is almost employed in every large computer system to compensate for the speed difference between main memory and processor logic; in another word, a cache is a hardware device used by the core of a chip to reduce the average time or energy to access data from the main memory [1, 2].

Through analyzing a large number of programs, it shows that the references to memory at any given interval of time tend to be confined within a few localized areas in memory, which is known as a phenomenon of "locality of reference." Although the cache is small comparing with the size of main memory, a large fraction of memory requests can be found here because of the locality of reference property of programs. In modern microchips, the improved performance puts a heavier burden on the memory interface since the processors demand more instructions and data [1]. Therefore, data

This work is supported by HGJ under Grant 2018ZX01029-103.

© Springer Nature Singapore Pte Ltd. 2019
W. Xu et al. (Eds.): NCCET 2019, CCIS 1146, pp. 112–121, 2019.
https://doi.org/10.1007/978-981-15-1850-8_10

cache is usually organized as a hierarchy of more cache levels, such as L1, L2, L3, etc. [3]. For the large chip manufacture companies, such as Intel, AMD, etc., all their chips include third-level cache(L3cache) [4–6]. L3cache is used between the cores and the memory, and purpose of designing L3cache is to increase the performance of the whole system [3]. Therefore, designing a high-performance L3cahce is very important for a microchip.

Moreover, A multi-core multi-socket processor is currently designed by a large number of companies. According to Moor's law that computer performance will double every 18 months [7]. The traditional single-core chip cannot be improved in the performance, because adding more transistors on a single-core chip generates heat that exceeds the advancements rate of the cooling techniques which is known as "the power wall" problem [8]. However, integrating two or more processors not only can enhance performance, but also largely reduce power consumption and efficiently process simultaneous multiple tasks; therefore, it is a growing industry trend replacing single-core processors that is rapidly reaching the physical limits of structure and speed [9–11].

In a multi-core multi-socket processor, a designer faces an issue that is the communication between core processors and the main memory. We can choose to use a single communication bus "shared memory model" or an interconnection network "distributed memory model". The single bus approach has an upper limit of 32 cores, after that the bus will be overfilled with transactions that lower the performance of the system [9, 12].

For the distributed memory model, every core has its own memory, the data in the memory might not be always updated, which will result in a cache coherence problem. Reaching a non-consistent value in the memory may result in a fatal error. Currently, there are two schemes that resolving the problem of cache coherence, i.e. the snooping protocol and a directory protocol. The snooping protocol is designed only for a bus-based system, it uses a number of states to determine whether or not there is a need to update the cache entries or not and also if it has control over writing to the block [9, 13]. Besides, the directory protocol has the scalability to work on any arbitrary network. A directory is used to hold information about which of the memory locations are being used exclusively by one core, and which are shared among multiple cores [9, 14]. Therefore, researching the cache system is important for a multi-core multi-socket microchip.

YinHe FeiTeng is a serials of high-performance and high-reliable microchips that are entirely designed and developed by the National University of Defense Technology in China [15, 16]. Among FeiTeng serial chips, for example, FT2000 uses ARMv8 structure and manufacture technology of 16 and 28 nm, and it includes a 128 MB L3cache [17, 18]. Besides, a recent FeiTeng serial chip applies a new systemic structure, i.e. multi-socket structure. To improve the performance of the chip, it includes an L3cache to increase the systemic performance.

Learnt from the literature review above, how to design the cache for a multi-core system needs to be researched. In this article, we research the L3cache system in a multi-core multi-socket microchip. First, we discuss the design of the L3cache, then we research the performance of the L3 cache in this chip. The innovation of this article is that we research the influence of the L3cache to a multi-core multi-socket chip with detailed data and comparison, and we provide useful data and results for microchip designers.

2   Design of the L3cache in the Microchip

The researched chip is a multi-socket system. Figure 1 shows the whole structure of the chip. It is consists of 6 panels and each panel contains 8 cores. Every panel connects with the local memory unit (LMU). Every panel is connected with other panels, LMU and IOU using a net protocol that is running on the Network On Chip (NOC) systems.

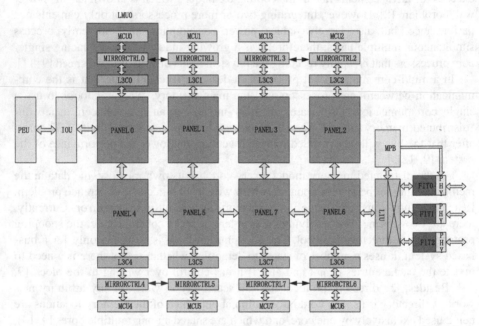

Fig. 1. General view of the chip

The L3cache is located in the LMU, and it directly connects with Mirror part. Figure 2 shows the structure of the L3C in the chip. In this structure, every L3C has 8 MB, and it has twelve stacks. L3cache is separated into two pipelines. Relevant part can access each of two pipelines using the lowest bit of the cacheline address in parallel. Every pipeline has 4 MB data array and it organizes as 8-way set associative. Moreover, in the L3cache, the cacheline is 64 Bytes. The frequency of the L3cache is 1.2 GHz, which is half of the NOC frequency. Third, tag array is consists of eight SRAM, and every SRAM corresponds to a one-way cacheline. The access cycle of tag and data is set as the multicycle. The strategy of the cacheline replacement is random placement. In the chip, the L3cache applied to write-back strategy. Fourth, L3cache supports inclusive and non-inclusive cache. L3cache can handle partial-word commands. Finally, L3cache supports read-after-write conflict, write-after-write conflict, write–after-write conflict and write-after-read conflict.

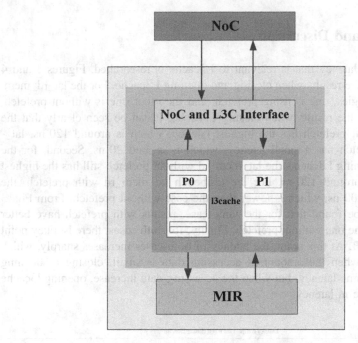

Fig. 2. Structural design of L3cache in the chip

3 Dataset and Simulation

The simulation of the system is performed on an eight-panel and 64-cores hardware accelerator. The usage of the testbench is mainly lmbench. Lmbench is a suite of simple, portable benchmarks, and it compares different Unix systems performance. In the lmbench, we chose lat_mem_rd and bw_mem to separately evaluate systemic latency and bandwidth of the whole system when closing and opening l3cache.

Besides, to quantitatively compare the latency and bandwidth under the situation of closing and opening L3cache, we use Eqs. (1) and (2) to calculate the difference of the latency and bandwidth.

$$PLRatio = (C(L) - O(L))/abs(C(L)) \tag{1}$$

$$PBRatio = (C(B) - O(B))/abs(O(B)) \tag{2}$$

Where $C(L)$ is the latency when closing l3cache, and $O(L)$ is the latency when opening l3cache. $C(B)$ is the bandwidth when closing l3cache, and $O(B)$ is the bandwidth when opening l3cache.

Finally, for evaluating the bandwidth, we use three kinds of commands that are read, read-write and initialization (write-zeros) commands. Three commands are evaluated using 1, 2, 3, 4, 8, 16, 32, 128, 256, 512, 1024 MB data.

4 Evaluation and Discussion

First, the systemic latency that is relevant to L3cache is researched. Figures 3 and 4 show the comparative results when closing and opening L3cache. For the lat_rd_mem, we have two strategies, one is using prefetch, and the other one is without prefetch. First, Fig. 3 shows the results when closing L3cache. It can be seen clearly that the lat_mem_rd without prefetch has the highest latency, which is around 120 ns, lat_-mem_rd with prefetch has a small latency, which is around 20 ns. Second, for the lmbench when opening L3cache, the lat_mem_rd without prefetch still has the highest latency, which is around 120 ns. For the testbench lat_mem_rd with prefetch, the latency is around 200 ns, which is lower than the case without prefetch. From Fig. 3 and Fig. 4, it can be found that for the same case, results with prefetch have better performance than the one without prefetch. Finally, for both cases, there is a key point that is about 50 MB. At this point, the latency of both cases increases sharply, which demonstrates that when the amount of accessing data is small, closing or opening l3cache have the same latency, but when the accessing data increase, opening l3cache shows its advantage in latency.

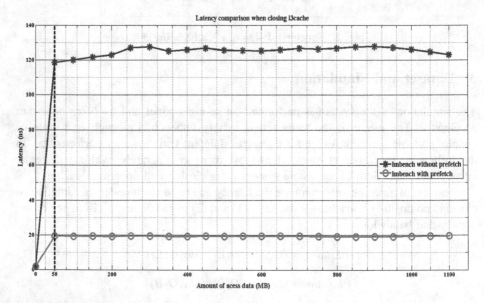

Fig. 3. The latency comparison when closing l3cache using lmbench with and without prefetch

However, from Figs. 3 and 4, it still cannot be found that the influence of the l3cache does not show clearly. For both figures, it is difficult to analyze the difference

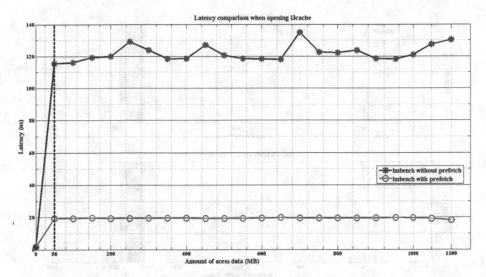

Fig. 4. The latency comparison when opening l3cache using lmbench with and without prefetch

of the latency when closing and opening l3cache. Therefore, we need to quantitatively compare two cases. We separated the result into two datasets, one is lower half of the group, and other one is the higher half of the dataset. The PLRatio of both groups are calculated through Eq. (1).

Figure 5 gives results about the performance of the system including and non-including l3cache. As the discussion above, we calculate PLRatio to quantize the difference of the latency when closing and opening L3cache. From this figure, it can be clearly found that when opening l3cache, the improvement of the performance is large. When the amount of the data is small (Dataset A), the PLRatio is lower than 1%, which proves that closing l3cahce or not will not obviously affect the performance when the amount of accessing data is small. Furthermore, when the accessing data is large (the dataset B), opening l3cache has a big improvement in system performance. For the lat_mem_rd with prefetch, the average PLRatio is around 6%, and for the testbench without prefetch, this ratio reaches 10%. Therefore, L3cache shows obvious advantage for the whole system.

Third, the bandwidth of the memory access when closing and opening l3cache is researched. Figures 6 and 7 show the comparison results when closing and opening L3cache. From both figures, it can be found that for the all three types of commands, before around 50 MB, the bandwidth changes sharply, and after this point, the bandwidth changes very slightly. Moreover, it can be found that read-write command has the worst bandwidth and the initialization command has the highest bandwidth for both cases.

Finally, Figs. 6 and 7 cannot demonstrate the performance difference when closing and opening L3cache. Therefore, we use Eq. (2) to further compare the difference of the bandwidth for both cases, and the simulation results are shown in Fig. 8. From the discussion above, after 50 MB, the bandwidth does not have an obvious change; therefore, we mainly compare the bandwidth difference under 1, 2, 3, 4, 8, 16 MB. First,

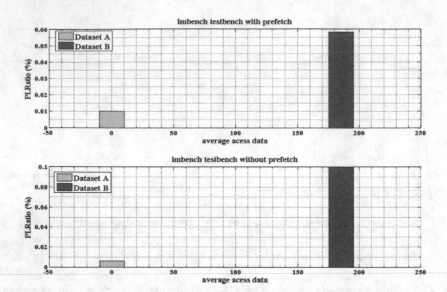

Fig. 5. Systemic latency comparison when closing and opening L3cache

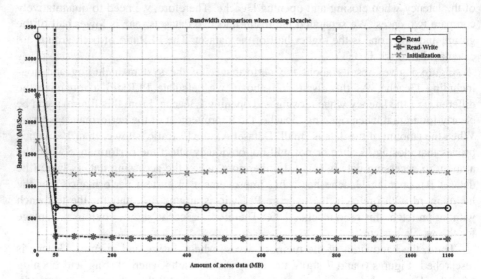

Fig. 6. The bandwidth comparison when closing l3cache using lmbench with three kinds of commands

read_write command has the highest bandwidth difference when the amount of data access is small, i.e. 2 Mb or 4 Mb, and the PBRatio can reach140%, which is a huge increase of the bandwidth. However when increasing the amount of the data, the bandwidth begins to fall, when the amount of the data reaches 16 MB, the PBRatio is 40%, which is still considerable in the increase of the bandwidth. Similarly, read command has the similar trend, but the increase of the bandwidth is not obvious than the

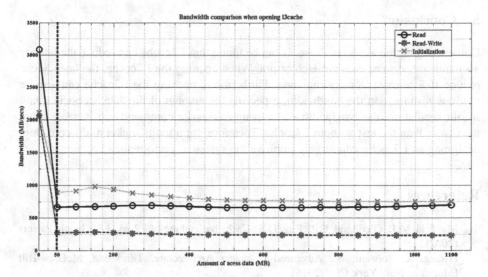

Fig. 7. The bandwidth comparison when opening l3cache using lmbench with three kinds of commands

one using read-write command. Besides, the initialization command has a slight fluctuation in the beginning, and the bandwidth begins to fall after 20 MB, and finally it reaches a plateau of PBRatio around - 20%. This result shows that when the amount of data is large, l3cache does not show considerable improvement when using initialization commands. Considering all the cases, it can be concluded that when the amount of the access data is small, opening L3cache can acquire significant increase in the bandwidth.

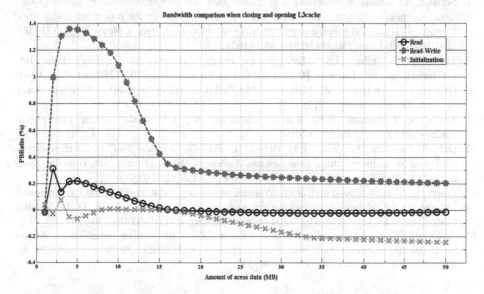

Fig. 8. Systemic bandwidth comparison when closing and opening L3cache

5   Conclusion

Considering all the analysis above, it can be found that L3cache can reduce the latency no matter the system uses prefetch or not. When opening the L3cache, the latency can reduce 10% at most in our simulation. Furthermore, opening the L3cache can acquire obvious advantage in the bandwidth, especially the amount of the data access is small. In our simulation, the bandwidth when using read-write command can increase more than twice than the test without L3cache. Therefore, for a multi-socket multi-core chip, designing an L3cache can largely improve the systemic performance.

References

1. Mayfield, M.J., O'connell, F.P., Ray, D.S.: Cache prefetching of L2 and L3. Google Patents (2002)
2. Hwang, K., Jotwani, N.: Advanced Computer Architecture, Third edn. McGraw-Hill Education, New York City (2016)
3. Hennessy, J.L., Patterson, D.A.: Computer Architecture: A Quantitative Approach, Sixth edn, pp. 78–148. Morgan Kaufmann Publishers Inc., San Francisco (2017)
4. Chang, M.T.: Technology implications for large last-level caches. Dissertation, University of Maryland at College Park 2013 (2013)
5. Chang, M.T., Rosenfeld, P., Lu, S.-L., Jacob, B.: Technology comparison for large last-level caches (L3Cs): low-leakage SRAM, low write-energy STT-RAM, and refresh-optimized eDRAM. In: 2013 IEEE 19th International Symposium on High Performance Computer Architecture (HPCA), pp. 143–154 (2013). https://doi.org/10.1109/hpca.2013.6522314
6. Ahn, H.K., Choi, S., Jung, S.: Evaluation of STT-MRAM L3 cache in 7 nm FinFET process'. In: 2018 International Conference on Electronics, Information, and Communication (ICEIC), pp. 1–4 (2018)
7. Schauer, B.: Multicore processors–a necessity, pp. 1–14. ProQuest discovery guides (2008)
8. Guo, X., Ipek, E., Soyata, T.: Resistive computation: avoiding the power wall with low-leakage, STT-MRAM based computing. SIGARCH Comput. Archit. News **38**(3), 371–382 (2010). https://doi.org/10.1145/1816038.1816012
9. Sirhan, N.N., Serhan, I.S.: Multi-core processors: concepts and implementations. Int. J. Comput. Sci. Inf. Technol. **10**(1), 1–10 (2018). https://doi.org/10.5121/ijcsit.2018.10101
10. Dropps, F.R., Anderson, M., Malewicki, M.: Packet tunneling for multi-node, multi-socket systems. Google Patents (2019)
11. Tsien, B., Broussard, B.P., Kalyanasundharam, V.: Multi-node system low power management. Google Patents (2019)
12. Deb, S., Ganguly, A., Pande, P.P., Belzer, B., Heo, D.: Wireless NoC as interconnection backbone for multicore chips: promises and challenges. IEEE J. Emerg. Sel. Top Circ. Syst. **2**(2), 228–239 (2012). https://doi.org/10.1109/JETCAS.2012.2193835
13. Louri, A., Kodi, A.K.: An optical interconnection network and a modified snooping protocol for the design of large-scale symmetric multiprocessors (SMPs). IEEE Trans. Parallel Distrib. Syst. **15**(12), 1093–1104 (2014). https://doi.org/10.1109/TPDS.2004.75
14. Sokolinsky, L.B.: Analytical estimation of the scalability of iterative numerical algorithms on distributed memory multiprocessors. Lobachevskii J. Math. **39**(4), 571–575 (2018). https://doi.org/10.1134/S1995080218040121

15. Xie, M., Lu, Y.T., Wang, K.F., Liu, L., Cao, H.J., Yang, X.J.: Tianhe-1A interconnect and messagepassing services. IEEE Micro **32**(1), 8–20 (2012). https://doi.org/10.1109/mm.2011.97
16. Liao, X.K., et al.: High performance interconnect network for Tianhe system. J. Comput. Sci. Technol. **30**(2), 259–272 (2015). https://doi.org/10.1007/s11390-015-1520-7
17. Liao, X., Xiao, L., Yang, C., Lu, Y.: MilkyWay-2 supercomputer: system and application. Front. Comput. Sci. **8**(3), 345–356 (2014). https://doi.org/10.1007/s11704-014-3501-3
18. Yang, X.J., Liao, X.K., Lu, K., Hu, Q.F., Song, J.Q., Su, J.S.: The TianHe-1A supercomputer: its hardware and software. J. Comput. Sci. Technol. **26**(3), 344–351 (2011). https://doi.org/10.1007/s02011-011-1137-8

An Efficient and Reliable Retransmission Mechanism for On-Chip Network of Many-Core Processor

Jianmei Luo[1], Hongwei Zhou[2(✉)], Ying Zhang[2], Nan Li[2], and Ying Wang[1]

[1] Phytium Technology Co., LTd., Tianjin 300131, China
[2] School of Computer, National University of Defense Technology,
Changsha 410073, China
zhou.hongwei@139.com

Abstract. Building a reliable and efficient Network-on-chip(NOC) system has always been an important part of the research on many-core processor architecture. In this paper, we propose a retransmission mechanism for many-core processor using dynamic pipeline and static flow control, which can break the deadlock caused by sharing channel on 2D mesh NOC. The configuration of key parameters in this retransmission mechanism is given by modeling. The modeling analysis and actual test results show that, the retransmission mechanism can not only avoid congestion and deadlock in NOC, but also effectively satisfies network bandwidth and memory access performance by properly set the depth of retransmission sender queue and retransmission receiver queue in different address mapping modes and transmission delays.

Keywords: Many-core processor · Network-on-chip · Retransmission mechanism

1 Introduction

With the rapid development of integrated circuit technology and the higher demand for application, the development of many-core processor based on NOC has become increasingly mature [1]. While many-core processors bring powerful parallel computing ability, they also take new challenges to the design of the architecture. It is important to provide efficient storage management and reliable interconnection communication protocol for designing and implementing high performance many-core processor.

The retransmission protocol is mainly used for implementing error-free data link layer communication [2]. It has great significance and is widely used in data transmission systems. Classic retransmission protocols mainly include Stop and Wait, Go-back-N and Selective-Retry [3]. The Stop and Wait is the simplest to implement but less efficiency, as shown in Fig. 1. The transmitting station must wait for a positive acknowledgement after sending a frame. It has to resend the

© Springer Nature Singapore Pte Ltd. 2019
W. Xu et al. (Eds.): NCCET 2019, CCIS 1146, pp. 122–135, 2019.
https://doi.org/10.1007/978-981-15-1850-8_11

frame after receiving a negative acknowledgement (NACK) or not receiving any acknowledgement within a certain time. Wang has provided some initial results on an investigation concerning the application of three tailored Stop-and-Wait Automatic Repeat reQuest (SW-ARQ) schemes to a diffusion based molecular communications system [4]. In the Go-back-N each frame has a sequence number, which is sent and received in sequence according to the sliding window protocol. The sender does not have to wait the acknowledgement from the receiver, but a large number of frame retransmissions will reduce channel utilization rate. As shown in Fig. 2, when frame 2 fails, the frames 2, 3, 4, and 5 must be retransmitted. Jianjun Hu has proposed an improved GBN protocol [5,6]. Obviously, Selective-Retry is more flexible as shown in Fig. 3. When the sender receives NACK2, only frame 2 is retransmitted and it's not necessary to retransmit all frames from the errors, which can greatly improve the transmission efficiency with more complex implementation.

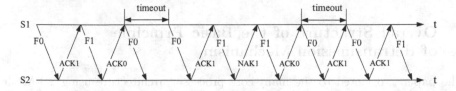

Fig. 1. Stop and wait

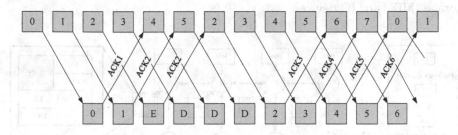

Fig. 2. Go-back-N

This paper proposes a retransmission protocol for the many-core processor using 2D-Mesh NOC [7,8]. The retransmission protocol has been improved and optimized on the basis of traditional retransmission protocol by adopting the Automatic Repeat Request (ARQ) technology and the static flow control based on credit [9]. The efficient and reliable flow control mechanism between the source node and the destination node on NOC is implemented, which can not only avoid congestion and deadlocks on network-on-chip but also ensures the memory bandwidth and performance [10,11].

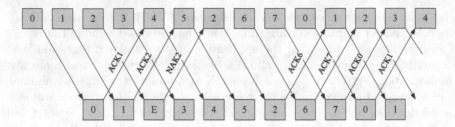

Fig. 3. Selective-Retry

The content behind the paper is organized as follows: The second chapter introduces the overall structure of NOC in our many-core processor and the basic principle of the proposed retransmission mechanism. The third chapter introduces the specific implementation of the retransmission mechanism proposed in this paper. The fourth chapter conducts experiments and analyzes the experimental results. The fifth chapter is the summary of the full text.

2   Overall Structure of the Basic Principle of Retransmission Mechanism

The paper is oriented to the many-core processor architecture using 2D-Mesh NOC [12], and its structure is shown in Fig. 4. Each processing unit (PE) includes a processor core (Core), a first-level instruction cache (L1I) and a first-level data cache (L1D), a second-level shared cache (L2C), and a consistency protocol directory control unit (DCU) and a Network Interface (NI). Each PE is linked to a routing node (Router). The edge routing node is able to mount memory storage (MEM) or IO devices.

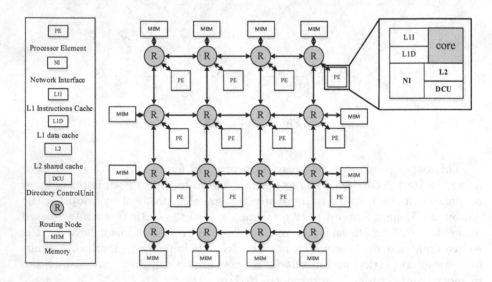

Fig. 4. Schematic diagram of multicore processor architecture based on 2D-mesh NoC

The processor cores get required instructions and data through the memory hierarchy [13]. L1ICache and L1DCache are the first level of accessible storage. If L2C access is failed, the access request is sent to DCU unit in order to maintain consistency. Then DCU will produce cache coherence packets in accordance with the state of the directory in DCU and Cache consistency protocol and send them to the NoC network. A copy of the latest data is obtained either from L2C of other PE or by accessing the MEM. The process of source node sending request packets to destination node is a combination of routing algorithm, address mapping mode and arbitration strategy on the basis of the address information in the header packet. Packet switching technology is used to transmit packet to destination node via network in the form of flit. Assume that the NoC channel contains 4 independent CC coherent physical channels: Request (Req), Response (Rsp), Snoop (Snp), and Acknowledge (Ack), and only Rsp and Ack can carry data. According to the communication requirements in our system, the memory access request from the DCU to the MEM is allocated to the downlink Rsp channel, and the memory access response is allocated to the uplink Rsp channel as shown in the Fig. 5. Since the request from DCU to MEM is also conducted through the Rsp channel on NoC, deadlock may occur once the channel is shared with cache coherence packet during channel allocation.

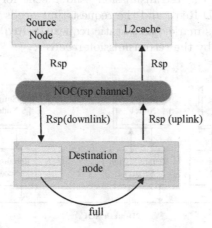

Fig. 5. Channel allocation diagram

In order to break the deadlock, this paper design the retransmission mechanism in the downlink Rsp channel, preventing the memory access requests from blocking the Rsp channel. The retransmission mechanism can ensure that the receiver is able to handle all requests sent from source node and avoid blocking between the cache coherence packets and the memory access response packets. At the same time, we put the retransmission acknowledgments to dedicated channel (RAck). So the retransmission acknowledgments can completely solve the deadlock problem and ensure memory access bandwidth.

According to the address mapping mode, a node where a MEM is located may correspond to a DCU in multiple PE cells. Here we define DCU as the source node and MEM as the destination node. Any DCU to any MEM needs to support retransmission mechanism. The resource nodes related to the retransmission mechanism on NoC of this paper can be abstracted into a model as shown in Fig. 6. There are 16 MEMs in the whole chip, and each MEM can support up to 16 DCUs for memory access operation. In order to maintain the memory access sequence, the communication between the same DCU and the same MEM must be in order. The communication between different DCU and the same MEM can be out of order, that is, the requests sent by different DCUs to the same MEM are not affected by each other.

According to the above requirements, for each specific sender and receiver, we design a retransmission mechanism combining dynamic pipeline and static flow control. When the receiver has not sent any negative acknowledgement packet (NACK) to the sender, the sender continues to send dynamic request to receiver. Once the NACK is received, it enters the static flow control mode. In this control mode, each time the sender receives a credit, it retransmits a static request until all accumulated static requests are retransmitted. The basic principle is shown in Fig. 7:

(1) Mark the request the retransmission sender sent for the first time as a dynamic request (D-Req), and the request that needs to be sent again due to retransmission is marked as a static request (S-Req). The static requests must be absorbed by the retransmission receiver.

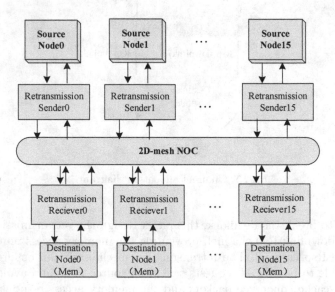

Fig. 6. Schematic diagram of resource nodes for retransmission on-chip network mechanism

(2) For dynamic pipeline, the receiver needs to return an ACK acknowledgement packet to the sender after receiving a dynamic request. If it has no space to receive any dynamic request, the receiver discards it and returns a NACK acknowledgement packet to the sender. The discarded requests (such as numbers D-Req3 and D-Req4) need to be retransmitted. Before the sender receives any NACK acknowledgement packet, the sender can continuously send a dynamic request. But once it receives a NACK, the sender must stop sending any dynamic request.

(3) When there is an idle item at the receiver, a PGrant acknowledgement packet (i.e., a credit for sending static request) is generated and returned to the sender for each of the previously discarded dynamic requests. After receiving the PGrant acknowledgement packet, the sender can send the previous request that needs to be retransmitted as a static request (that is, the s-req3 and s-req4). After receiving all PGrant (PGrant3 and PGrant4) and sending out all static requests, the sender turns to dynamic pipeline and proceeds to send the next dynamic requests.

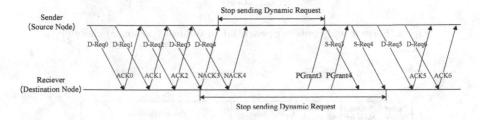

Fig. 7. Schematic diagram of the retransmission protocol process

For any receiver, while there is a request from a source node is retransmitted currently, it can only receive static requests from the source node before all PGrants are sent to its sender, but it can receive dynamic requests from other source nodes which has no retransmitted request at that time. In this way, the requests sent by different source nodes to the same destination node will not be affected by each other.

The retransmission mechanism can effectively avoid congestion between source node and destination node in the on-chip network, break the deadlock which may be caused by channel dependence [14].

3 Retransmission Mechanism Design

3.1 Packet Format Design

In NOC, the source node and the destination node is communicated in the form of micro-packets which is consist of flits. The retransmission module includes the request packet (the downlink Rsp channel from the PE to the MEM), the data response packet (the uplink Rsp channel from the MEM to the PE), and the retransmission acknowledgement packet (the dedicated RAck channel). The above channels allocated are independent physical channels. The request packet can be divided into two forms: a header flit and two data flits, as shown in Fig. 8. For read request, it just has a header flit and the write request has a header flit and two data flits. The retransmission acknowledgement packet has only one flit, as shown in Fig. 9. The data response packet's format is the same as the request packet's since they belong to the same channel.

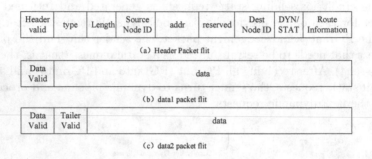

Header valid	type	Length	Source Node ID	addr	reserved	Dest Node ID	DYN/ STAT	Route Information

(a) Header Packet flit

Data Valid	data

(b) data1 packet flit

Data Valid	Tailer Valid	data

(c) data2 packet flit

Fig. 8. Format and content of each flit in request (response) channel

Packet Valid	Source Node ID	Dest NodeID	type	reserved	Route Infomation

Fig. 9. Format and content of each flit in retransmission acknowledgement channel

The request from the source node firstly arrives at the retransmission sender module, and then it is forwarded by the intermediate routing node and reaches the retransmission receiver of the destination node. If the destination node is capable of handling the current request, the retransmission receiver sends the request smoothly to the destination node. If the destination node is too busy to process the current request and the retransmission receiver has no space to buffer any request, it will discard the current request. Whether receiving or discarding the request, the key information of the request will be recorded for generating a retransmission acknowledgement packet (ACK/NACK/PGrant) to the source node. According the retransmission protocol rules described in Sect. 1 of this paper, the source node will make a judgment whether to send a dynamic request or a static request according to the information of the received acknowledgement packet. Above is a complete transmission process of the destination node receiving request packet, writing data flits to MEM or read data flits from MEM.

3.2 Retransmission Sender Design

The retransmission sender is consist of a dynamic request sender queue, a static request sender queue, ACK/NACK acknowledgement packet receiving counter, and transmission control logic. The working process is shown in Fig. 10.

(1) When the sender has not yet received any NACK acknowledgement packet returned from the receiver, the sender sends a dynamic request from the sender queue in the first-in-first-out order and its valid status bit is marked as 0. At the same time, for each ACK acknowledgement packet received by the sender, it's ACK acknowledgement packet receiving counter is incremented by 1 and the earliest dynamic request whose valid status bit is 0 in the sender queue is cleared out of the dynamic request sender queue.

(2) Once the sender receives a NACK acknowledgement packet, it's NACK packet receiving counter is incremented by 1, and the sender stops sending dynamic requests right now. At the same time, the earliest request in the sender queue whose valid status bit is 0 will be transferred to the static request sender queue and marked as a static request.

(3) Upon receiving a PGrant acknowledgement packet, the request in the static request sender queue can be send. Each time a PGrant packet is received, a static request can be sent. The sender can continue to send other dynamic requests until all PGrant packets are arrived and the static request queue is empty.

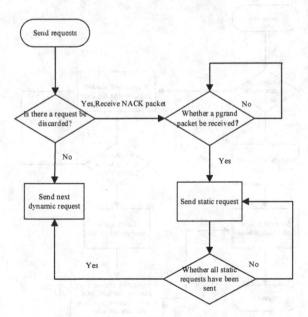

Fig. 10. Working process of retransmission sender

3.3 Retransmission Receiver Design

The retransmission receiver is consist of the receiver queue and item counters for each kind of flit, the NACK counter, the PGrant counter, and control logic. There are up to 16 different source nodes for each destination node in NOC. We set 16 retransmission response packet queues, 16 NACK counters and 16 PGrant counters at retransmission receiver, corresponding to 16 source node id in the system. The working process is shown in Fig. 11.

(1) When the request packet reaches the retransmission receiver and the receiver queue is not full, the retransmission receiver can absorb the request packet including the header flit and the data flit respectively into the header flit queue and data flit queue. For each request packet received, the receiver queue counter is incremented by 1. At the same time, the key information of the request will be recorded and written to its corresponding acknowledgement queue for generating an ACK packet to the sender.

(2) When the receiver queue is full, the request packet from network can no longer be buffered into the receiver queue, so it must be discarded and retransmitted. At the same time, the key information of the request will be recorded and written to its corresponding acknowledgement queue for generating a NACK packet to the sender. For each request packet discarded, the NACK counter is incremented by 1.

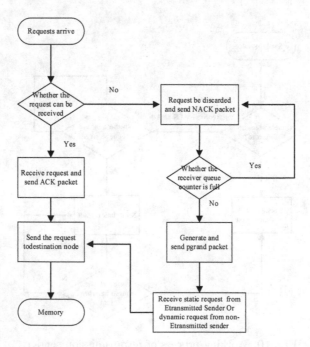

Fig. 11. Working process of retransmission receiver

(3) When the receiver queue has extra idle entries, the receiver can allocate PGrant packets according to the remarked counters of each source node. Each time a PGrant packet is allocated, an item is reserved in the receiver queue(i.e., reserved item) so that the corresponding static packet can be received. Meanwhile, the receiver item counter is also incremented by 1. For different source nodes, the arbitration strategy for PGrant is Round-Robin scheduling algorithm according to the current status of each NACK counter to avoid starving of any source node.

(4) It is worth noting that each time the receiver queue receives a static request, the receiver item counter stays the same, the NACK counter and the PGrant counter of the corresponding source node are decremented by 1, and no ACK/NACK acknowledgement packet is generated at this time.

(5) All requests that are buffered into the receive queue will be sent to the destination node for memory access operations using handshake protocol.

3.4 Flow Control Parameter Description

The retransmission mechanism proposed in this paper aims to solve deadlock. When the receiver is in lack of resource, the retransmission mechanism turns to the mode of static-flow-control. In this mode, the sender can only retransmit the static request from the previous first NACK breakpoint when receiving the PGrant, so the sending of dynamic request is interrupted. The dynamic mode can only be restored when the sender receives all PGrants. To eliminate the impact of interruptions on memory bandwidth, the receiver must ensure that sufficient requests are available for processing during the interruptions. To achieve this goal, the configuration of flow control parameters is critical. Next, we analyze the optimal settings of the relevant flow control parameters through modeling [15, 16].

(1) The transmission delay—T_p

The transmission delay is defined as the number of clock cycles required for the sender to send the first request packet to the retransmission receiver in NOC. The transmission delay of the on-chip network is decided by the distance of the transmission path.

(2) Depth of the sender queue—D_{tx}

The retransmission sender is the master component of the flow control. It has to make ensure that the request is sent continuously every cycle. The depth is closely related to the transmission delay and determines the maximum number of requests that can be retransmitted.

(3) Depth of the receiver queue—D_{rx}

The retransmission receiver is the slave part, its depth reflects the maximum capacity of the receiver queue. Its depth depends on the transmission delay and the depth of the transmission queue. If it is too small, the read data from MEM cannot be continuously returned every cycle, or it will occupy too many physical resources if it's too large.

When the receiver queue is full, the number of requests buffered is equivalent to D_{rx}. At this point, the retransmission mechanism changes from dynamic pipeline to static flow control. The sender continues to send requests before receiving NACK. The subsequent request number is equal to D_{tx}. The receiver can start to generate the PGrant packet after all the requests are retransmitted. The PGrant starts to be sent and reaches the sender after T_p clock cycles. The retransmission sender then sends the static request for another T_p clock cycles and reach the receiver. That is, in the above $(2D_{tx} + 2T_p)$ clock cycle, the destination node processes a total number of D_{rx} valid requests with $3D_{rx}$ cycles, wherein the data response packet each read request returns includes a header flit and two data flits. The bandwidth utilization can be calculated as follows:

$E = 3D_{rx}/(2D_{tx} + 2T_p)$

4   Experiments and Analysis of Results

4.1   Experimental Environment Construction

In this paper, the UVM platform is used to construct the test environment of the retransmission mechanism for functional verification and performance analysis. In this environment, the retransmission sender is connected between the destination node and NOC, and the retransmission receiver is connected between NOC and MEM. In order to analyze the behavior of the source node and MEM, we write an simulation model for sending requests and a memory model for memory access operation. This environment is also able to record packets in each channel, automatically compare requests both at the sender and receiver queue, and check the results of the memory access operation.

4.2   Experiments and Analysis of Results

(1) Effect of transmission delay on the depth of sender queue and receiver queue in the case of single source node

Consider the retransmission flow control of a single source node with MEM. For the transmit receiver, the longer the transmission delay, more time it takes for the ACK/NACK sent from the receiver and reach the sender. Also, the inflighting requests continuously to be retransmitted makes the timing of the PGrant and the timing of the static message to be sent longer. For the sender, it is necessary for the sender queue to ensure that the request is continuously sent each cycle in dynamic mode, so the depth of the sender queue must not be less than the round-trip time between the sender and the receiver. At the same time, in order to ensure that the receiver has enough buffered requests to be handled during the time of retransmitted request reaching receiver queue, the depth should not be less than the round-trip time between the sender and the receiver. Assume that the depth of sender queue and receiver queue are the same. We have made a series of experiments for getting 100% memory access bandwidth. The minimum value for the depth of sender queue and receiver queue in different transmission delays is as shown in Fig. 12.

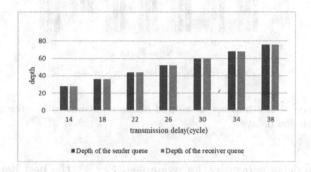

Fig. 12. Effect of different transmission delay on the depth of the sender queue and receiver queue

The transmission distance between the sender and the receiver is related to their location in many-core processor. Theoretical analysis combined with tests under different address configuration mode show that, when the physical distance between the source node and the destination node is the closest, we get the minimum value of the transmission delay which is 18 cycles. In contrary, when the physical distance between the source node and the destination node is the farthest, we get the maximum value of the transmission delay which is 38 cycles. Obviously, when the number of retransmission requests reaches the maximum, the depth of the sender queue and receiver queue must be 76 for 100% bandwidth utilization according to the above formula.

(2) Performance analysis for multiple source nodes and destination nodes

Consider multiple source nodes continuously sending requests to the same destination node each cycle. Since the requests from different source node is independently sent on NOC and the arbitration strategy at routing node is round-robin, each request has the same chance to reach receiver queue. For example, if a request from source node A is retransmitted, the receiver queue can also receive dynamic requests from source node B if there still has extra entries. It is not necessary to wait for the static request from source node A comparing with the situation of single source node. In this case, the utilization of the receiver queue is more sufficient, and the utilization bandwidth of the destination node is higher. The test results is shown in Fig. 13. Assume the depth of sender queue and receiver queue is 64. If the value of transmission delay is less than 32, the bandwidth of memory bandwidth can fully be used with a single source node continuously sending requests. Not even for multiple source nodes. If the value

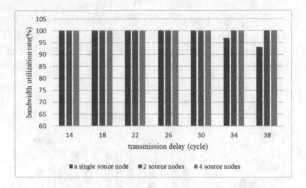

Fig. 13. Influence of the number of source nodes on bandwidth interest rate under different transmission delays

of transmission delay is over 32, for example, 34 or 38, the best bandwidth utilization with a single source node continuously sending requests is 96% or 93%. At this point, the response bandwidth can only be fully used by sending requests concurrently through more source nodes.

5   Summary

This paper proposes and implements an efficient and reliable retransmission mechanism between memory access request node and destination node for NOC in many-core processor. This retransmission mechanism is combined with dynamic pipeline and static flow control, which can successfully avoid congestion and deadlock in NoC. The modeling analysis and test results show that the retransmission mechanism has a good performance on satisfying the demand of bandwidth utilization and efficient communication between source node and destination node with reasonable configuration under different transmission delays. The research results of this paper have been applied to a 64-core independently-designed processor, which has achieved the expected results.

Acknowledgements.   This work is supported by HGJ under Grant 2018ZX01029-103.

References

1. Kong, D., Shi, H.: Research on the design of 2D-Mesh on-chip network based on multi-core system. Microelectron. Comput. **32**(04), 75–78 (2015). (in Chinese)
2. Liu, H.: Research and implementation of high speed Interconnection Network link layer protocol. National University of Defense Technology 2007. (in Chinese)
3. Matthews, J.: Computer Networks: Intermet Protocols in Action. Wiley, Hoboken (2005)
4. Wang, X., Higgins, M.D., Leeson, M.S.: Stop-and-wait automatic repeat request schemes for molecular communications (2013)

5. Jianjun, H.: Study on an improved Go-Back-N ARQ policy. Comput. Appl. Softw. **28**(07), 230–232 (2011). (in Chinese)
6. Tian, Y., Zhou, H.: Design and verification of link layer retransmission mechanism for direct interface of microprocessor[D]. National University of Defense Technology, National University of Defense Technology (2009). (in Chinese)
7. Liao, X.-K., et al.: High performance interconnect network for Tianhe system. J. Comput. Sci. Technol. **30**(2), 259–272 (2015)
8. Pang, Z.B., et al.: The TH Express high performance interconnect networks. Front. Comput. Sci. **8**, 357–366 (2014)
9. Anonymous. An Overview of ARQ Technology and Principles. Streaming Media Magazine (2016)
10. DeOrio, A., Fick, D., Bertacco, V., et al.: A reliable routing architecture and algorithm for NoCs. IEEE Trans. Comput. Aid. Des. Integr. Circuits Syst. **31**(5), 726–739 (2012)
11. Yung-Chou, T., Yarsun, H.: Study of dynamically-allocated multi-queue buffers for NoC routers. In: Proceedings of the International Conference on Parallel and Distributed Processing Techniques and Applications (2014)
12. Shahnawaz, T.: Improving router efficiency in network on chip triplet-based hierarchical interconnection network with shared buffer design. In: Proceeding of the Fifth International Conference on Intelligent Systems (2014)
13. Poluri, P., Louri, A.: Shield: a reliable network-on-chip router architecture for chip multiprocessors. IEEE Trans. Parallel Distrib. Syst. **27**(10), 3058–3070 (2016)
14. Liu, L.: Reserch on High-performance Mapping algorithm for network on-chip. Xidian University (2017). (in Chinese)
15. Ma, S., Wang, Z., Jerger, N.E., et al.: Novel flow control for fully adaptive routing in cache-coherent NoCs. IEEE Trans. Parallel Distrib. Syst. **25**(9), 2397–2407 (2013)
16. Wang, P.: Analysis and implementation of key technologies of flow control in on-chip interconnection networks. National University of Defense Technology (2014). (in Chinese)

Anti-vibration Performance and Electromagnetic Compatibility Design for the Shipborne Reinforced Computer

Guangle Qin[✉]

Jiangsu Automation Research Institute, Lianyungang, China
k8.k8@163.com

Abstract. The ability of the shipborne computer to withstand harsh environments plays a very important role in ensuring the stability of the warship's system. This paper discusses design ideas of shipborne computer deeply, by using ANSYS to analysis the vibration of equipment modal, and elaborating on the electromagnetic compatibility design of the reinforcement computer. Through computer simulation and experiment, it is shown that the design of this type of shipborne reinforcement computer can guarantee its resistance to vibration shock and electromagnetic compatibility, and make sure that it has good comprehensive protection performance.

Keywords: Shipborne · Reinforced computer · Anti-vibration · Electromagnetic compatibility

1 Introduction

With the development of modern naval warfare in the direction of over-the-horizon, non-contact, and electronic information, the use environment of military electronic equipment is more varied, harsh and demanding [1]. Therefore, the ability of military equipment to withstand harsh environments is becoming stronger. The birth of the reinforced computer provides an effective means to help solve the problem of electronic computers, which is the core component of modern warships. The computer is reinforced to ensure that the computer can continue to operate normally for a long time in an extremely harsh and varied environment, so that it can withstand strong vibration shocks, electromagnetic interference and other harsh weather conditions to improve the reliability of the computer [2–4].

In this paper, the modal analysis of vibration and shock resistance in the structural design of the reinforced chassis and the electromagnetic compatibility design of the reinforced computer are described in detail, focusing on the board-level signal suppression, filtering and shielding of the whole machine.

© Springer Nature Singapore Pte Ltd. 2019
W. Xu et al. (Eds.): NCCET 2019, CCIS 1146, pp. 136–143, 2019.
https://doi.org/10.1007/978-981-15-1850-8_12

2 Structure Design

The reinforcement computer designed in this paper adopts multi-bus module structure, and the equipment is divided into reinforcement box, computer module and external equipment module. As a basic equipment to protect the internal components, the reinforced cabinet plays an important role in ensuring the stable and reliable operation of the internal computer modules. It also has a certain protective effect against strong vibration shocks and electromagnetic interference caused by harsh environment [5–7].

As shown in Fig. 1, the reinforced box body is designed with a split-sector structure. The computer module is located at the center of the box as the core of the protection. It is mainly used for loading control computers and other important electrical equipment. The external equipment modules mainly include the outer panel and fixed. On the series of high-performance electrical connectors on it, each bin is separated to avoid mutual interference.

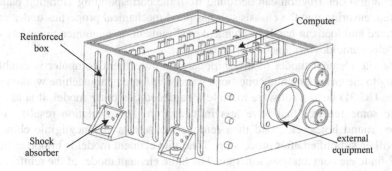

Fig. 1. The structure of the reinforced computer

3 Design and Simulation of Anti-vibration Impact Performance

The harsh environment in which a shipborne computer is working shows that different forms of vibration and shock are inevitable during its life cycle. First of all, it is necessary to determine the source of vibration and shock [8]. The vibration of the ship mainly comes from the power machinery such as the propeller operation. In addition, the harsh weather conditions of the ship during the navigation on the Sea may cause the ship to bump and shake [9–11]. Then the reinforcement computer in the ship's warehouse will be subject to different degrees of vibration and shock. For a Shipborne computer, the vibration it receives will not be exactly the same because of the installation location and the vibration and shock received by the ship itself. Vibration and shock are situations that are expected to be avoided as much as possible during the course of a ship's navigation, as its reliability and stability to the computer may be unpredictable. Therefore, how to reasonably avoid the damage and interference of the vibration environment to computer products is one of the key factors to strengthen the computer design.

3.1   Modeling

In this paper, based on the vibration and impact environment of the shipborne computer, the analytic analysis is carried out by using ANSYS to determine whether the designed chassis can withstand harsh environments and impacts, and verify whether the designed computer structure is feasible. The modality is the inherent vibrate characteristic of the structure. It is independent of whether there is load outside. Each modality corresponds to a specific parameter, namely the natural frequency and the mode shape. Finding the eigenvectors is the fundamental purpose of modal analysis. The features are the frequencies corresponding to the fundamental modes of the structure. They are far from these frequencies in order to avoid resonance when the structure is designed. If the rigidity of the structure needs to be strengthened, the part with the largest deformation can be found from the corresponding vibration pattern to strengthen, ensuring that the chassis still has good mechanical properties under various complicated and loads in harsh mechanical environment, to guarantee the safety of the various electronic devices inside the chassis.

The finite element model of the shipboard reinforcement computer is established according to the environmental conditions where reinforcement machine worked in. By using the UG 3D design software to build a hardened computer model, it is necessary to delete some features that have less influence on the calculation results, such as chamfers, round holes, etc., and then remove the screws and negligible chips, etc., which will be simplified after processing. The finite element model is imported into the ANSYS finite element analysis software. The finite element model of the reinforcement computer is shown in Fig. 2.

Fig. 2. The finite element model of the reinforcement computer

3.2   Modal Analysis

According to the established three-dimensional model, reinforced computer model is mainly composed of a casing shell, an internal module and a shock absorber, and the internal connection mode is screw fixing [12, 13]. Keep the shock absorber for vibration simulation. By meshing the chassis shell, the minimum unit size is set to 3 mm, and the PCB and the cold plate are modeled by a tetrahedral element. The other contact portions are set to rigid body contact and have no relative sliding tendency. The 6th-order frequency of the shipboard reinforced computer is extracted as shown in the Table 1, and its sixth-order mode and its natural mode are extracted. The frequency varies from 510.71 Hz to 1439.1 Hz.

Table 1. Modals from 1 to 6

Modal	Frequency/Hz
1	510.71
2	735.94
3	925.93
4	1008.6
5	1424.1
6	1439.1

This modal analysis has a total of 6 steps. Since no obvious deformation occurred in the latter two-stage chassis, so not all modal clouds are displayed, but the first four stages are selected, as shown in Figs. 3 and 4.

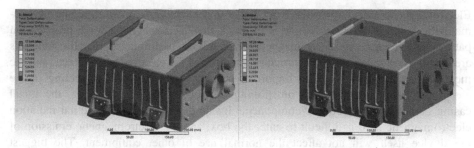

Fig. 3. The modal clouds since 1 to 2 stages

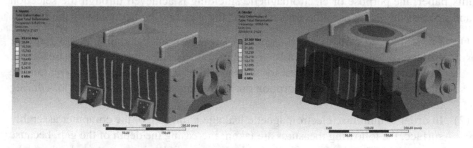

Fig. 4. The modal clouds since 3 to 4 stages

It can be seen that the main deformation part of the first-order modal device occurs in the rubber damper, and the box body is hardly deformed, which is consistent with the actual situation. According to the results of the above modal analysis, the resonance phenomenon can be avoided during the design of the prototype chassis, and the ability of the reinforced computer to resist vibration and impact can be improved.

4 Electromagnetic Compatibility Design

With the increasing use of shipborne computers in the military industry, other devices with different functions are also integrated into the ship cabin, and the electromagnetic environment of the cabin is very complicated [8]. Therefore, in addition to considering the effects of the computer on heat dissipation, vibration, and impact, the improvement of the reliability of the shipboard reinforced computer has become an important technical indicator that must be fully considered during design and development. Space radiation and cable transmission are two basic ways of electromagnetic interference. For the two interference modes and related electromagnetic compatibility requirements, this paper mainly uses filtering and shielding methods to suppress and loss electromagnetic interference, and through reasonable wiring and low impedance grounding. The circuit introduces electromagnetic interference into the reference ground to meet the requirements of electromagnetic compatibility indicators.

4.1 Shield Design

Electromagnetic shielding is the most basic and effective way to eliminate electromagnetic interference. Its principle is to block the electromagnetic wave propagation path, so as to remove the electromagnetic compatibility performance, metallic materials are usually selected as the main structural member of the electronic equipment, and the metal casing not only plays an important role for supporting and protecting of the electronic equipment, but also functioning as electromagnetic shielding, the metal casing closes all the electronic components inside the box, and the external radiation electromagnetic field is difficult to enter the box, and the electromagnetic emission of the device itself will not affect the normal use of other equipment. The biggest advantage of electromagnetic shielding is that it can improve electromagnetic compatibility without changing the circuit structure when the device function is used. In this paper, the purpose of electromagnetic shielding is achieved through the selection and processing of the box, the processing of the gap and the treatment of the holes.

(1) The reinforced computer case is made of low-resistance aluminum alloy, and the surface of the structural member is subjected to conductive oxidation treatment. The shielding effect is caused by the reflection of electromagnetic waves on the surface of the shield, the absorption during internal absorption, and the loss during transmission.

(2) In order to minimize electromagnetic leakage in the gap of the computer assembly surface, the following measures are taken: increasing the depth of the gap, because according to the electromagnetic field theory, a slit having a certain depth can be

regarded as a waveguide, and the waveguide can transmit electromagnetic waves inside the waveguide under certain conditions. Attenuation, the deeper the depth, the more the attenuation; the mounting surface is designed with grooves and filled with conductive rubber strips as shown. When the cover plate is fastened, the conductive rubber strip is 10%–25% compressed, which can play the role of shielding and sealing; the screw spacing of the motherboard cavity cover in the reinforced computer is designed to be 18 mm, which is about the highest working frequency. Figure 5 shows the typical gap between the processing cabinets.

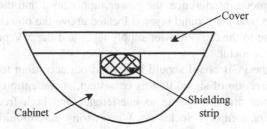

Fig. 5. The typical gap between the processing cabinets

4.2 Filter Design

In order to solve the EMI conduction interference of the reinforced computer, the filtering technology design method is adopted to filter the power input and the panel indicator.

The EMI power filter is a low-pass filter that delivers 50 Hz AC to the ruggedized computer without attenuation, greatly attenuating EMI interference signals into and out of the chassis. The AC-DC power module in the rugged computer is an inductive load, and a two-stage π-type filter is selected to achieve better filtering. The opening of the indicator light is an important factor that causes the electromagnetic leakage of the computer [14]. Therefore, the reinforced filter is selected by the reinforced filter indicator for filtering. The filter circuit is composed of a single-capacitor low-pass filter, which can couple the inside of the chassis to the indicator signal line. The EMI interference is introduced into the chassis to achieve EMI filtering.

In the process of assembling and reinforced computer, the following auxiliary measures have been taken to enhance the filtering: the filter component housing is sufficiently grounded so that electromagnetic interference can be introduced into the reference ground through the casing; the filter should be placed in the interior of the chassis close to the input port.

4.3 PCB Electromagnetic Compatibility Design

For electronic equipment, mechanical structure design and circuit design play a key role in the electromagnetic compatibility of the product. In the design process of similar equipment, it is often considered to use the mechanical properties of the chassis to achieve the purpose of shielding, while the electromagnetic compatibility of the PCB circuit board level can be designed to solve the electromagnetic compatibility performance. One of the means, this article will explain the specific measures of PCB board-level electromagnetic compatibility design from the following aspects.

The multi-layer printed board design is the main measure to reach the electromagnetic compatibility standard. According to the actual function, the motherboard in the shipboard reinforcement computer is designed as an eight-layer board. It is required to allocate a separate 3.3 V power supply layer and 5 V to the main board. The power supply layer and the ground layer help to reduce the power supply impedance and suppress common mode interference; the power supply layer and the ground layer are as close as possible, and the ground layer is located above the power supply layer; the wiring layer is close to the 3.3 V power supply layer and the 5 V power supply layer containing the whole metal.

The layout of the PCB board should be carried out according to the circuit signal flow, so that the direction of signal flow is consistent, and attention should be paid to isolating devices that are susceptible to interference and high frequencies, such as network transformers, memory, clocks, etc. When wiring, care should be taken to avoid paralleling the long distance between the input and output wires. Inserting the ground wire between the parallel traces reduces signal crosstalk. In addition, proper grounding between the connector pins on the board also helps to reduce The loop area of the pin signal and the ground impedance. In addition, reduce the length of the wire and differentially wire some sensitive signals: serial signals, LVDS display signals, network signals, etc.

4.4   Test Verification

By examining the radiation, conduction and other testing items of the electromagnetic compatibility performance of the shipboard reinforcement machine during operation, one of the test results is listed. As shown in Fig. 6, the test proves that the signal of the hardened computer is more effectively suppressed.

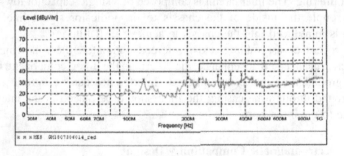

Fig. 6. The electromagnetic compatibility test results

5   Conclusion

In this paper, the modal analysis of the impact and vibration of the ship-borne computer is carried out, and the 6th-order modal cloud image of the box is obtained through simulation. The main deformation part of the first 4th modal device occurs in the rubber damper, and the box is hardly deformed, it can avoid the occurrence of resonance and improve the ability of the computer to resist vibration and shock. By adopting the box shielding design, filtering design and board level signal suppression, the electromagnetic compatibility of the rugged computer is designed, and the test results show well.

References

1. Anonymous: Rugged Computers for Harsh Conditions. Engineering and Mining Journal, No. 8, pp. 34–38 (2018)
2. Jiangfeng, H.: Structural design of a fully enclosed airborne reinforcement computer. Ind. Control Comput. **7**, 21–23 (2018)
3. Li, Y.: A small cabinet structure and strengthening protection design. Modern Manuf. Eng. **7**, 123–125 (2012)
4. Lei, H.: A certain type of structural design of reinforced mainframe computer chassis. J. Mech. Manag. Dev. **22**(5), 7–9 (2010)
5. Haijun, Z., Jian, J.: The construction design about a military ruggedized cabinet. In: Proceedings of the Conference on Mechanical and Electrical Engineering for the Year 2005. Electronic Industry Press, Nanjing (2005)
6. Zheng, Z., Wang, Y.: Introduction of parameters in random vibration and their calculation. J. Electr. Prod. Reliab. Environ. Test. **27**(6), 45–48 (2009)
7. Yingbao, D.: Design on a new type of reinforced computer cabinet. Comput. Netw. **29**(10), 42–44 (2011)
8. Liu, Z., Guo, J., Yang, L.: Random vibration analysis of airborne electronic equipment structure. J. Aeronaut. Comput. Tech. **41**(4), 91–93 (2011)
9. Yong, Z., Ma, L., Liu, S., et al.: The coupling effects of thermal cycling and high current density on Sn58Bi solder joints. J. Mater. Sci. **48**(6), 2318–2325 (2013)
10. Hongmin, L., Zhiyong, Y., Wanyu, L.: Engineering Electromagnetic Compatibility. Xi'an University of Electronic Science and Technology Press, Xi'an (2012)
11. Putin, E., Asadulaev, A., Ivanenkov, Y.: Reinforced adversarial neural computer for de novo molecular design. J. Chem. Inf. Modeling **58**(6), 1194–1204 (2018)
12. Hou, H., Wang, J., Yi, X., et al.: Computer electromagnetic radiation carcinogenic doses based on Monte Carlo algorithm. Cluster Comput. **9**, 1–8 (2018)
13. Wang, Q., Chen, M.: Emulation and analysis of random vibration. Electro-optic Technol. Appl. **24**(5), 77–80 (2009)
14. Jinghui, C.: Construct collectivity design of ship borne electronic equipment. J. Ship Electr. Eng. **26**(2), 163–166 (2006)

Effect of Passivating and Metallization Layers on Low Energy Proton Induced Single-Event Upset

Ruiqiang Song, Jinjin Shao[✉], Bin Liang, Yaqing Chi, and Jianjun Chen

College of Computer, National University of Defense Technology, Changsha 410073, Hunan, China
shaojinjin308@163.com

Abstract. Using Monte Carlo and TCAD simulation, we investigate the effect of passivating and metallization layers on low energy proton induced SEU in the commercial SRAM cell. Simulation results indicate metallization layers and tungsten contacts significantly reduce proton energy and enhance the energy distribution. Therefore, they can decrease the SEU percentage of the commercial SRAM cell.

Keywords: Single-event upset · Low energy proton · Passivating layer · Metallization layer

1 Introduction

Single-event upset (SEU) has become an important reliability concern for nanoscale technologies [1,2]. Reduced nodal capacitance and supply voltage decrease the critical charge to cause SEU [3]. Close proximity of transistors results in charge sharing at multiple nodes [4]. These phenomena increase the SEU sensitivity of the commercial static random access memory (SRAM) by orders of magnitude. Some works have reported an incident particle can induce more than 10 bits upset in the commercial SRAM [5]. Therefore, it is vital to investigate the SEU sensitivity of SRAMs at advanced CMOS technologies.

Many previous works have studied the SEU sensitivity of SRAMs under heavy ion radiation environment [6–8]. Recently, low energy proton-induced SEU has become a key issue for the commercial SRAM [9–11]. Because of the decreased critical charge, low energy protons can significantly increase the SEU cross sections by orders of magnitude. Passivating and metallization Layers significantly affect low protons when they pass through semiconductor devices. However, few works study the effect of passivating and metallization layers on low energy proton induced SEU.

Project supported by the National Natural Science Foundation of China (Grant No. 61804180) and the Hunan Natural Science Foundation of China (Grant No. 2019JJ50740).

© Springer Nature Singapore Pte Ltd. 2019
W. Xu et al. (Eds.): NCCET 2019, CCIS 1146, pp. 144–150, 2019.
https://doi.org/10.1007/978-981-15-1850-8_13

In this paper, we investigate the effect of passivating and metallization layers on low energy proton induced SEU in the commercial SRAM cell. Simulation results indicate metallization layers and tungsten contacts significantly decrease the SEU percentage of the commercial SRAM cell. Simulation results are useful for radiation hardened by design. Designers can add additional metallization layers and tungsten contacts to mitigate low energy proton-induced SEU.

2   Simulation Setup

2.1   Proton Transportation Setup

In previous works, Monte Carlo simulation tools have been widely used to handle the radiation transportation and energy deposition in matter [12,13]. In this paper, we use Monte Carlo simulation tool Geant4 to determine low proton-induced energy deposition at the silicon substrate. Three simulation structures are built in Geant4 simulation tool, as shown in Fig. 1. The first simulation structure consists of the silicon substrate and passivating layers (Sim1). The second simulation structure adds metallization layers, which is used to investigate the effect of metallization layers on proton-induced energy deposition (Sim2). The last simulation structure adds tungsten contacts between two metallization layers (Sim3). It is used to investigate the effect of tungsten contacts on proton-induced energy deposition.

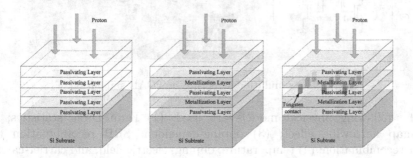

Fig. 1. The simulation structures in Geant4 simulation tool.

The following physics processes are used in Monte Carlo simulation: ionization, nuclear elastic, inelastic reactions and coulombic scattering. The proton energy is from 0.5 MeV to 10 MeV. For each proton energy, the number of incident proton is set to 100. When an incident proton passes through the silicon substrate, the energy deposition is determined and the equivalent linear energy transfer (LET) is calculated during Monte Carlo simulation.

2.2   Charge Collection Simulation Setup

After determining the energy deposition and the equivalent LET in the silicon substrate, TCAD simulation tool is used to investigate SEU in the commercial SRAM cell. In our previous works, TCAD simulation tool has been a useful means to investigate the physical mechanism of SEU [14–17]. In this paper, we use TCAD simulation tool to simulate the charge collection and transient voltage after proton striking. The simulation circuit is shown in Fig. 2. The PMOS and NMOS transistors in two inverters are represented as the TCAD model. The rest transistors use the corresponding SPICE model. The TCAD model is firstly calibrated to match electrical characteristics obtained from standard compact models for 65 nm CMOS technology. The NMOS transistor size is $W/L = 210\,nm/60\,nm$ and the complementary PMOS transistor size is $W/L = 150\,nm/60\,nm$. The supply voltage is set to 1.2 V. The incident location is set to the center drain region of the P1 transistor. TCAD simulation is repeated 100 times with each proton energy to obtain a SEU percentage. The LET value in each TCAD simulation is based on Monte Carlo simulation results.

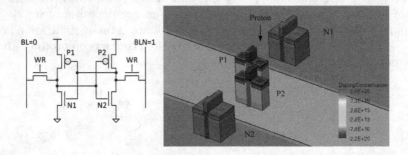

Fig. 2. The simulation structure in TCAD simulation.

The following physical models are used: (1) Fermi-Dirac statistics; (2) band-gap narrowing effect; (3) doping-dependent SRH recombination and Auger recombination; (4) temperature, doping, electric field, and carrier-carrier-scattering impact on mobility; (5) incident heavy ions are modeled using a Gaussian radial profile with a characteristic $1/e$ radius of 50 nm and a Gaussian temporal profile with a characteristic decay time of 0.25 ps; and (6) a hydrodynamic model is used for carrier transportation. Unless otherwise specified, the default models and parameters provided by TCAD simulation tool are used.

3   Simulation Results

The SEU percentage with different proton energies is shown in Fig. 3. The SEU distributions show significant discrepancies with different passivating and metallization structures. When the simulation structure only consists of passivating layers, the proton energy in the peak region is 1.0 MeV and the SEU percentage is more than 90% (Sim1). However, when metallization layers are added in the simulation structure, the proton energy in the peak value is 2.5 MeV and the SEU percentage is only about 80% (Sim2). Similar with the Sim1 and Sim2 results, when tungsten contacts are also added in the simulation structure, the proton energy and the SEU percentage in the peak region also change. The proton energy in the peak value is 3.0 MeV and the SEU percentage is no more than 60% (Sim3). Simulation results indicate passivating and metallization layers increase the threshold energy in the peak region. It needs higher proton energies to cause SEUs at the worst case. Moreover, passivating and metallization layers can decrease the SEU percentage. They can be used to mitigate low proton-induced SEUs.

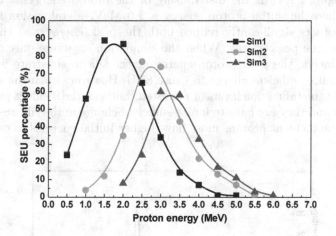

Fig. 3. The simulated SEU percentage with different proton energies.

4   Discussion

Simulation results confirm metallization layers and tungsten contacts significantly affect proton energies and SEU percentages in the peak region. The reduced proton energy and the enhanced energy distribution at the silicon substrate is the main mechanism to cause different simulation results.

When an incident proton passes through passivating or metallization layers, it interacts with the electrons of atoms in the material. This interaction excites or ionizes the atoms and it leads to an energy loss of the incident proton. When the incident proton arrives at the silicon substrate, the proton energy is smaller than the initial value. Therefore, although the initial energy is same, incident protons will have different energies and they are consisted of an energy distribution at the silicon substrate. The ionizing interaction is strongly dependent on the material types. Different materials have different ionization capabilities, which significantly affect the proton energy at the silicon substrate. Generally, the ionizing interaction between particles and materials can be expressed by the following equation [18]:

$$\frac{dE}{dx} = \frac{4\pi}{m_e c^2} \frac{nz^2}{\beta^2} \frac{e^2}{4\pi\varepsilon_0} \left[\ln(\frac{2m_e c^2}{I(1-\beta^2)}) - \beta^2\right] \tag{1}$$

Based on the equation, the ionizing interaction is related to the incident particle energy E, the electron number density n of the target material and the mean excitation potential I. Metallization layers and tungsten contacts increase the electron number density compared with passivation layers. Incident protons will loss more energy when they pass though metallization layers and tungsten contacts. Figure 4 reveals the distributing of the proton energy at the silicon substrate when the initial proton energy is 1.0 MeV. Metallization layers and tungsten contacts significantly reduce both the peak energy and the number of protons at the peak energy. When the simulation structure only consists of passivation layers, the peak proton energy at the silicon substrate is 0.8 MeV and it can ionize sufficient charge to cause SEU. However, when the simulation structure adds metallization layers or tungsten contacts, the incident protons loss more energy and they are hard to ionize sufficient charge in the silicon substrate. Therefore, the incident protons must have higher initial energies to cause SEU.

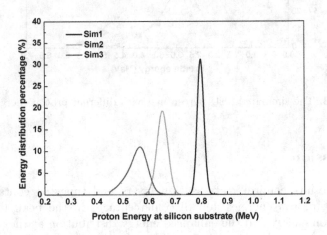

Fig. 4. The distributing of the proton energy at the silicon substrate when the initial proton energy is 1.0 MeV.

Besides reducing the proton energy, metallization layers and tungsten contacts also enhance the energy distribution at the silicon substrate. Figure 5 shows the energy distributions when the initial energy is 1.0 MeV and 3.0 MeV, respectively. Although the peak values of the proton energy between two simulation structures are same, the energy distribution in Sim3 is larger than that in Sim1. When the simulation structure only consists of passivation layers (Sim1), the energy distribution is from 0.75 MeV to 0.85 MeV. Most of the proton energies are larger than the critical energy and the SEU percentage is more than 90% in TCAD simulation. However, when the simulation structure adds metallization layers and tungsten contacts (Sim3), many incident protons do not exceed the critical energy because of the enhanced energy distribution. These incident protons can not cause SEU and they significantly decrease the simulated SEU percentage. Therefore, the SEU percentage is only about 60% and it is smaller than Sim1 results in TCAD simulation.

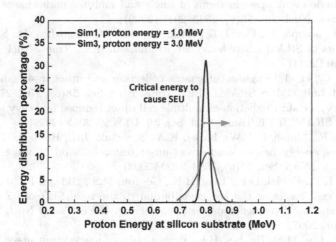

Fig. 5. The distributing of the proton energy at the silicon substrate when the initial proton energy is 1.0 MeV and 3.0 MeV, respectively.

5   Conclusion

We have combined realistic Monte Carlo simulations and TCAD simulation to study the effect of passivating and metallization layers on low energy proton induced SEU. Three simulation structures with different passivating and metallization layers are investigated and the simulation results are compared.

Simulation results indicate metallization layers and tungsten contacts significantly increase the threshold energy and decrease the SEU percentage in the peak region. The higher ionizing interaction in metallization layers and tungsten contacts is the reason to increase the threshold energy. The incident protons must have higher initial energies to cause SEU. Metallization layers and tungsten contacts also enhance the energy distribution at the silicon substrate. It is the reason to decrease the simulated SEU percentage.

References

1. Du, T., ChaoHui, H., YongHong, L., Hang, Z., Cen, X., JinXin, Z.: Soft error reliability in advanced CMOS technologies-trends and challenges. Sci. China Tech. Sci. **57**(9), 1846–1857 (2014)

2. Massengill, L.W., Bhuva, B.L., Holman, W.T., Alles, M.L., Loveless, T.D.: Technology scaling and soft error reliability. In: Proceedings of IRPS, 3.C.1 (2012)
3. Dodd, P.E., Shaneyfelt, M.R., Felix, J.A.: Production and propagation of single-event transients in high-speed digital logic ICs. IEEE Trans. Nucl. Sci. 51(6), 3278–3284 (2004)
4. Black, J.D., Dodd, P.E., Warren, K.M.: Physics of multiple-node charge collection and impacts on single-event characterization and soft error rate prediction. IEEE Trans. Nucl. Sci. 60(3), 1836–1851 (2013)
5. Uznanski, S., Gasiot, G., Roche, P., Autran, J.L., Tavernier, C.: Characterizing SRAM single event upset in terms of single and multiple node charge collection. IEEE Trans. Nucl. Sci. 55(6), 2943–2947 (2009)
6. Avner, H., Joseph, B., David, D., Eitan, K., Nati, R., Shimshon, R.: Single event hard errors in SRAM under heavy ion irradiation. IEEE Trans. Nucl. Sci. 61(5), 2702–2710 (2014)
7. Indranil, C., et al.: Single-event charge collection and upset in 40-nm dual- and triple-well bulk CMOS SRAMs. IEEE Trans. Nucl. Sci. 58(6), 2761–2767 (2011)
8. Correas, V., et al.: Prediction of multiple cell upset induced by heavy ions in a 90 nm Bulk SRAM. IEEE Trans. Nucl. Sci. 56(4), 2050–2055 (2009)
9. Heidel, D.F., Marshall, P.W., LaBel, K.A., Schwank, J.R., Rodbell, K.P., Hakey, M.C.: Low energy proton single-event-upset test results on 65 nm SOI SRAM. IEEE Trans. Nucl. Sci. 55(6), 3394–3400 (2008)
10. Rodbell, K.P., Heidel, D.F., Tang, H.K., Gordon, M.S., Oldiges, P., Murray, C.E.: Multiple cell upsets as the key contribution to the total SER of 65 nm CMOS SRAMs and its dependence on well engineering. IEEE Trans. Nucl. Sci. 54(6), 2474–2479 (2007)
11. Liu, H.Y., Liu, M.S., Hughes, H.L.: Proton induced single event upset in 6 T SOI SRAMs. IEEE Trans. Nucl. Sci. 53(6), 3502–3505 (2006)
12. Song, R.Q., Chen, S.M., Du, Y.K., Huang, P.C., Chen, J.J., Chi, Y.Q.: PABAM a physics-based analytical model to estimate bipolar amplification effect induced collected charge at circuit-level. IEEE Trans. Device Mater. Rel. 15(4), 595–603 (2015)
13. Song, R.Q., Chen, S.M., He, Y.B., Du, Y.K.: Flip-flops soft error rate evaluation approach considering internal single-event transient. Sci. China Inf. Sci. 58(6), 062403 (2015)
14. He, Y.B., Chen, S.M.: Experimental verification of the parasitic bipolar amplification effect in single event transient. Chin. Phys. B 23(7), 079401 (2014)
15. Qin, J.R., Chen, S.M., Li, D.W., Liang, B., Liu, B.W.: Temperature and drain bias dependence of single event transient in 25 nm FinFET technology. Chin. Phys. B 21(8), 089401 (2012)
16. Ruiqiang, S., et al.: Experimental characterization of the dominant multiple nodes charge collection mechanism in metal oxide-semiconductor transistors. Appl. Phys. Lett. 110, 232106 (2017)
17. Song, R.Q., Chen, S.M., Liang, B., Chi, Y.Q., Chen, J.J.: Modeling the impact of process and operation variations on the soft error rate of digital circuits. Sci. China Inf. Sci. 60(12), 129402 (2017)
18. Segr, E., Bethe, H., Ashkin, J.: Experimental nuclear physics. Annual Report of China Institute of Atomic Energy (1996)

Design and Realization of Integrated Service Access Gateway (ISAG) for Integrated Fusion Shipboard Network

Qilin Wang[✉]

The Equipment Manufacturing Department,
Jiangsu Automation Research Institute, Lianyungang, China
wangqilin@jari.cn

Abstract. Shipboard network is a bearing platform for the ship's information processing system, and it is composed of control network, service related network, public computing platform network, and communication network. Integrated fusion of multiple networks is a trend for Shipboard network, however there are some challenges: how to ensure uniform business bearer, how to guarantee service quality, and how to realize layered safety protection and availability. In this paper, features and design requirements of the integrated fusion Shipboard network are analyzed first, and then an integrated network architecture based on ISAG and a model to realize the ISAG are put forward. Works concerned with GW80, a ISAG oriented to design of Shipboard network integrated fusion are described at last.

Keywords: Shipboard network · Integration · ISAG

1 Preface

Shipboard network is an important part of ship's comprehensive information platform. The traditional Shipboard network includes on-site control network, computer network, and communication network in respect to different data type and application the network carried.

The access objects of the on-site control network are various intelligent sensors and controllers onboard the ship used to ensure information exchange in real-time and be reliable. For big ships, there are normally several different on-site control networks such as the power (boiler) control system network, power station and power supply control system network, propulsion system network, and steering control system network. Normally these on-site control networks are developed by different departments, adopt different on-site bus technology, have different data formats and protocols, and they are connected with computer network via special gateways, which bring complexity and poor efficiency not only in information interaction, but also in system management and maintenance [1].

Ethernet features versatility and high bandwidth, especially in recent years IEEE has started a work focusing on standardization of time sensitive network (TSN) which has solved the problem of uncertainty in Ethernet exchange, so using Ethernet to

© Springer Nature Singapore Pte Ltd. 2019
W. Xu et al. (Eds.): NCCET 2019, CCIS 1146, pp. 151–159, 2019.
https://doi.org/10.1007/978-981-15-1850-8_14

replace on-site bus has become an irreversible trend for on-site control network in fields such as industrial control, aerospace, automobiles, and rail transit, and brought some new changes to Shipboard network development: speeding up fusion of on-site control network and computer network to reduce complexity of connectivity between different onboard networks as well as the cost to realize it; providing efficient data exchange foundation for deployment of onboard public computing platforms to support low cost IT service by the way of using data center and cloud computing onboard the ship.

However, under Ethernet Shipboard network fusion, the problem of security will be more severe. On the one hand external attack through the ship's communication network against the ship's internal computer network and on-site control network shall be avoided to prevent the attack from penetrating the ship's core control system and remotely controlling the ship; on the other hand effective isolation ensuring security domain between the internal networks of the ship shall be applied to avoid information flowing from higher levels of confidentiality to lower one. As a result, it is necessary to place security gateways in the fused Shipboard networks to realize efficient security protection at boundaries of different security domain.

The paper studies the composition of the ship's network under integrated fusion tendency, its security protection requirements, and the mechanism realizing the gateway equipment, and its major innovation includes:

(1) Proposing a composing architecture of integrated and fused future Shipboard network including communication network, on-site control network, service network, and public computing platform, and analyzing features of security protection, service quality assurance, high availability, and forward compatibility of the integrated gateways connecting these networks;
(2) Proposing a model to realize the integrated gateway of the Shipboard network, supporting loading and layout of various networks and security protection function per requirement on the gateway platform through mechanisms such as scalable hardware streamline and network function arrangement to satisfy networking requirement of the integrated fusion network;
(3) A FAST architecture [5] based integrated gateway GW80 with a throughput of existing 80 Gbps was designed and realized, and the test shows that GW80 can meet the design requirements in aspects of hardware resource usage rate, network interface performance and security function layout.

In the second part of the paper, the ship integrated network architecture based on the integrated gateway is put forward; in the third part of the paper, design requirement and realization model of the integrated gateway are introduced; in the fourth part of the paper, the overall structure, key technology realization and initial test results of GW80 – the integrated gateway of Shipboard network we realized on the base of FAST architecture [5] are described; and in the final part, we look to the future development trend of the integrated Shipboard network.

2 Ship Integrated Fusion Network Based on Integrated Gateway

With the standardization and gradual development of TSN technology, the on-site control network will change from real-time bus technology into Ethernet technology little by little, and form a foundation for building ship integrated fusion network. We think that on the future informational platform of the ship, there are four (4) types of networks basically: on-site control network, service network, public computing platform network, and communication system network, and their characteristics are given in Table 1.

Table 1. Major types and characteristics of Shipboard network

Network type	Access node	Data exchange requirement	Network technology
On-site control network	Programmable logic controller (PLC), sensor, actuator	Time sensitive service, bandwidth sensitive service	On-site bus, TSN etc.
Service network	User terminal, service related sensor, controller, etc.	Time sensitive service, bandwidth sensitive service, best effort service	On-site bus, TSN etc.
Public computing platform network	High performance server, storage server etc.	Best effort service, network virtualization	Data center network
Communication system network	Satellite communication node, GPS/Beidou terminal node	Best effort service	Special transmission channel

In the future ship integrated fusion network, the four (4) networks mentioned above will be thoroughly connected with standard Ethernet technology to realize connectivity based on TCP/IP. However, different types of networks demand different transmission quality and security protection, it is necessary to use gateway between the networks for controlled data exchange. The structure of gateway-based ship integrated fusion network is shown in Fig. 1.

For the integrated fusion network shown in Fig. 1, the integrated gateway shall have the following capabilities:

- Security control capability. Realize controlled communication based on whitelist mechanism between different networks, realized intrusion detection mechanism between the external network and internal network. The gateway shall support functions such as information security zone division, important information transmission protection, network user access authentication, and network intrusion detection.

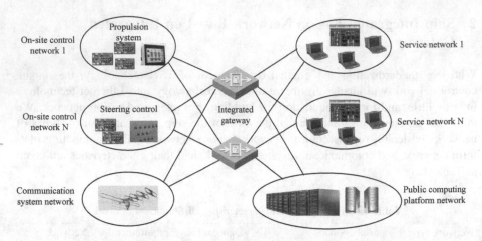

Fig. 1. Structure of gateway-based ship integrated fusion network

- Multiple services bearing and service quality assurance capability. The gateway shall be able to mark multiple services transmission across networks via VLAN to support all kinds of services onboard the whole ship, especially effective transmission for real-time data and voice. Network routing, exchange performance and bandwidth, time delay, and jitter guideline shall be satisfied, and service isolation shall be realized as well to avoid influence between dataflow.
- Forward compatibility capability. The traditional on-site control system normally adopts CAN bus or RS485 bus for data exchange between nodes, though the technical trend is using TSN instead of the on-site bus, still forward compatibility for existing on-site bus network shall be considered in the gateway design, so changing from several on-site buses to Ethernet will be required.
- Redundant operation capability. The integrated network is the whole ship information service bearing platform, once there is a failure, operation of several systems will be affected, so the network shall be highly robust and available. To avoid single node failure caused by gateway, failure detection between gateways shall be supported, and service fast auto protection and switch shall be available.
- Visualization management capability. The network after fusion will have bigger scale and more complicated configuration, and the difficulty for its management will be increased, so simpler visualized management method will be required to make the administrator realize multiple-layered management for equipment, links and services easily and intuitively.

3 Integrated Gateway Realization Model

Existing gateway products mainly include security gateway, protocol gateway and various application layer gateways, and they basically have three (3) ways to realize: pure software NFV method, dedicated hardware-based method, and FPGA-based software and hardware coordination method.

For the gateway adopting NFV architecture, on a standard server its network functions are all realized by software based on the virtualized mechanism of the platform. By this way the arrangement and layout can be flexible, but the performance will be difficult to improve, especially when the core of the future Shipboard network is required to support 10G network interface, and the way of gateway realization with standard server based NFV can't meet the performance demand; the gateway adopting dedicated hardware will have high performance but poor scalability, which will make it difficult to realize forward compatibility for existing bus, nor support data exchange demand for quickly developing TSN exchange and data center exchange;

Software and hardware coordination gateway realization is mainly based on coordinated realization of FPGA based common multiple-core processor, which can bring both performance and flexibility, such as VFP [5] and UniSec [6] etc. The paper proposes an integrated gateway realization model based on software and hardware coordination, as shown in Fig. 2.

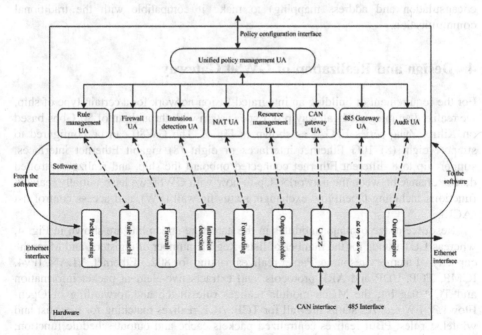

Fig. 2. Integrated gateway realization model

The model shown in Fig. 2 has three (3) features. One feature is that it is based on the scalable hardware processing streamline. Packets received by network interface are first parsed and rule matched (for example the five-element model rule), the parsing and matching results are transferred to the follow-up network process modules with packets for processing; complicated functions difficult to completely realize by hardware will be realized by software, for example the deep packet inspection (DPI) function in intrusion detection. Under FAST architecture support, the hardware streamline can send these packets to relevant software application (briefly UA) for realization. Another feature is the separated network function controller, each hardware functional module correspond to a controller at the software end responsible for management and configuration of the hardware functional module, and decoupling of the control flat can support dynamic deployment of network functions conveniently. The third feature is the unified policy management interface provided, and it can support separation of mechanisms and policies during network function realization.

The software and hardware coordination in the gateway model mainly takes software and hardware coordinated extensible switch architecture (ESA) put forward in reference [7] for reference, so its details are not given here. Please note though CAN bus and 485 bus interface process logics are not network functions, they can be integrated in the hardware streamline, data received and sent by CAN/485 bus can be encapsulated in packets and communicate with corresponding software UA, and the software UA can realize change from the tradition bus to Ethernet (including data encapsulation and address mapping) to make it compatible with the traditional communication.

4   Design and Realization of GW80 Gateway

For the requirement of building an integrated fusion network for a certain type of ship, we realized an integrated gateway prototype system with throughput of 80 Gbps based on Xilinx Zynq series FPGA, as shown in Fig. 3. The GW80 can be configured to support eight (8) 10G Ethernet interfaces or eight (8) gigabit Ethernet interfaces, support up to 8 different Ethernet connected onboard the ship, and realize controlled data exchange between the networks. Up to now with GW80 we have initially realized functions including OpenFlow exchange, status firewall (FW), and access control list (ACL).

Resource usage of major modules in the hardware streamline are shown in Fig. 4, whereas LUT stands for the number of lists, Reg the number of registers, and Mem the capacity of memory resource. Parser realizes parsing for 802.3 Ethernet, VLAN, IPv4, ICMP, TCP, UDP and ARP protocols, and extracts five-element packet information and TCP flag bit; the Match module realizes rule match and forwarding of OpenFlow1.3; FW realizes status firewall for TCP; ACL realizes matching for blacklist and whitelist rules; PBuf realizes centralized packets cache and output schedule function; Others logic mainly realizes switch control for software and hardware packets.

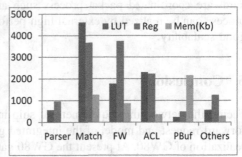

Fig. 3. Physical picture of GW80

Fig. 4. Streamline hardware resource usage

Besides the hardware streamline, inside FPGA there are also some common logics irrelevant with specific network functions, and they include MAC logic for network interface receiving and sending, receiving packet buffer at each port, DMA engine for communication between the hardware streamline and the CPU. These logics totally use about 24,000 LUTs, 40,000 registers and 3.6 Mb on-chip memories.

Results of GW80 basic exchange and FW performance tests are shown in Fig. 5. Whereas the 10G interface can realize line speed packet forwarding, the maximum delay for head-in-head-out packets is about 8us, and TCP connection setup rate supported by the firewall can be up to 40,000 per second.

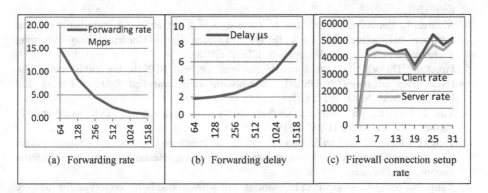

Fig. 5. Initial performance test results

We have realized OpenFlow1.3 channel controller, ACL controller and status firewall controller on FPGA embedded ARM CPU. Whereas the OpenFlow channel configures rule list of the Match module by preset rules, FW and ACL module only realize configuration of relevant security policies, so ARM CPU doesn't realize packet data flat forwarding operation.

PCIe 2.0x4 interface has also been realized on FPGA, external high performance computing board can be connected through back plane to perform software and hardware coordinated packet process such as intrusion detection, complex software process can be realized by external high performance computing board, so GW80 has good scalability.

5   Conclusion

Facing the networking requirement of ship integrated fusion network, the paper puts forward request and model of the integrated gateway, as well as design and prototype realization of GW80. At present the GW80 gateway is still a prototype system needs to be further developed and improved to satisfy networking requirement of ship integrated fusion network, and the major works involve supporting TSN function, network virtualization function, and on-site bus forward compatibility. The initial test results have proved availability of the integrated gateway realization model and performance based on FAST hardware streamline. Future works will be done to further improve functions of GW80, and further tests will be taken under physical networking environment.

References

1. Bai, Y., Zhao, X., Shen, W.: Design of embedded shipboard network integrated gateway. Ship Sci. Technol. (9) (2016)
2. Finn, N.: Introduction to time sensitive networking. IEEE Commun. Stan. Mag. **2**, 22–28 (2018)
3. Su, Y., Liu, Y., Long, F.: Overview of shipboard network security. Mar. Electr. Electron. Eng. (2018)
4. Alvarez, I., Barranco, M., Proenza, J.: Towards a fault-tolerant architecture based on time sensitive networking. In: 2018 IEEE 23rd International Conference on Emerging Technologies and Factory Automation (ETFA) (2018)
5. Firestone, D.: VFP: a virtual switch platform for host SDN in the public cloud. In: Proceedings of the 14th USENIX Symposium on Networked Systems Design and Implementation (NSDI 2017) (2017)
6. Yan, J., Tang, L., et al.: UniSec: a unified security framework with SmartNIC acceleration in public cloud. In: ACM TURC (2019)
7. Tang, L.: Research and realization of software & hardware coordinated extensible packet process technology. Doctoral Dissertation in Engineering, National University of Defense Technology, December 2017
8. Yang, X., Sun, Z., et al.: FAST: enabling fast software/hardware prototype for network experimentation. In: IWQoS 2019 (2019)
9. Yan, G., Zhang, Y., et al.: The design technique for shipborne network based on ethernet ring. Command Control Simul. **3**, 32 (2013)
10. Zheng, J.: Research and simulation of unknown protocol identification method based on carrier network. Ship Sci. Technol. **3** (2015)
11. Liu, Y., Shao, H., et al.: DAG task scheduling integrating with security and availability in cloud environment. Comput. Eng. **40**(12), 12–18 (2014)

12. Cheng, Y.: Design and implementation of an integrated network routing algorithm for ship navigation. Ship Sci. Technol
13. Liu, F., Wang, Y.: Architecture of unified network based on programmable control gateway. J. Beijing Univ. Aeronaut. Astronaut. (10) (2015)
14. Wang, Q., Yang, D., et al.: A DNS compatible resource resolving system in universal network. Comput. Technol. Dev. (01), 2 (2013)
15. Bai, Y., Zhao, X.: Design of embedded ship integrated network gateway. Ship Sci. Technol. (17) (2016)
16. Ma, X., Li, Y., Lu, J.: Research and algorithm improvement of the mobile routing protocol of the Shipboard network node. Ship Sci. Technol. (6) (2016)

A Convolutional Neural Networks Accelerator Based on Parallel Memory

Hongbing Tan[1], Sheng Liu[2(⊠)], Haiyan Chen[2], Honghui Sun[1], and Hongliang Li[1]

[1] Jiangnan Institute of Computing Technology, Wuxi 214125, China
tanhongbing1993@163.com, hhsun0703@163.com,
hongliangli@263.net
[2] National University of Defense Technology, Changsha 410073, China
liusheng83@nudt.edu.cn, hychen608@163.com

Abstract. Convolutional Neural Networks (CNNs) is one of the core algorithms for implementing artificial intelligence (AI), which has the characteristics of high parallelism and large amount of computations. With the rapid development of AI applications, general purpose processors such as CPU/GPU can't meet the requirements for performance, power consumption and real-time performance of CNN. However, ASIC can fully exploit the parallelism of CNN and improve resource utilization to meet its requirements This paper has designed and implemented a new CNN accelerator based on parallel memory technology, which can support multiple parallelisms. A super processing unit (SPU) with kernel buffer and output buffer is proposed to make computation and data fetching more streamline then ensure the performance of accelerator. In addition, a two-dimensional buffer which can provide conflict-free non-aligned block access with different steps and aligned continuous access to meet the data requirements of varies parallelisms. The synthesis results show it can work at 1 GHz frequency with area overhead of 4.51 mm^2 and on-chip buffer cost of 192 KB. We evaluated our design with varies CNN workloads, the efficiency of our design over 90% in most cases. Compared with the state-of-the-art accelerator architectures, the hardware cost of our design is smaller under the same performance.

Keywords: Convolution · 2-D buffer · Super processing unit · Non-aligned block access · Data-reusing

1 Introduction

Recently, Convolutional Neural Network (CNN) has been widely used in image analysis, speech recognition, web search, etc [1–3], promising great opportunities for artificial intelligence (AI). Due to the intrinsic properties of CNN algorithm, the training and inference processes are computationally intensive with vast multiplication and addition operations. Although extensive attempts have been carried out to accelerate the computation process by utilizing high performance CPU and GPU [27, 28], the acceleration for CNN is insufficient due to the versatile architectures of the above

© Springer Nature Singapore Pte Ltd. 2019
W. Xu et al. (Eds.): NCCET 2019, CCIS 1146, pp. 160–176, 2019.
https://doi.org/10.1007/978-981-15-1850-8_15

two processors. To further exploit the intensive parallelisms in feature map, neuron, and synapse, various dedicated accelerators have been proposed for CNN.

The parallelism of CNN includes feature map inter-parallelism (FM-Ie-P), feature map intra-parallelism (FM-Ir-P) and kernel parallelism (KP). To maximize the efficiency for each parallelism, Systolic [4, 21], 2D-Mapping [13] and Tiling [10, 11] have been reported for KP, FM-Ir-P and FM-Ie-P, respectively. However, each of these three dedicated architectures can only exploit one parallelism. Thus, superior architecture is imperative to exploit more than one parallelism of convolution for better comprehensive efficiency. Furthermore, parallelism and data reuse are two correlative factors in CNN algorithm. As matter of fact, the data reuse of input feature map is prominent in FM-Ie-P and FM-Ir-P, while it turns to KP for kernel. In general, the demand of bandwidth could be significantly reduced if the rate of data reuse is increased. However, the coexistence of different parallel mechanisms (i.e., FM-Ie-P, FM-Ir-P and KP with different demands for data accessing) in CNN will dramatically increase the difficulty of memory design. Therefore, specialized memory must be designed to ensure the parallelism of CNN.

In this paper, a CNN accelerator with parallel memory is proposed. The accelerator supports all parallelisms mentioned above and the rate of data reuse is increased significantly. Specially, this paper makes the following contributions.

1. A mixture parallel mechanism was proposed to improve the utilization of computing resource and data reusability.
2. A 2D memory architecture was proposed which can support both aligned continuous access and non-aligned block access with different steps.
3. A super processing unit (SPU) with local buffer was proposed which makes the data fetching and calculation more efficiency.
4. Comprehensive evaluations of the accelerator were performed. The figure of merits, such as the utilization of computing resource and the amount of read/ write data, of our design indicate superior performance than the state-of-art accelerators.

The rest of this paper is organized as follows. Section 2 discusses the related works. Section 3 analyzes the parallelism and data reusability of CNN. Section 4 represents the design of CNN accelerator. Section 5 evaluates the CNN accelerator, and make comparisons with other designs. Finally, Sect. 6 makes some conclusions.

2 Related Works

With the rapid developments of AI applications, CNN hardware accelerators have also ushered in a boom. Compared to the low energy efficiency of general-purpose processors in AI applications, the development of AI dedicated hardware has reached consensus in academia and industry.

Domestic research team Chen Yunqi, Chen Tianshi and others have proposed a series of custom chips dedicated to AI—Cambrian, including six themes: DianNao [10] (prototype processor for multiple artificial neural networks), DaDianNao [11] (multi-core processor for large-scale artificial neural networks), PuDianNao [12] (supports multiple machine learning algorithms), ShiDianNao [13] (dedicated chips for CNN), and Cambricon-X [14] (an accelerator for sparse neural networks).

DianNao is the first prototype processor of the Cambrian series,it consists of a single-core processor with the same average performance as the mainstream GPU (NVIDIA K20M). However, its power consumption and area are two orders of magnitude lower than that of mainstream GPU. DianNao meets the needs of computing functions with limited memory bandwidth to achieve high performance ratios. DaDianNao is designed to meet the needs of a rapidly growing neural network scale, it uses a multi-core architecture to expand the size of the processor. There are 16 cores, and the on-chip resources are much larger than DianNao, but DaDianNao has weak scalability. DaDianNao's 64-cores cascading system delivers 450 times better performance than the GPU, while power consumption is only 0.67% of the GPU. However, if the number of cores is further increased, it will lead to performance degradation, so DaDianNao is still not suitable for handling large-scale tasks. Based on DianNao, PuDianNao also supports other classical machine learning algorithms (k-NN, k-Means, SVM, deep neural network, naive Bayes and classification tree) while processing neural networks. Because it is more versatile than DianNao, its pipeline is further subdivided into six stages by DianNao's three stages, and a hierarchical memory architecture based on data reuse distance is proposed, which greatly reduces the access cost. ShiDianNao further reduces power consumption for embedded CNN applications while still delivering more than 30 times the performance of GPU. What's more, ShiDianNao loads the CNN model into the on-chip SRAM cache, which reduces the overhead of accessing DRAM. However, because all the data needs to be placed on the internal memory, the application range of ShiDianNao is limited, and large-scale neural network calculation cannot be performed. Then Chen proposed a deep learning accelerator —Cambricon-X, which can process sparse neural networks effectively. Cambricon-X reduces its size by compressing the neural network, thereby accelerating the calculation. Cambricon-X first marks non-zero neurons one by one, filters out zero-valued neurons, and then sends the neurons to the computational units for processing. Cambricon-X eliminates unnecessary computation and weight storage and then processes non-sparse neural networks, so it is more versatile. At the same time, Cambricon-X provides a companion programming framework with ease of use.

Another more influential architecture in dedicated chips is Google's TPU [15]. TPU works at 700 MHz, consumes only 40 W, supports up to 95TFlops with 8-bit data width, and 23TFlops with 16-bit data. Although the total computing power of the TPU is not comparable to the V100 of NVIDIA, it is equivalent to the power consumption per unit. The heart of TPU is the Matrix Multiply Unit, which is a 256×256 systolic array, and the rest of the chip is mainly for systolic array services. The underlying goal is to maximize the performance of the systolic array and achieve relatively low I/O bandwidth (30 GB/s). The realization of these two points benefits from the characteristics of the systolic array: balanced I/O and operation, and relatively simple processing element. Of course, there is another reason that TPU uses an 8-bit fixed-point multiply and accumulate cell (MAC) (supports 16-bit operations).

In addition to the "Cambrian" series of chips and TPU, there are also some more energy-efficient ASICs, such as Eyerss [16, 17], EIE [18] and so on. Eyeriss proposed a CNN hardware accelerator that uses a new data movement model (called RS in the paper) to replace the SIMD/SIMT architecture accelerators such as GPUs. The advantage of RS over traditional SIMD is that it takes advantage of the data multiplexing contained in the CONV operations to move the data less. Compared with the existing accelerators, the accelerator has achieved 1.5 to 3 times higher energy efficiency in AlexNet [6]. EIE compresses the neural network, so that the neural network parameters obtained after compression can be completely allocated to the SRAM, thereby greatly reducing the number of DRAM accesses, and the DRAM access is the most energy-intensive operation in the traditional CNN accelerators, so the EIE can achieve good performance and power consumption. Compared with the uncompressed neural network accelerator DaDianNao, EIE's throughput is increased by 2.9 times, power consumption is increased by 19 times, and the area is only 1/3 of DaDianNao.

3 Design Analysis for CNN Accelerator

3.1 Convolutional Layer Algorithms

CNN usually consist of convolutional layers (CONV), pooling layers, and fully connected layers. CONV layers are highly computation intensive. For a typical CNN application, CONV layers take up more than 90% of the computation volume in both inference and training procedures. So, accelerating CONV layer is the key to accelerate CNN. The operation of CONV layer is shown in Fig. 1. The operation data includes three-dimensional input feature maps, three-dimensional kernels and generated output feature maps. The batch-size of the input feature maps, the numbers of channel is N, C, respectively, so the size of each input feature map is H × W × C, the number of kernels is M, and the size of each kernel is R × S × C. A three-dimensional kernel acts on a three-dimensional input feature map, obtaining a two-dimensional output feature map whose size is E × F. M kernels act on an input feature map to obtain a three-dimensional output feature map with M channels. M kernels act on N three-dimensional input feature maps obtain N three-dimensional output feature maps whose number of channels is M.

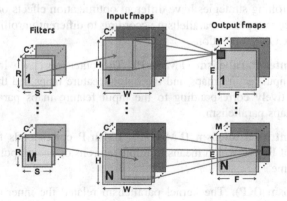

Fig. 1. CONV operations in general form

Corresponding to the operations of CONV layer, Fig. 2 shows the pseudo code of CONV operation, which composed of six loops.

```
for(m=0; m<M; m++)       { // Output Feature maps
  for(c=0; c<C; c++)      { // Input Feature maps
    for(j=0; j<H; j++)     { // The j-th row of output feature maps
      for(i=0; i<W; i++)    { // The i-th column of output feature maps
        for(u=0; u<R; u++)   { // The u-th row of kernels
          for(v=0; v<S; v++) { // The v-th column of kernels
          Loop:              //multiplication and addition
            output_fm(m, j, i)+=Kernel(m, c, u, v)*input_fm(c, Sh*j+u, Sw*j+v);
}}}}}}
```

Fig. 2. The pseudo code for CONV operation

In the above figure, S_w denotes the stride size in the horizontal direction of the CONV operation, and S_h denotes the stride size in the vertical direction of the CONV operation; C denotes the number of channels of the input feature maps; *Output_fm*(m, i, j) denotes the neuron value at location (m, j) in the m-th output feature map, *Input_fm* (c, i, j) denotes the neuron value at location (i, j) in the c-th channel of a input feature map. *Kernel*(m, c, u, v) denotes the synapse value at location (u, v) in the kernel which between n-th input and m-th output.

The main purpose of the CNN accelerator designed in this paper is to accelerate the CONV operation in Fig. 2. How to exploit the parallelism of CONV operation, improve the reuse rate of data, and reduce the data movement are our concerned.

3.2 Parallelism Analysis for CONV Layer

As Fig. 2 shown, CONV operations consist of multiple loops, which means it has a lot of potential parallelism. Exploiting the most of loops parallelism is the key to accelerate calculation. As we know, loop unrolling is a common way of loop optimization, and different loop unrolling strategies have different optimization effects on the algorithms [25]. There are three types of parallelism according to different unrolling strategies for related loops in CONV operations.

Feature Map Inter-Parallelism (FM-Ie-P). The outer-most two loops related the traversal of the input feature maps and the output feature maps,and the two unrolling loops are respectively corresponding to the input feature maps parallelism and the output feature maps parallelism.

Feature Map Intra-Parallelism (FM-Ir-P). FM-Ir-P corresponds to the middle 2 unrolling loops of Fig. 2, which means multiple neurons of one output feature map are processed at a time.

Kernel Parallelism (KP). The kernel parallelism related the inner-most two loops, which means multiple synapses of one kernel are processed at a time.

Although there are 2^3 combinations in FM-Ie-P, FM-Ir-P and KP, it is not easy to fully exploit these parallelism because of the distinct dataflow in different processing styles. In most architectures, only one of FM-Ie-P, FM-Ir-P, and KP is implemented, such as DC-CNN [19], CNP [20], and NeuFlow [20] just considering KP,Diannao [10], DaDiannao [11] FPGA15 [22] only considers FM-Ir-P; ShiDiannao [13] only considers FM-Ie-P. Although choosing one of them can improve the performance of CONV operations, the potential parallelism of CONV operations is not fully utilized. Moreover, to achieve all the three types parallelism at the same time, the loops need to be fully unrolled, which would increase dataflow complexity a lot, and more bandwidth and computing resources are required in hardware design. In this paper, FM-Ie-P and FM-Ir-P are implemented to fully exploit the parallelism of the CONV operations.

3.2.1 Parallelism Analysis for CONV Layer

According to the definition of FM-Ie-P, FM-Ie-P can be divided into input feature map parallelism (IFMP) and output feature map parallelism (OFMP). The implementation of the two ways is shown in Fig. 3.

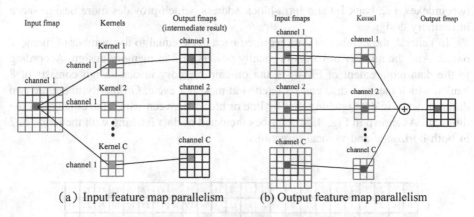

(a) Input feature map parallelism   (b) Output feature map parallelism

Fig. 3. Two kinds of parallel mechanism of FM-Ie-P

OFMP refers to convolving a channel of the input feature map with corresponding channels of the plurality of kernels to obtain an intermediate result of the plurality of output feature maps, and the plurality of output feature maps obtained until all channels of all the input feature maps are traversed. IFMP refers to convolving all channels of an input feature map with a kernel to obtain an output feature map. These two mechanisms have different hardware requirements. The former needs to configure a dedicated output buffer for each output feature map and a sharing input buffer for input feature maps, the other needs to configure a dedicated input buffer for each input feature map and a sharing output buffer for output feature map. IFMP needs to repeatedly read the same input feature map during multiple iterations, which will cause a low data reuse. OFMP also needs to read the intermediate result of the output feature image repeatedly and accumulate the calculated result, but the CONV operations only need to read/write the buffer in both the first clock cycle and the last clock cycle, so the frequency of buffer access is low. Therefore, we choose OFMP.

3.2.2 Analysis for FM-Ir-P

FM-Ir-P indicates multiple neurons of one output feature map are processed simultaneously, which means multiple input feature map data need be read at each clock cycle. CONV operations have steps in both horizontal and vertical directions. Fetching multiple data in one cycle may cause memory conflicts due to the discrete data distribution. Therefore, it is necessary to design a dedicated memory unit to avoid the memory conflict.

As a general rule, there are two different addressing methods in memory design, one-dimensional (1-D) addressing and two-dimensional (2-D) addressing. Because of the complicated stride in CONV operations, those data required for each cycle is discrete in input feature map. Memory which adopt 1-D addressing often need complicated pre-processing for the data, or a memory conflict occurs, but a 2-D addressing memory has better effect. Firstly, the feature map is natural in 2-D form, 2-D addressing can make the memory access more intuitive. Secondly, a 2-D memory has two indexes, i.e., bank ID and intra-block address, which provides more design space in memory design.

In general, the number of data required each cycle equal to the number of memory banks. And the number of banks is usually powers of 2 in memory design. According to the data requirement of FM-Ir-P, the on-chip memory in our design consists of 8 banks, which means 8 data can be fetched at most per cycle. Ordinarily, there are two different ways in data fetching that by line or block, between which the efficiencies are different. As shown in Fig. 4, it describes the detail of data fetching with the stride of 2 in both horizontal and vertical directions.

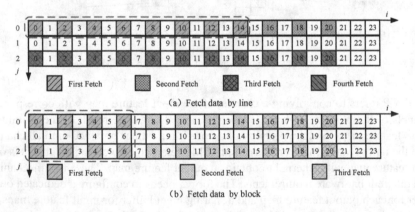

Fig. 4. Two kinds of access modes in 2-D buffer

To get the required data, it takes 4 operations in fetching data by line, and only 3 operations in fetching data by block. In contrast, b fetching data by block are more suitable for data requirement in CONV operations.

3.3 Analysis for Data Reusability Analysis

In CONV operations, there is a large number of repetitions in data access, and most operation-related data need to be read repeatedly. Repeated reading causes unnecessary waste of bandwidth, but the multiplexing of data can effectively reduce the bandwidth requirement.

Considering the kernels, multiple synapses parallel processing in FM-Ir-P mechanism can effectively multiplex the kernel data. Considering the feature maps, the FM-Ie-P mechanism can effectively multiplex the input feature map data. In addition, during the CONV operations, the kernel slides in the horizontal/vertical direction of the maps according to the stride, and the smaller the stride, the more data is repeated between the two adjacent sliding, especially when the stride is 1. Assuming that the kernel size is K × K, the repeated data in the adjacent sliding is K × (K − 1) with the stride being 1. As shown in Fig. 5, the kernel size is 3 × 3, and 6 pixels in the adjacent sliding need to be reused. The bandwidth requirements can be greatly reduced as soon as the data reusability improved. Therefore, this paper focuses on how to eliminate the reading of duplicate data and improve data reusability in the memory design.

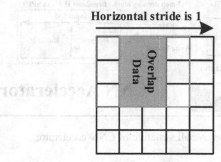

Fig. 5. Data overlapping of kernel adjacent sliding

4 Design and Implementation of CNN Accelerator

4.1 Architecture Analysis

At present, the common architectures of CNN accelerators are as follows: Systolic, 2D-Mapping and Tiling. Systolic can only support KP [4, 21], 2D-Mapping can only support FM-Ir-P [13], and Tiling can only support FM-Ir-P [10, 11]. Those architectures can not meet the requirements of this paper to support mixture parallelism. Therefore, this paper designed a specialized architecture and implemented a CNN accelerator.

The overall structure of the CNN accelerator designed in this paper is shown in Fig. 6, which consists of input buffer, control logic, and process unit. In order to realize FM-Ie-P, CNN accelerator has multiple super process units (SPUs), each of them is responsible for all calculations of a channel of output feature map. What's more, there is a other benefit that the performance of CNN accelerator can be further improved by increasing the number of SPUs without additional hardware overhead. Each SPU contains multiple MACs, one kernel buffer and one output buffer. Multiple MACs can simultaneously process multiple neurons in order to achieve FM-Ir-P. In addition, a sharing input buffer is designed to provide input feature map data for all SPUs. The CNN accelerator can connect to different external memory units through the AXI protocol. The calculation process of the CNN accelerator can be depicted as follows. Firstly, the operation data was read from the external memory unit. Secondly, the master logic sends the data to the corresponding module and then controls each module to work. Finally, the result was written back to the external memory unit.

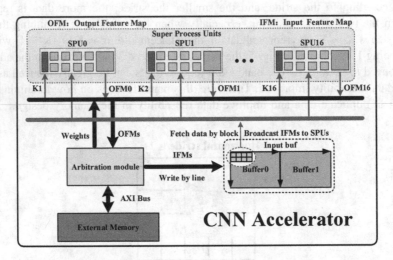

Fig. 6. The overall structure of CNN accelerator

4.2 Memory Design

According to the parallel mechanism determined in Sect. 2.2, the input feature maps should be stored in the input buffer, and shared by multiple SPUs. In the process of CONV operations, we adopt broadcast mechanism to provide map data to all SPUs. 2.2.2 indicates input buffer consists of 8 banks, which means it must provide 8 map data to SPUs per cycle. Because of the convolution stride, the map data required each cycle is discrete in input feature map. It is necessary to design a specialized buffer to realize conflict-free access.

In traditional matched parallel memory schemes, it is impossible to simultaneously support both parallel unit-stride and arbitrarily stride block access orders [26]. However, this paper proposes a 2-D addressing scheme which can support non-aligned block (4 * 2 block) access with different strides (stride in the horizontal direction is s and the stride of vertical direction is h) and aligned continuous access.

Gou et al. [23] proposed an addressing scheme that guarantees arbitrary stride access in a 1-D memory. We have improved and innovated his solutions and then proposed a 2-D addressing scheme to provide conflict-free access for non-aligned block access. 2-D addressing has two indexes, Bank ID and intra-bank address, and we only need to ensure that the locations accessed each cycle has different Bank ID. This paper proposes a function of Bank ID, the neurons in feature maps whose location is (i, j) can be map to a specific bank $f(w)$:

$$f(w) = \left(w + \left(\frac{w}{8}\right)\%s'\right)\%8$$
$$w = i + ((j/h)\%2) * 4s'$$

(1)

In the above formula, i and j represent the abscissa and ordinate of the neuron in feature map respectively. "/" means the floor operation; "%" means the remainder operation; s' is an addressing parameter and can be divided into 4 groups, its values are listed in Table 1. An addressing scheme example of memory is shown in Fig. 7.

Table 1. The value of s' in different stride

Groups	s $(1 \leq s \leq 15)$	s'
1	1, 3, 5, 7, 9, 11, 13, 15	1
2	2, 6, 10, 14	2
3	4, 12	4
4	8	8

The intra-bank address of neuron whose location is (j, i):

$$g(i,j) = i/8 + j*(X_m/16) + (i/(X_m/2))*(X_m*Y_m/16)$$

(2)

X_m and Y_m represent the input buffer length and width respectively. Input buffer can support ping-pang access in the horizontal direction, because it consists of memory banks

In addition, considering that there are a large number of data repetitions in adjacent sliding, we add a compare logic to avoid repeat access. The adjacent two access addresses are compared and if the next access address is the same as the previous one, reusing the result of the previous read.

4.3 SPU Design

We propose a super processing unit (SPU) to provide computing power for the CNN accelerator. FM-Ir-P means that the processing of multiple neurons is performed simultaneously, so we design 8 MACs in the SPU. Each MAC consists of an adder and a multiplier, which can perform one multiplication and one addition per cycle. What's more, each SPU also contains a local output buffer (Obuf) and a kernel buffer (Kbuf). The Kbuf adopts 1-D addressing mechanism and responsible for providing weight data. The Obuf also adopts 2-D addressing mechanism, but it just supports conflict-free block access without stride. Obuf is used to store the intermediate result of the CONV operation, and the final result is written back to the external memory unit after it is calculated. The internal structure of the SPU is shown in Fig. 8.

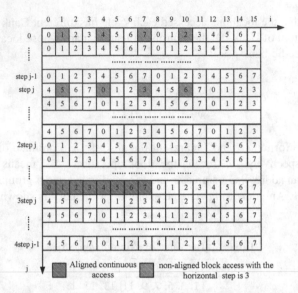

Fig. 7. Our addressing scheme that provides conflict-free non-aligned block access with different steps and aligned continuous access ($s' = 1$)

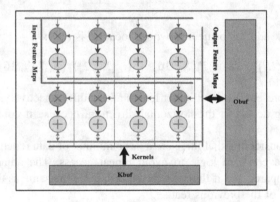

Fig. 8. The internal structure of SPU

The internal pipeline of SPU is shown in Fig. 9, which is divided into six stages. The logic shown by the solid box should be performed for each input data. In order to ensure the timing target of the whole system, the multiplication operation is completed in two cycles, and the addition operation is completed in one cycle. The logic shown by the dashed box and the dashed arrow is selectively executed as the data gradually enters. In our design, the Kbuf is accessed every four cycles (the interval time load next kernel). The Obuf reading only occurs when the first data input in a CONV operation except the operation of first map. The Obuf writing only occurs when the last data is calculated in a CONV operation. The selector of the E3 mainly selects one valid data from the four data which read out in the Kbuf, and then send them to multiplier. The selector of the E5 mainly selects the other operand of the corresponding adder. When the first data, in the first feature map, is input into a CONV operation, the operand is zero. When the first data, not in the first feature map, is input into a CONV operation, the operand is the value returned by the Obuf corresponding position. In other cases, the operand is the result of the output of the adder at the last cycle.

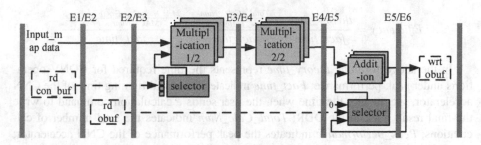

Fig. 9. The internal pipeline structure of SPU

4.4 Circuit Synthesis

In CNN accelerator, the Ibuf capacity is 32 KB, the total Obuf capacity is 128 KB, and the total Kbuf capacity is 32 KB. We synthesized our design under the 40 nm process by using complier tool. The result indicates that the circuit can work at 1 GHz. The area of each component is shown in Table 2. The total area is 4.512 million μm^2, of which the control logic accounts for 41.9%.

Table 2. Systhesis result of CNN accelerator

	Area ($\times 10^4$ um^2)	Ratio
Total	451.2	100%
Ibuf	22.2	4.9%
Obuf	191.8	42.6%
Kbuf	47.8	10.6%
else	189.4	41.9%

5 Evaluation and Comparison

This paper adopted simulation tools to simulate the CNN accelerator at 1 GHz. We selected DDR3 IP model as external memory unit, which reflects DDR page hits, page conflicts, refreshes, etc., and is almost identical to real DDR behavior. The default rate of DDR3 is 2133 Mbps, and using Matlab to generate test stimulus and standard results. During the simulation, we sample and count the access situation of DDR, the efficiency of SPU, etc. to generate the final test results.

5.1 Efficiency Calculation

The CNN accelerator designed in this paper has 16 SPUs, a total of 128 MACs. The system frequency is 1 GHz and the peak performance is 256 GOPs. However, the real performance needs to be calculated according to the actual efficiency of the SPU, and the efficiency can be obtained by formula (3):

$$Efficiency = \frac{theory\_time}{fact\_time} = \frac{\frac{Total\_Calc\_Num}{Peak\_performance}}{fact\_time} = \frac{\frac{M \times N \times C \times E \times F \times R \times S}{MAC\_Num \times Freq}}{fact\_time} \quad (3)$$

In the above formula, *theory_time* represents the time required for CONV operations under peak performance; *Fact_time* indicates the actual running time of the CNN accelerator, specifically the time when the user sends a calculation command to write the final result back to the DDR; *Total_Calc_Num* indicates the total number of calculations; *Peak_performance* indicates the peak performance of the CNN accelerator; *MAC_Num* indicates the total number of MACs of the CNN accelerator; *Freq* indicates the work frequency of the CNN accelerator; M, N, C, E, F, R and S refer to Fig. 1.

5.2 Results

In order to fully test the CNN accelerator, we adopted some classic CNN models, such as AlexNet [6], GoogleNet [7], VGGNet [8], ResNet [9] etc., as test stimulus. Although the structure and scale of these models are quite different, the parameters of their CONV layers are similar, such as the number of input/output feature maps, the size of the kernels, and the size of the stride. Therefore, we selected AlexNet and VGGNet as representative test sets.

In addition, because we didn't design data compression logic specifically, the efficiency on sparse network processing is general. Moreover, the CONV layers which closer to the FC layer are often sparse and have many zeros. Taking AlexNet as an example, the proportion of zeros in the input feature maps of the last three CONV layers is nearly 80%, and data needs to be compressed to further improve the efficiency of the accelerator, so this paper mainly tests the convolution layer with less zeros in the data. In addition, we also select some practical application networks as test samples, such as face recognition neural network [24], speed sign recognition neural network [24]. The specific parameters of those CNN models are listed in Table 3.

According to the model parameters in Table 3, we use MATLAB to generate test stimulus and convert it into hexadecimal format. Test results as shown in Table 4.

CNN accelerator performs well when processing the group 1, 2, 4, 5, 8 and 9, the efficiency of SPU over 90%. The reason why the SPU efficiency of the 6th and 7th groups is less than 90% is that there are only 14 output feature maps, and only 14 SPUs work at this time, resulting in a decrease in SPU efficiency. The efficiency of group 3 is less than 90%, because the input feature map only has 3 channels, the calculation finished very quickly, and the result needs to be written back and the next period of data also needs to be read, resulting in the memory bandwidth cannot meet the computational requirements.

Table 3. Model parameters

	AlexNet [13]		VGGNet [15]			Face recognition neural network		Speed sign recognition neural network	
Groups	1	2	3	4	5	6	7	8	9
Input	3	48	3	128	256	4	14	6	16
Output	48	128	64	128	256	14	14	16	80
H × W	224 × 224	55 × 55	224×224	112 × 112	56 × 56	640 × 360	320 × 180	640 × 360	320 × 180
E × F	55 × 55	27 × 27	224×224	112 × 112	56 × 56	320 × 180	320 × 180	320 × 180	320 × 180
R × S	11 × 11	5 × 5	3×3	3 × 3	3 × 3	6 × 6	6 × 6	6 × 6	5 × 5
$S_w × S_h$	4, 4	2, 2	1,1	1, 1	1, 1	2, 2	1, 1	2, 2	1, 1

Table 4. Various network model test results

Groups	1	2	3	4	5	6	7	8	9
Reading DDR data (MB)	4.0	6.8	4.3	90.4	88.8	5.2	4.7	8.2	26.9
Writing DDR data (MB)	1.1	0.4	17.3	8.6	3.8	4.4	3.4	5.0	18.5
DDR Performance (Gbits/s)	97	63	105	62	55	78	19	71	24
PE Performance (GOPs)	239.8	236.8	209.4	251.4	243.0	190.8	218.8	250.6	239.6
Efficiency	93.7%	92.5%	81.8%	98.2%	94.9%	85.1%	85.5%	97.9%	93.6%
Runtime (us)	439.7	945.4	821.8	14366.8	14614.8	1047.8	3554.1	1560.3	15377.8

The actual DDR performance of group 7 and group 9 is lower, because the stride of the two groups is small, both are (1, 1), and the size of their kernels is relatively large. Each pixel of the output feature needs more computation, resulting in longer operation time of the SPU, so the performance requirement for the DDR is low, and the DDR is idle for a long time, which reduces the efficiency of the DDR.

The total amount of DDR write data is slightly larger than the theoretical value. The main reason is that the output result is written back to the DDR, and the address is not aligned,but he DDR only supports the alignment access. At this time, some invalid data is written, but the invalid data of the multiple writes will be overwritten by the next period of write data. It does not affect the final result of writing back to DDR.

The data amount of reading DDR includes input feature maps, kernels and parameters. When the number of output feature map is large, only 16 output feature maps can be calculated in one period, so it is necessary to repeatedly read input feature map, and non-aligned access is read. Take some invalid data, plus the kernels, and finally make the total amount of data read DDR larger.

5.3 Comparison

Table 5 compares our design with Eyeriss [16, 17] and EIE [18]. Eyeriss supports data processing with a precision of 16-bit, an on-chip buffer of 183.3 KB, a peak performance of 33.6-84GOPs, and it's average buffer capacity per GOP is 2.18 KB. EIE supports data processing with a precision of 4-bit fixed-point, an on-chip buffer of

Table 5. Comparison between this design and related research

Index	Eyeriss	EIE	This Design
Technology (nm)	65	45	40
Clock Frequency	200 MHz	800 MHz	1 GHz
MACs	168	64	128
Peak performance (GOPs)	33.6–84.0	102	256
On-Chip Storage (KB)	183.3	162	192
Word Bit-width (Fixed)	16 Fixed-Point	4	32 Fixed-Point
Storage/Performance (16-bit) Fixed-Point)	4.36 KB/GOPs	6.35 KB/GOPs	0.75 KB/GOPs
Area (mm^2)	12.25	40.8	4.51
Power (mW)	278	590	985

162 KB, a peak performance of 102GOPs, and it's average buffer capacity per GOP is 6.35 KB (Converted to 16-bit). In contrast, our design supports 32-bit fixed-point, 192 KB on-chip buffer, a peak performance of 256GOPs, and the average buffer capacity per GOP is only 0.75 KB. Overall, our design has less hardware overhead.

6   Conclusions

This paper designs and implements a new CNN accelerator,which can fully exploit the parallelism of CNN. In order to meet the data requirements of parallel mechanisms, this paper design a 2-D buffer, it can support non-aligned block access with different steps and aligned continuous access. Moreover, A dedicated super processing unit is designed, which includes output buffer, kernel buffer, and MACs, and it makes the calculation and data fetching more streamline then ensure the performance of the accelerator. Compared with other designs [16–18], the hardware cost of the proposed accelerator is smaller under the same performance. In addition, this paper does not design a special hardware circuit for sparse neural networks, which needs further study.

Acknowledgment. This paper is supported by the National Science and Technology Major Project—intelligent computing unit for data center (cloud platform) and cluster computing (No. 2018ZX01031101) and the National Nature Science Foundation of China (No. 61602493, name: researches on efficient parallel memory techniques for wide vector dsps).

References

1. Ji, S., Xu, W., Yang, M., et al.: 3D convolutional neural networks for human action recognition. IEEE Trans. Pattern Anal. Mach. Intell. **35**(1), 221–231 (2013)
2. Khalil-Hani, M., Sung, L.S.: A convolutional neural network approach for face verification. In: International Conference on High PERFORMANCE Computing & Simulation, pp. 707–714. IEEE (2014)

3. Wang, C., Zhang, H., Yang, L, et al.: Deep people counting in extremely dense crowds. In: ACM International Conference on Multimedia, pp. 1299–1302. ACM (2015)
4. Chakradhar, S., Sankaradas, M., Jakkula, V., et al.: A dynamically configurable coprocessor for convolutional neural networks. ACM Sigarch Comput. Architect. News **38**(3), 247–257 (2010)
5. Rumelhart, D.E., Hinton, G.E., Williams, R.J.: Learning internal representations by error propagation, pp. 318–362. MIT Press (1988)
6. Krizhevsky, A., Sutskever, I., Hinton, G.E.: ImageNet classification with deep convolutional neural networks. In: International Conference on Neural Information Processing Systems, pp. 1097–1105 (2012)
7. Szegedy, C., Liu, W., Jia, Y., et al.: Going deeper with convolutions, pp. 1–9 (2014)
8. Simonyan, K., Zisserman, A.: Very deep convolutional networks for large-scale image recognition. Comput. Sci. (2014)
9. He, K., Zhang, X., Ren, S., et al.: Deep residual learning for image recognition, pp. 770–778 (2015)
10. Chen, T., Du, Z., Sun, N., et al.: DianNao: a small-footprint high-throughput accelerator for ubiquitous machine-learning. ACM Sigplan Notices, vol. 49, no. 4, pp. 269–284 (2014)
11. Chen, Y., Luo, T., Liu, S., et al.: DaDianNao: a machine-learning supercomputer. In: IEEE/ACM International Symposium on Microarchitecture, pp. 609–622. IEEE (2014)
12. Liu, D., Chen, T., Liu, S., et al.: PuDianNao: a polyvalent machine learning accelerator. In: Twentieth International Conference on Architectural Support for Programming Languages and Operating Systems, pp. 369–381 (2015)
13. Du, Z., Fasthuber, R., Chen, T., et al.: ShiDianNao: shifting vision processing closer to the sensor. In: ACM Sigarch Computer Architecture News, vol. 43, no. 3, pp. 92–104 (2015)
14. Zhang, S., et al.: Cambricon-X: an accelerator for sparse neural networks. In: The 49th Annual IEEE/ACM International Symposium on Microarchitecture, MICRO (2016)
15. Jouppi, N.P., Young, C., Patil, N., et al.: In-datacenter performance analysis of a tensor processing unit. In: International Symposium on Computer Architecture, pp. 1–12. ACM (2017)
16. Chen, Y.H., Emer, J., Sze, V.: Eyeriss: a spatial architecture for energy-efficient dataflow for convolutional neural networks. IEEE Micro **PP**(99), 1 (2016)
17. Chen, Y.H., Krishna, T., Emer, J.S., et al.: Eyeriss: an energy-efficient reconfigurable accelerator for deep convolutional neural networks. IEEE J. Solid-State Circ. **52**(1), 127–138 (2017)
18. Han, S., Liu, X., Mao, H., et al.: EIE: efficient inference engine on compressed deep neural network. In: ACM Sigarch Computer Architecture News, vol. 44, pp. 3, pp. 243–254 (2016)
19. Chakradhar, S., Sankaradas, M., Jakkula, V., Cadambi, S.: A dynamically configurable coprocessor for convolutional neural networks. In: SIGARCH Computer Architecture News, vol. 38, no. 3, pp. 247–257, June 2010
20. Farabet, C., Poulet, C., Han, J.Y., et al.: CNP: an FPGA-based processor for convolutional networks. In: International Conference on Field Programmable Logic and Applications, pp. 32–37. IEEE (2009)
21. Farabet, C., Martini, B., Corda, B., et al.: NeuFlow: a runtime reconfigurable dataflow processor for vision. In: Computer Vision and Pattern Recognition Workshops, pp. 109–116. IEEE (2012)
22. Zhang, C., Li, P., Sun, G., et al.: Optimizing FPGA-based accelerator design for deep convolutional neural networks, pp. 161–170 (2015)
23. Gou, C., Kuzmanov, G.K., Gaydadjiev, G.N.: SAMS: single-affiliation multiple-stride parallel memory scheme, pp. 350–368. ACM (2008)

24. Peemen, M., Setio, A.A.A., Mesman, B., et al.: Memory-centric accelerator design for convolutional neural networks. In: IEEE International Conference on Computer Design, pp. 13–19. IEEE (2013)
25. Lu, W., Yan, G., Li, J., et al.: FlexFlow: a flexible dataflow accelerator architecture for convolutional neural networks. In: IEEE International Symposium on High Performance Computer Architecture, pp. 553–564. IEEE (2017)
26. Lang, T., Valero, M., Peiron, M., et al.: Conflict-free access for streams in multimodule memories. IEEE Trans. Comput. **44**(5), 634–646 (1995)
27. Chetlur, S., Woolley, C., Vandermersch, P., et al.: cuDNN: efficient primitives for deep learning. Comput. Sci. (2014)
28. Vanhoucke, V., Senior, A., Mao, M.Z.: Improving the speed of neural networks on CPUs. In: Deep Learning and Unsupervised Feature Learning Workshop, NIPS 2011 (2011)

RCTS: Random Cyclic Testing System

Wang Liyi[⊠], Wang Xingyan, Zheng Yan, Shen Li, and Tan Jian

Jiang Nan Institute of Computing Technology, Wuxi 214083, China
wangliyi1979@hotmail.com

Abstract. In order to fully verify the correctness of the design, random test generators are usually used in microprocessor verification. In this paper, a random cyclic testing system called RCTS is designed for multi-core and heterogeneous many-core processors. RCTS supports FPGA verification and can verify hardware logic and integrated implementation at design stage. RCTS also supports the verification of prototype chips. Especially in the system-level hardware-software co-verification, it can find hard-to-expose hardware design problems. RCTS can completely eliminate the need for architectural simulators to compare the results, so it can reduce the verification time and improve the verification efficiency.

Keywords: Random test · Function verification · System-level

1 Introduction

Random testing is very important in pre-silicon verification and post-silicon verification, which can expose many critical errors at design time. Pseudo-random test generators can be tuned to produce streams of valid instructions with a wide range of properties. Randomized tests are most commonly focused on system-level aspects and interactions, subjecting the design to a variety of stressful stimuli [1]. But the drawback of random testing in post-silicon verification is that the results must be compared with the output of a golden architectural model.

In this paper, a random cyclic testing system is proposed. The random test generator used in this system can generate a test program with self-checking function, and it can support cyclic generation of test programs and cyclic testing, which can reduce the time overhead of random test generation.

The rest of the paper is organized as follows. Section 2 reviews the related work. Section 3 overviews a random cyclic testing system. Section 4 describes an experiment. Section 5 concludes the paper and outlines future research directions.

2 Related Work

Verification engineers leverage pseudo-random test generators (also called RTGs) that can be tuned to produce streams of valid instructions with a wide range of properties, e.g., focused activity on certain functional units, specific inter-instruction dependencies, and so on [1].

© Springer Nature Singapore Pte Ltd. 2019
W. Xu et al. (Eds.): NCCET 2019, CCIS 1146, pp. 177–185, 2019.
https://doi.org/10.1007/978-981-15-1850-8_16

Genesys-Pro is a typical random test generators in industry. Genesys-Pro is based on a generic engine that receives Test specification and Design model as it's input. The design model is specified in a declarative language that contains special constructs for describing the architecture and micro-architecture-including instructions, registers, cache structure, and translation mechanisms. Genesys-Pro is also integrated with two deep-knowledge test generators, FPgen and DeepTrans. This allows Genesys-Pro to create sophisticated and difficult to create scenarios in the areas of floating point and memory management unit (MMU) verification. Genesys-Pro uses a reference model to track the state of the processor throughout the test generation [2].

Genesys-Pro is a model-based approach, where a microprocessor model is separated from a platform-independent generation core. In fact, developing a microprocessor model is rather difficult and usually requires deep knowledge of the inner-core structure and interfaces [3].

Reconfigurable test program generator is customized with the help of architecture specifications and configuration files, which describe parameters of the microprocess or subsystems (pipeline, memory, and others). So it eases the model development and makes it possible to apply the model-based testing in the early design stages when the microprocessor architecture is frequently modified [4].

MicroTESK is a reconfigurable model-based test program generator (TPG) for microprocessors and other programmable devices. MicroTESK uses machine-readable ISA specifications as a source of knowledge about the design under test (DUT). This approach allows the TPG to be applied to a wide range of ISAs. Two main constructs, generic operations and revision annotations, can reduce code duplication and ease development of specifications with multiple ISA revisions and implementation-defined features [5]. However, whether the test program generated by MicroTest supports self-checking has not been mentioned.

The simulation of the golden model is several orders of magnitude slower than the hardware execution, therefore, the computation of the final state becomes a bottleneck for random testing or Pseudo-random testing. The strategy to solve this problem is based on reversible methods. Reversi is such a solution, which generates random programs in such a way that their correct final state is known at generation time, thus completely eliminating the need for architectural simulation. This allows Reversi-based post-silicon flow to bypass the simulation step and speed up the overall validation. However, this approach has a few limitations. The most important one stems from the fact that Reversi relies on the existence of inverse functions. So if the integer division operation were implemented in such a way that the remainder was discarded, the value of the dividend could not be restored precisely. Similarly, floating point instructions do not always provide high precision. Unfortunately, input and output operations are inherently irreversible and cannot be easily validated through a Reversi solution [1].

Multicore hardware validation is often handled by randomly generated testcases. This is useful for initial verification effort, but might not necessarily mirror real-world patterns of communication traffic. MINIME-Validator is a toolset for generating synthetic parallel testcases from a newly defined Parallel Pattern Markup Language (PPML) that uses the concept of parallel patterns. The technique allows for the generation of concise real world testcases to stress a system's inter-processor communication architecture [6].

3 Random Cyclic Testing System Overview

Most realistic test programs are large and slow to run via simulation and sometimes even too large for emulation. Fast and small synthetic tests are needed to catch more complex hardware bugs. Based on the idea of reversibility, a random cyclic test system with self-checking function can be realized.

3.1 Main Composition

The system consists of five parts: control center, program framework, random test generator, compiler environment and test management system. The composition of the random cyclic test system is shown in the Fig. 1.

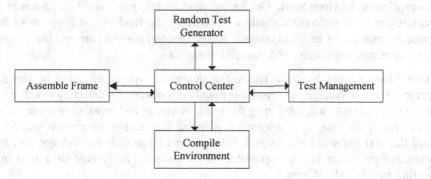

Fig. 1. The Five components of the random cyclic test system and their relationships are presented.

Control Center. The control center is mainly responsible for calling the random test generator, then embeds the assembly instructions into the program framework, and then calls the compiler to compile the assembly program into an executable program, and then calls the test management system to perform one or more tests. After completing the test, it returns to the control center and waits for the next random test. This cycle repeats until it reaches a certain degree of test satisfaction. When an error occurs in a program, the assembly program that caused the error is saved to help to diagnose the root cause of the error.

Program Framework. The program framework includes C program framework and assembly program framework. C program framework has nothing to do with architecture. It's main function includes initializing data and comparing results. Multi-core C program framework also includes task allocation. In addition to these functions, many-core C program framework also includes creating threads and recycling threads. The structure of assembly program framework is determined by different architectures, and the assembly instruction formats under different architectures are also different. The assembly framework of multi-core and single-core test programs is different, because functions such as synchronization are needed to generate multi-core parallel test programs. The assembly framework of heterogeneous many-core testing programs is also different, because heterogeneous many-core testing programs often contain a variety of instruction set architecture (ISA), so a variety of assembly frameworks are needed.

Random Test Generator (RTG). Random test generator generates random assembly instruction sequences according to instruction template. There are many kinds of instruction templates, such as reversible instruction template, cache conformance test template, register file test template and so on. Instruction templates are written according to predetermined rules. For example, integer registers are denoted by $A, floating-point registers are denoted by $FA, and quantitative registers are denoted by $VA. When the random test generator parses the instruction template, it allocates it with the corresponding register.

Compilation Environment. Generating random test programs with different architectures requires different compilers. Especially, the random test program of heterogeneous many-core needs to compile the program of control core and the program of operation core separately, and then link them up.

Test Management System. The test management system is called by the control center. The test management system is mainly responsible for detecting whether the test resources can be tested, submitting the test if available, and monitoring the test status in real time. If the hang-up phenomenon is found, the current test process will be killed and the next test will be continued. When testing large-scale parallel systems, the test management system is also responsible for the statistical analysis of test results in order to find out the rule of error.

3.2   Support Multi-core and Heterogeneous Many-Core

With the increasing number and complexity of processor cores, the problem of "state space explosion" is a difficult problem that can not be solved by multi-core and many-core processor verification technology. Likewise, increasing capabilities of formal verification tools in the future will be outpaced by the complexity of critical modules requiring formal analysis [1, 7]. Random test generation for multi-core and many-core processors needs to be further studied [8]. Ristretto is a random test generator for multicore microprocessor cache coherence verification. The solution scheme deals with the adaptation of some available stochastic testing approaches to multicore testing tool [9]. Some solutions need use a small amount of hardware logic to log information relevant to memory accesses [10, 11]. McVerSi and MTraceCheck both are aimed at validating non-deterministic behavior of memory consistency models [12, 13].

Our solution uses random test generation to verify cache coherence of the shared memory microprocessor without any hardware area penalty. The assembly instruction sequence generated by the random test generator supported by RCTS can be embedded in different assembly sub-functions, and these sub-functions can be executed concurrently on multiple cores. Task allocation is performed in the C program framework.

In the assembler, $16 passes the first address of the source space, and $17 passes the first address of the destination space (see Fig. 2).

```
sub0:
      vldd $f9,0*32($16)
      vstd $f9,0*32($17)
      addl $16,128,$16
      addl $17,128,$17
      flds $f2,0*4($16)
      fsts $f2,0*4($17)
      ......
      flds $f6,7*4($16)
      fsts $f6,7*4($17)
      ......
```

```
sub1:
      vldd $f9,1*32($16)
      vstd $f9,1*32($17)
      addl $16,128,$16
      addl $17,128,$17
      flds $f2,8*4($16)
      fsts $f2,8*4($17)
      ......
      flds $f6,15*4($16)
      fsts $f6,15*4($17)
      ......
```

```
sub2:
      vldd $f9,2*32($16)
      vstd $f9,2*32($17)
      addl $16,128,$16
      addl $17,128,$17
      flds $f2,16*4($16)
      fsts $f2,16*4($17)
      ......
      flds $f6,23*4($16)
      fsts $f6,23*4($17)
      ......
```

```
sub3:
      vldd $f9,3*32($16)
      vstd $f9,3*32($17)
      addl $16,128,$16
      addl $17,128,$17
      flds $f2,24*4($16)
      fsts $f2,24*4($17)
      ......
      flds $f6,31*4($16)
      fsts $f6,31*4($17)
      ......
```

Fig. 2. The graph represents a parallel memory access assembly program.

It can be seen from the assembly program that the randomly generated assembly program can greatly improve memory access density, so it can be used to verify cache coherence of the shared memory. The self-checking of test results can be accomplished by means of XOR and summation, i.e. summing data in Cache rows, and then XOR the summation results of Cache rows. These two steps act on the source space and the destination space respectively, and the result is correct if the hash values obtained are equal. To test multi-core cache consistency, multiple cores must access the same Cache Line at the same time. In order to cover more consistency states, each core can randomly access different locations of the same Cache Line.

For heterogeneous many-core, the control core and the operation core can access the same Cache line at the same time. The memory access instructions contained in the parallel program must be supported by both cores. Some memory access instructions only support the control core or the operation core, so when the random generator generates the sequence of access instructions, some difficulties will be encountered, such as the need to add memory fence instructions between the Cache access instructions and the Cache access instructions.

3.3   Advantages of RCTS

Because the design of the random cyclic testing system adopts a loosely coupled modular design, its scalability is relatively good. It is mainly reflected in the following aspects: supporting multiple random test generators and supporting multiple architectures. Because the instruction templates of different architectures are different and the assembly formats are different, the random cyclic testing system needs to support different random test generators.

The rules of instruction templates under different instruction set architectures are unified, so the establishment of instruction templates does not require much effort. The main work is to generate algorithm in random test generator. However, the general instruction generation algorithm for each architecture has little change, mainly because some accelerated instructions need a special generation algorithm. Moreover, acceleration instructions often do not have corresponding reversible instructions, so these instructions cannot be added to instruction templates in reversible random test generation. In order to improve the randomness of the program, multilevel reversible instruction segments can be linked randomly. Multilevel reversible instruction segments can not contain instructions with different data granularity, otherwise it is not easy to reverse them.

The control center, C program framework and test management system have nothing to do with the architecture, so the system also has good scalability.

The advantage of stopping immediately after an error occurs in a random test is that you can see the scene of the error and start checking for it (see Fig. 3). But the result of this is that the test cannot be carried out continuously, and someone must check the test situation at any time. In order to improve the efficiency of testing, we can save the error scene when the result is wrong, such as data and assembly program (see Fig. 4).

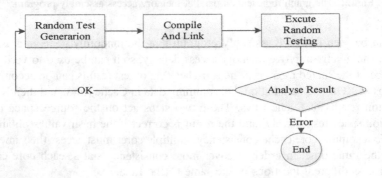

Fig. 3. Stop and check the scene when errors are found in random test.

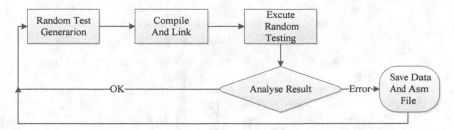

Fig. 4. When errors are found in random tests, data and assembly program are retained to reproduce the scene and locate errors.

Using the retained data and assembly program, the error scene can be reproduced to locate the error.

4 Experiment

To compare RCTS with Reversi, we created one reversible instruction block databases of the Extended DEC Alpha instruction set. The reversible instruction template we created contains 35 distinct blocks for arithmetic and logic functions, testing a range of instruction formats (register/register and register/immediate). In addition to that, the instruction template included 13 blocks for load and store instructions, 8 unconditional jump block and 14 branch blocks.

The following Table 1 gives a comparison of various types of reversible instruction numbers.

Table 1. This is a comparison between RCTS and Reversi with various reversible instructions.

Reversible instruction type	RCTS	Reversi
Arithmetic and logic	35	17
Load and store	13	3
Unconditional jump	8	1
Branch	14	16

The random test generator used in RCTS supports both scalar instructions and vector instructions. Instructions of different data lengths mixed in a multilevel reversible instruction block can cause incorrect reversal results. The solution is to put different data length instructions and their inverse instructions into different instruction templates. Random reversible instructions can not contain different data length instructions. When multiple random reversible instructions link, they need to be reserved and restored.

Test generation for RCTS was performed on Intel(R) Xeon(R) CPU E5-2640 v3 @ 2.60 GHz. The relationship between the length and time of generating random instruction segments is shown in the Fig. 5.

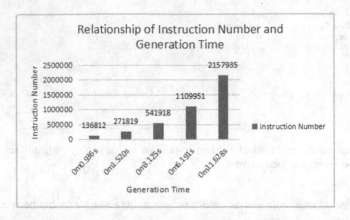

Fig. 5. The graph shows the relationship between instruction number growth and generation time.

As can be seen from Fig. 5 and Table 2, the time required to generate 2 million instructions is only about 9 s, which can be overlaid with the run time of the random test program.

Table 2. The generating and running time of parallel random test program is recorded.

Instruction number	Generation time (seconds)	Running time (seconds)
116390	0.552	8.090999
242758	1.092	14.656082
482086	2.089	27.374942
988238	4.567	55.056814
1941374	8.897	116.552643

5 Conclusion

This paper presents a random cyclic testing system-RCTS. RCTS combines the reversible idea and realizes the self-checking of random testing. The running time of random testing program is used to hide the generating time of testing program, which can improve the efficiency of random testing for post-silicon verification. The future research directions include combining other random test generators, such as reconfigurable random test generators, and studying other self-checking methods besides reversibility.

References

1. Wagner, I., Bertacco, V.: Post-Silicon and Runtime Verification for Modern Processors. Springer, Heidelberg (2011)

2. http://www.research.ibm.com/haifa/projects/verification/genesys_pro/. Accessed 29 July 2019
3. Adir, A., et al.: Genesys-pro: innovations in test program generation for functional processor verification. IEEE Des. Test Comput. **21**(2), 84–93 (2004)
4. Kamkin, A., Kornykhin, E., Vorobyev, D.: Reconfigurable model-based test program generator for microprocessors. In: International Conference on Software Testing Verification and Validation Workshops, pp. 47–54. IEEE, Berlin (2011)
5. Chupilko, M., Kamkin, A., Kotsynyak, A., Protsenko, A., Smolov, S., Tatarnikov, A.: Maintaining ISA specifications in MicroTESK test program generator. In: 2017 18th International Workshop on Microprocessor and SOC Test and Verification (MTV). IEEE, Austin (2017). https://doi.org/10.1109/MTV.2017.13
6. Sen, A., Deniz, E., Kahne, B.: MINIME-validator: validating hardware with synthetic parallel testcases. In: Design, Automation & Test in Europe Conference & Exhibition (DATE), pp. 386–391. IEEE, Switzerland (2017)
7. Pelánek, R.: Fighting state space explosion: review and evaluation. In: Cofer, D., Fantechi, A. (eds.) FMICS 2008. LNCS, vol. 5596, pp. 37–52. Springer, Heidelberg (2009). https://doi.org/10.1007/978-3-642-03240-0_7
8. Ludden, J.M., Rimon, M., Hickerson, B.G., Adir, A.: Advances in simultaneous multithreading testcase generation methods. In: Barner, S., Harris, I., Kroening, D., Raz, O. (eds.) HVC 2010. LNCS, vol. 6504, pp. 146–160. Springer, Heidelberg (2011). https://doi.org/10.1007/978-3-642-19583-9_15
9. Smirnov, A.V., Chibisov, P.A.: Random test generator for multicore microprocessor cache coherence verification (Ristretto). In: MES (2018). https://doi.org/10.31114/2078-7707-2018-2-31-38
10. DeOrio, A., Bauserman, A., Bertacco, V.: Post-silicon verification for cache coherence. In: Proceedings of the International Conference on Computer Design, ICCD, pp. 348–355, October 2008
11. Mammo, B.W., Bertacco, V., DeOrio, A., Wagner, I.: Post-silicon validation of multiprocessor memory consistency. IEEE Trans. Comput.-Aided Des. Integr. Circ. Syst. **34**(6), 1027–1037 (2015)
12. Elver, M., Nagarajan, V.: McVerSi: a test generation framework for fast memory consistency verification in simulation. In: International Symposium on High Performance Computer Architecture (HPCA) (2016)
13. Lee, D., Bertacco, V.: MTraceCheck: validating non-deterministic behavior of memory consistency models in post-silicon validation. In: ACM/IEEE International Symposium on Computer Architecture. IEEE Computer Society (2017)

Evaluation and Optimization of Interrupt Response Mechanism in RISC-V Architecture

Kefan Xu, Yong Li[⊠], Bo Yuan, and Dongchu Su

School of Computer Science, National University of Defense Technology,
Changsha 410073, China
kefan9969@163.com,
{yongli, yuanbo18, sudongchu18}@nudt.edu.cn

Abstract. RISC-V (Reduced Instruction Set Computer-Five) is an emerging universal open ISA, targeting to become as popular for processors as Linux for operating systems. Currently, many research institutions and companies publish various RISC-V processor cores. One of the most important feature of processors is the ability to response to interrupt events. This paper studies the interrupt mechanism of Hummingbird e203, which is an open-source RISC-V processor. By analyzing the existing interrupt mechanism, we propose a new mechanism of interrupt vectorization, which can achieve faster interrupt response. We also carry out simulation and logical synthesising for these two different response mechanism. Theoretical analyzing and evaluation results show that our design is feasible and efficient, improving the response speed to 1.6x–3.5x.

Keywords: RISC-V · Privileged architecture · Interrupt response mechanism · Interrupt vectorization

1 Introduction

RISC-V is an open source instruction set architecture designed and developed by a team at the University of California, Berkeley. It is designed to be open, free, simple, extensible to use and has better internal structure [1]. As an emerging open-source software and hardware ecosystem, RISC-V has gained popularity in both industry and academia [2, 3]. The ecosystem provides rich open-source software and hardware toolchains that enable computer architects to quickly leverage RISC-V in their research. On the hardware side, several RISC-V prototypes have been published on open source websites such as GitHub and PULP platform.

Hummingbird e203 [4] core, the first open-source processor in China, was published to support RISC-V instruction set, which implements instructions such as RV32IEAMCFD and provides a mature GCC compiler toolchain. Therefore, we take Hummingbird e203 as the prototype to analyze the interrupt mechanism of RISC-V architecture in this paper.

There are two types of interrupt with the same handling mechanism. A synchronous internal exception is caused by the actions of instruction in the currently executing program. An asynchronous external interrupt is generated by external hardware devices [5]. We will discuss these two concepts in a unified way. The privileged architecture of

© Springer Nature Singapore Pte Ltd. 2019
W. Xu et al. (Eds.): NCCET 2019, CCIS 1146, pp. 186–197, 2019.
https://doi.org/10.1007/978-981-15-1850-8_17

RISC-V specifically defines two ways to transfer control to the interrupt handler and implements a simple interrupt mechanism, supporting query mode and vector mode. If the processor needs to enter the interrupt handler routine, it must access the special registers to get the interrupt number and then find the interrupt service routine based on the interrupt number [6].

An ongoing challenge in interrupt mechanism design is the problem of delay in response function. Hummingbird e203 adopts the query mode in interrupt mechanism that needs software to polling the handler address, which leads to long and unify response time, that means various interrupt events have different response time. We analyze the disadvantage of the query mode of Hummingbird and implement vector mode to speedup interrupt response speed. The simulation and logical synthesising results for these two different response mechanisms show that our design can achieve high and unify response speed at fairy hardware cost.

2 Related Works

The Instruction Set Architecture (ISA), the interface between hardware and software, is the major portion of an architecture. With the straight-forward and modular ISA, RISC-V can be designed for variety of processors, from extremely small implementations to large, high-performance implementations [7].

Currently, many RISC-V cores were published from different research institutions and companies based on RISC-V Instruction Set Manual Volume, which analyses ISA features and brings out the technical specification. There are several typical cores listed as follows. The fully open hardware system, Rocket chip [8] and Boom [9] which was designed in the hardware construction language Chisel, based on RISC-V has been published by the University of California, Berkeley. SHAKTI [10], from the Indian institute of technology, aiming to design series open-chip processor for full-range applications has published its SDK in 2019. Processors in SHAKTI series has published with Bluespec System Verilog, consisting of ultralow power processor E-Class, out of order processor I-class with 200-1 GHz, and multi-threaded with 32-100 cores processor in H-class etc. PULP is a joint project between the Integrated Systems Laboratory (IIS) of ETH Zurich and the Energy-efficient Embedded Systems (EEES) group of UNIBO, which aims to develop an open, scalable Hardware and Software research platform. It offers us series efficient implementations of RISC-V cores.

The Workshop on Computer Architecture Research with RISC-V (CARRV) offers the opportunity to computer architecture, compilers, and systems for technical exchange on using RISC-V in computer architecture research. In the past 3 meetings, various research institutes and companies have introduced their own work on both software and hardware toolchains such as Simulation Infrastructure [11], cycle-level simulation platform [12], and method for developing SoCs [13] etc. The prosper of ecosystem provided us with sufficient resources for research.

For each computer system, interruption is a very important technology, and it is an effective extension of microprocessor functions [14]. Interrupt can interfere with the normal execution of the program and have a certain impact on the performance of the processor. Interrupt mechanism has been discussed a lot in the previous architecture, such as ARM. That provides us with a convenient way to deeply learning the merits and optimizing the function in our studies. CortexM3 [15] achieved the priority arbitration, interrupt nesting and preemption techniques. CortexM4 [15, 16] provide the interrupt vector table structure, which has certain reference significance for our future research. The interrupt mechanism in the RISC-V architecture allows users to customize and extend. Research on interruption is beneficial to achieve a more complete, real-time and efficient interrupt mechanism to improve the performance of the processor.

3 Introduction of RISC-V Privilege Architecture

Machine mode is the most privilege mode that a RISC-V hardware thread can execute in, running the most trusted code. It is the only privilege mode that all standard RISC-V processors must implement [17–20]. The most important feature of machine mode is the ability to intercept and handle interrupts [17]. Therefore, this paper mainly studies the machine mode.

3.1 CSRs in Machine Mode

At the center of the RISC-V privilege system are a number of Control and Status Registers (CSRs) [18], which are different from general purpose registers. Each CSR has a unique name and specialized functions. Some hardware behaviors are specified in the architecture to implement response and processing. The CSR is used to reflect the interrupt information [19]. CSRs are integral to machine-mode exception handling, which listed as follows:

Machine Exception Program Counter (mepc): when the processor enters to the interrupt processing, mepc will record the current pc of the instruction that encountered the exception.

Machine Status Register (mstatue): It holds global interrupt enable and controls the harts current operating statue. In the case of machine mode, the valid fields are MIE and MPIE. MIE indicates that the interrupt is globally enabled, and an interrupt can only be generated when this bit is valid. The MPIE is used to save the status of the MIE before entering the interrupt processing and returning to the scene.

Machine Cause Register (mcause): when the processor enters to the interrupt processing, mcause will be written with a code indicating which exception occurred. The highest bit is the interrupt filed, and the lower 31 bits are the exception number field. If there is an interrupt event pending, the interrupt bit will be set. The Exception Code field holds the identification code of the pending event. The middle bits can be used as a reserved field to support field expansion for exception encoding. The format is shown in Fig. 1.

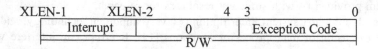

Fig. 1. Machine Cause register (mcause).

Machine Trap Vector Base-Address Register (mtvec): It holds the address where the processor will jump to when an exception occurs, [17] consisting of a vector base address (BASE) and a vector mode (MODE). The lowest two bits are mode bits, which can be set to different response strategies to ensure the flexibility of the processing mechanism. The bits from 2 to XLEN-1 is the base address of the BASE field representing the exception vector. The format is shown in Fig. 2:

Fig. 2. Machine trap-vector base-address register (mtvec)

Machine Scratch Register (mscratch): It is used to hold a pointer to a machine-mode hart-local context space and swapped with a user register upon entry to an M-mode trap handler [17]. The mscratch registers can be quickly saved and restored using specific instructions.

3.2 CSRs Behavior

Hummingbird e203 studied in this paper abides by the RISC-V privilege architecture specification and implements the related processing of interrupt exceptions. When the RISC-V core takes an interrupt or exception, the hardware atomically undergoes several status transactions:

1. Record the source number of events into the mcause register;
2. Update the status register mstatus to record the status before the interrupt processing and disable the MIE bit;
3. Save the exceptional instruction PC in mepc so that the processor can return to the main routine after processing the interrupt;
4. Stop the currently executing program flow and start to execute from the PC defined in the control status register mtvec.

The RISC-V architecture stipulates that there is no hardware automatically saving and recovering operation when processor enters and exits the interrupt mechanism, so we need to set software program to save the context [20]. To avoid overwriting the contents of an integer register before responding to an interrupt, the values in integer register will be swapped with mscratch by handler. Through the software settings, the context space pointer to the machine mode hardware thread is placed in the mscratch register to hold the integer registers that will be used in its handler. After the execution of the handler, the interrupt program restores the registers it has saved to memory, and then uses mscratch and integer register to swap again to restore the values of the two registers before the exception occurred.

The RISC-V architecture defines the instruction, mret, to exit the interrupt. When the exception processing has finished, mret is executed. The processor stops the current interrupt processing program flow and resumes the execution of main program from the PC address defined in the control status register mepc, as well as updates mastues.

4   Interrupt Mechanism of Hummingbird

4.1   Interrupt System of Hummingbird

Interrupt system contains the connection between different interrupt and exception source and the handling unit. The interruptions and exceptions in the Hummingbird e203 are handled in the commit module. ALU unit mainly issues instruction access fault and illegal instruction exception. When long instruction needs to be written back, a read/write memory exception will be issued from long instruction write back module. The ordinary interrupt consists of software interrupt, timer interrupt and external interrupt. After the arbitration of local interrupt controller and the platform level interrupt controller [17], the corresponding interrupt request will be sent to the exception/interrupt handling unit. The debug module will generate a debug interrupt. When an interrupt or exception meets the trigger condition, pipeline flush signal will be generated to cancel the subsequent unexecuted instructions and the value in flush pc will be sent to the fetch unit for fetching the next instruction. The interrupt system is shown in Fig. 3.

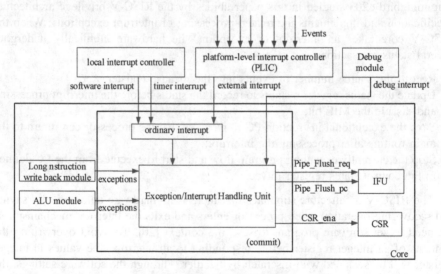

Fig. 3. Interrupt system

4.2   Interrupt Handling of Hummingbird

The design of the Hummingbird e203 is consistent with the RISC-V architecture in processing of interrupts and exceptions. It is mainly composed of the trigger module, detection module, priority arbitration module and processing module, as shown in Fig. 4.

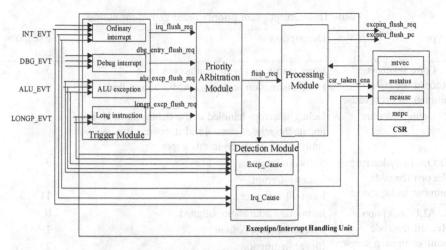

Fig. 4. Exception/Interrupt handling unit

Trigger module is the basis of interrupt processing. When an interrupt or exception event is detected, a trigger request signal of the corresponding type interrupt will be issued, indicating that kind of interrupt event occurs. The trigger request signal will then be sent to the priority arbitration module to determine which interrupt event should be processed first.

Priority arbitration module determines which type of interrupt event should be processed first based on the request signal received from the trigger module and the priority order illustrated in mcause. Long instruction type interrupt has the highest priority, debug interrupts have the second priority and then normal interrupts, ALU modules have the lowest priority. When the four types of interrupts occur at the same time, the long instruction type interrupt is processed first. The rest of the triggered interrupt signals are still pulled high waiting for the end of the higher-priority interrupt processing. The priority arbitration module finally issues a pending request to the processing module and records the exception event number according to the processing request in the reason register.

Detection module records the current pending interrupt or exception event number. When the interrupt request is detected and the corresponding enable bit is on, mcuse will directly be updated with the event number. The debug interrupt updates dcause according to the request signal. When the pending request is detected, the event number with corresponding type is directly recorded into the exception cause register. The event number also represents the priority order of different type of events. The interrupt event priority order and the event number are shown in Table 1.

Table 1. Interrupt event priority order and event number

Type	Description	Exception code
1. Long instruction Record the code number in excp_cause	Long instruction with load access fault	5
	Long instruction with store/AMO access fault	7
2. Debug interrupt	Debug interrupt handled in the debug mode. It will update the related control and status register. We only study machine mode in this paper	
3. Oridinary interrupt Record the code number in irq_cause	Software interrupt	3
	Timer interrupt	7
	External interrupt	11
4. ALU exception Record the code number in excp_cause	Instruction address misaligned	0
	Instruction access fault	1
	Illegal instruction	2
	Breakpoint	3
	Load address misaligned	4
	Load access fault	5
	Store/AMO address misaligned	6
	Store/AMO access fault	7
	Environment call from U-mode	8
	Environment call from S-mode	9
	Environment call from H-mode	10
	Environment call from M-mode	11
	Reserved	≥ 12

According to the current interrupt information, the processing module can identify the CSRs which should be updated, and then issue the pipeline flushing signal and PC value. For different type of interrupts and exceptions, there are slight differences in the update CSRs: when the exception to be processed is a long instruction type, the return value register mepc saves the pc value of the long instruction, and in other cases, the pc in the execution unit ALU is saved. If the processing signal sent by priority arbitration module is the exception type, mcause will be updated to exception reason number, otherwise to interrupt reason number.

4.3 Evaluate the Interrupt Response Mechanism of Hummingbird

Interrupt response is the process from receiving an interrupt request to jumping to the corresponding interrupt service routine. Similar with the conventional method, the processor can enter the processing program from the currently executed main program by querying mode and vector mode [21].

Hummingbird e203 implements query mode, setting the MODE filed of mtvec register to 0. This means when an exception or interrupt occurs, CPU will be informed by the hardware to jump directly to the entry of the exception handler, which specified by the BASE field in mtvec register. After entering the service program, software needs to save the context and then decode the type of pending event and exception code, identifying whether the pending event is the external interrupt or internal exception. It is caused by an external interrupt when the lowest bit in the mcause register is 1. Software program will read the exception code in mcause and polling to get the address of the corresponding handler. Otherwise, there is an internal exception event to be processed, which enters the corresponding handler by polling the number in the mcause register.

The existing interrupt response means to prioritize the query order through the software. This way is versatile because it requires no additional hardware support and allows the easy modification of the query priorities. The major disadvantage, however, is the delay introduced by low priority events. Even if it is the only event which occurs, the low-priority event must wait for the program to poll all the higher-priority orders. This may cause a delay that slows down the hardware speed during entering the handler process.

5   Optimization of the Interrupt Response Mechanism

5.1   The Interrupt Response Mechanism in Vector Mode

Handling interrupts in a quickly and efficiently way is an important indicator to assess the interrupt system. We add hardware (HW) design and change the way to obtain the interrupt service address. As the comparison shown in Fig. 5, RISC-V privilege architecture indicates that the address of interrupt service routine can be directly calculated according to the type of pending interrupts. The mechanism allows the processor to jump directly to the service routine rather than an entry point.

In terms of hardware design, considering to get the address of the interrupt service table, we add the interrupt service routine address register ISR_ADDR and interrupt service table on the processing module. The interrupt service table contains multiple sets of interrupt vectors. When an interrupt request is waiting for processing, the processor will generate an offset address according to the event number in mcause and acquire the base address of the service routine which defined in mtvec. The entry address of service program of interrupt vector is the summary of the base address and the offsets. Figure 5a shows the interrupt response process in query mode while Fig. 5b is vector mode.

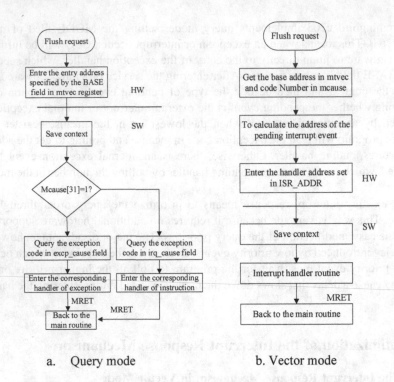

a. Query mode   b. Vector mode

Fig. 5. Interrupt response process in query mode and vector mode

Vector mode is a method to calculate the address of the interrupt handler in hardware (HW) side. The processor can quickly obtain the corresponding interrupt vector address rather than polling the code number in mcause with software (SW) method.

5.2 Comparison to Hummingbird

Interrupt vectorization brings lots of advantage. In the case of the query mode, response time depends on the position of the interrupt in the polling chain. While in vector mode, the procedure for reading and polling mcause is eliminated, which unifies the response time to enter different interrupt routine, speeds up the processing and reduces the response time when dealing with interrupts. We make a comparison between query mode and vector mode with the same interrupts.

In query mode, when the processor detects the most priority interrupt request from interrupt processing module, the relevant CSRs will be updated and the routine will switch to the interrupt handler entry address, which requires 12 clock cycles. Then the software must save context and query mcause to find the address of corresponding interrupt which need to be processed. Saving the context takes 36 clock cycles which is an inevitable step. Query and obtain the interrupt service routine address needs to polling mcause, which has different response time. In this way, the hardware design is relatively simple, but takes long times to response to interrupt and has certain impact on efficiency of the processor. The time-consuming of each interrupt querying to the service address is different and cannot be unified.

After vectorization, when the processor detects pending request, it can quickly enter to the interrupt service routine corresponding with the pending event. This method only cost 12 clock cycles regardless of the interrupt type. However, since the RISC-V architecture provides no hardware behaviours to save the context, the work of saving context still needs to be done in software. It will only cost 36 clock cycles at the beginning of every service routine. This kind of response mechanism allows different type of events to be completed in the same amount of time and the total time required for every event only takes 48 clock cycles.

The query mode requires different cycles for consulting the number in mcause to enter the corresponding service routine. After optimization, the responding speed boots a lot as shown in the Fig. 6. We take these 6 types events in Fig. 6 as example, comparing the time consumption of event response in query mode and vector mode.

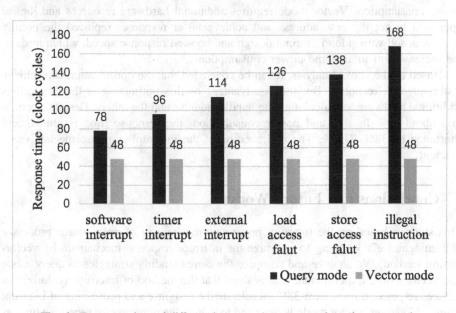

Fig. 6. Response time of different interrupts in query mode and vector mode

Software interrupt is the shortest time-consuming event in query mode, taking 30 clock cycles to decode mcause and get the software interrupt entry address. The whole process of entering the software interrupt handler routine costs 78 clock cycles. The longest query time appears when illegal instruction exception pending. It takes 120 clock cycles to query the entry address, the overall response time is 168 clock cycles. In vector mode, all events enter to the corresponding handler at 48 clock cycles.

By calculating the ratio of response speeds in query mode to vector mode, we can draw the conclusion that compared with query mode, the response speed in vector mode is improved to 1.6–3.5 times, which achieve the requirement of fast response.

The interrupt processing module has been logically synthesized using Design Compiler based on the same process library. We set same constraints for query mode and vector mode when synthesizing. The comparison of area, timing and power consumption were reported and shown in Table 2.

Table 2. DC results of different response mode

Mode/report	Area	Dynamic power	Leakage power
Query mode	2874.486084 μm^2	111.2383·μw	86.3235 μw
Vector mode	4139.292955 μm^2	155.6222 μw	142.3172 μw

Obviously, the area ratio after interrupt vectorization is increased to 48%, the static power consumption increased to 39.8% and the drain voltage power consumption increased to 64.9%. The larger the layout area, the higher the manufacturing costs and power consumption. Vector mode requires additional hardware resources and logical operation to get the new address and achieve faster response, replaced the polling process at software side in original design and boosted response speed, which leads to the increasement in area and power consumption.

Based on the above analysis, it can be concluded that the optimization can achieve faster interrupt response. But the disadvantage of this optimizing is that it requires additional hardware for calculating the handler address and the others. Despite a certain loss about 50% in area and power consumption, the response time is unified and shortened by 38%–71.4%. The optimization of the interrupt response mechanism is efficient.

6 Conclusions and Future Works

This study is based on the interrupt processing mechanism of open-source processor Hummingbird e203 aiming to optimize the interrupt response mechanism by vectorization method. We analyze and compare the corresponding strategies in query mode and vector mode. Experimental results show that the method of interrupt vectorization reduces response time at least 38%, accelerate the response and processing of interrupt events. Moreover, vector mode is designed to reduce the unnecessary repetitive queries in software and achieve optimization, which ensuring different interrupt can enter their service program in the same time. However, as hardware design increases, the area and power consumption are inevitably increased.

In future work, we plan to develop an open-source processor, which implements more privilege patterns. To facilitate our processor, we will achieve debug mode to support debug interrupt based on existing research.

References

1. Lei, S.: Research on open source processor and SoC based on RISC-V. J. Microcontrollers Embedded Syst. (2017)
2. Asanovic, K., Patterson, D.: Instruction sets should be free: the case for RISC-V. Technical Report UCB/EECS-2014-146, EECS Department, University of California, Berkeley, August 2014
3. RISC-V Foundation (2018). http://www.riscv.org. Accessed 17 Mar 2018
4. Hu, Z.B.: How to design CPU: RISC-V processor articles (2018)
5. Li, Y.: Exceptions and Interrupts Handling and Design in Verilog HDL. Computer Principles and Design in Verilog HDL. Wiley, Hoboken (2016)
6. Ye, Q.Y., Liu, Q.: Analysis and implementation of interrupt stack based on ARM in operating system. J. Wuhan Univ. Technol. **26**(1), 87–89 (2004)
7. Jan, G.: GRVI phalanx: a massively parallel RISC-V FPGA accelerator accelerator. In: Proceedings of the 2016 IEEE 24th Annual International Symposium on Field-Programmable Custom Computing Machines (FCCM), pp. 17–20 (2016)
8. Asanović, K., et al.: The rocket chip generator. Technical report UCB/EECS-2016-17, EECS Department, University of California, Berkeley, April 2016
9. Christopher, C., Patterson, D., Asanović, K.: The Berkeley Out-of-Order Machine (BOOM): an industry-competitive, synthesizable, parameterized RISC-V processor. Technical report UCB/EECS-2015-167.EECS Department, University of California, Berkeley (2015)
10. Gala, N., Menon, A., Bodduna, R., et al.: SHAKTI processors: an open-source hardware initiative. In: the 29th International Conference on VLSI Design and 2016 15th International Conference on Embedded Systems (VLSID). IEEE (2016)
11. Neethu, B.M., Cecilia, G.A., Trevor, E.C.: Flexible timing simulation of RISC-V processors with sniper. In: The Second Workshop on Computer Architecture Research with RISC-V (CARRV), Los Angeles, CA. USA (2018)
12. Tuan, T., Lin, C., Christopher, B.: Simulating multi-core RISC-V systems in gem5. In: The Second Workshop on Computer Architecture Research with RISC-V (CARRV), Los Angeles, CA, USA (2018)
13. Paul, R., Borivoje, N.: Designing digital signal processors with rocket chip. In: The Second Workshop on Computer Architecture Research with RISC-V (CARRV), Los Angeles, CA, USA (2018)
14. Xu, P.: Study of interrupt control IP core for embedded system. J. Inf. Technol. **11**, 121–123 (2006)
15. Joseph, Y.: The definitive guide to the ARM Cortex-M3 and Cortex-M4 (2015)
16. Shi, J., Wang, Y.H., Su, Y.: Design and interrupt program framework design of MQX interrupt mechanism based on ARM Cortex-M4. J. Comput. Sci. **40**(6), 41–44 (2013)
17. Andrew, W., Krste, A.: The RISC-V Instruction Set Manual VolumeII: Privileged Architecture. University of California, Berkeley, 7 May 2017
18. Harry, H.P.: RISC-V: An Overview of the Instruction Set Architecture. Portland State University
19. David, A.P., John, L.H.: Computer Organization and Design (2018)
20. David, P., Andrew, W.: The RISC-V Reader: An Open Architecture Altlas, First Edition, 1.0.0. (2018)
21. Li, Y.M.: Computer Organization and Design (2011)

Numerical Analysis and Experimental Study on Heat Dissipation Performance of Sealed Rugged Server

Miao Zhang$^{(\boxtimes)}$ and Fuge Wang

The Computer Department, Jiangsu Automation Research Institute,
Lianyungang, China
zm86325@126.com, wangfuge716@163.com

Abstract. With the rapid development of computer technology, the power density of the rugged server is getting larger and larger, so it must be reasonably designed to ensure that the temperature of the server is properly controlled within the scope. This paper introduces the structure of the rugged server and selects the appropriate fan through theoretical analysis and calculation. Based on Icepak thermal simulation software, the rugged server is simulated and optimized, getting the steady temperature field and the velocity field inside the server. The product prototype is tested at a high temperature of 55 °C. The test results show the scheme of thermal design is feasible. The working temperature meets the derating design requirements, and the reliability of the equipment is improved. The simulation results of the paper can provide calculation methods and reference for the thermal design of sealed rugged servers.

Keywords: Sealed rugged server · Numerical analysis · Thermal design · Thermal test

1 Introduction

With the continuous development of shipboard advanced electronic manufacturing technology, the multi-function ship-based electronic equipment for large-scale and ultra-large-scale integrated circuits has gradually increased, and in a limited space, the thermal design of electronic modules in the chassis has stricter requirements. Therefore, under the condition of various harsh mechanical environments, the thermal design of the electronic equipment chassis becomes a precondition for ensuring reliable operation of the equipment. The performance of the electronic equipment thermal design system affects directly the working performance and working life of the electronic equipment. Therefore, solving the problem of overheating of electronic equipment is one of the research hotspots in the field of thermal design technology of electronic equipment at home and abroad [1, 2].

The thermal design method of traditional electronic equipment is to first determine the design according to the experience of the designer, and then use the empirical formula to estimate and verify by the test, and optimize according to the test results, and finally redesign the production [3]. The design method has poor accuracy, long

© Springer Nature Singapore Pte Ltd. 2019
W. Xu et al. (Eds.): NCCET 2019, CCIS 1146, pp. 198–211, 2019.
https://doi.org/10.1007/978-981-15-1850-8_18

design cycle and high research and development cost. Front-end thermal design refers to solving the basic problems of thermal design in the pre-research and development stage of the product, comprehensively analyzing the feasibility of the thermal design scheme, accurately predicting the design results, and analyzing and optimizing the thermal design scheme [4, 5].

Based on this front-end thermal design idea, this paper applies modern computational fluid dynamics technology and numerical heat transfer technology to perform a system-level simulation analysis of a closed-type reinforcement server, which obtains the flow state of the cooling airflow in the chassis and gives the flow field distribution and temperature distribution of different profiles. It provides a theoretical basis for optimizing and improving the thermal design of the equipment that analyzes and discusses the calculation results, and effectively verifies the correctness of the optimization scheme through experimental measurements.

2 Modeling Method

2.1 Object Description

The reinforced server is a fully sealed reinforced chassis. The dimensions (mm) are: 482.6 (width) × 309.9 (height) × 260 (deep). The chassis consists of a frame, a front panel, and a rear panel. The front panel is equipped with a small door for easy operation of the debugging module, and the rear panel is equipped with a power switch, a fuse and a filter and connectors for the outer lead of the chassis. The computer uses conduction and forced air cooling to dissipate heat. The frame of the chassis adopts vacuum brazing technology. The welded frame can not only improve the vibration and shock resistance of the whole machine, but also meet the vibration requirements of the use environment, and increase the electrical continuity of the chassis and improve the shielding effectiveness of the whole machine. The specific dimensions of the hardening server are shown in Fig. 1.

2.2 Control Equation

The cooling method used by the research object is a typical forced convection heat transfer method using air as the heat transfer medium. In the Cartesian coordinate system, the symbolic rules of Einstein summation are used. The mass conservation, momentum conservation and energy conservation equations can be written as follows:

The expressions of the control equations are as follows [6, 7]:

Mass conservation equation

$$\frac{\partial \rho}{\partial t} + \frac{\partial}{\partial x_i}(\rho u_i) = 0 \tag{1}$$

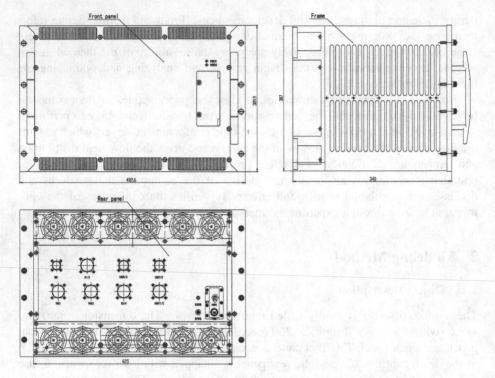

Fig. 1. The outline drawing of the reinforcement server

Momentum conservation equation

$$\frac{\partial}{\partial t}(\rho u_i) + \frac{\partial}{\partial x_j}(\rho u_i u_j) = -\frac{\partial p}{\partial x_i} + \frac{\partial}{\partial x_j}\left(\mu \frac{\partial u_i}{\partial x_j} - \rho \overline{u_i u_j}\right) \tag{2}$$

Energy conservation equation

$$\frac{\partial}{\partial t}(\rho E) + \frac{\partial}{\partial x_i}(u_i(\rho E + p)) = \frac{\partial}{\partial x_i}\left(k_{eff}\frac{\partial T}{\partial x_i} - \sum_{j'} h_{j'} J_{j'} + u_j \tau_{eff}\right) \tag{3}$$

2.3 Thermal Model

(1) Setting of external environment parameters

According to the highest working temperature requirements of the equipment environment, the ambient temperature of the chassis is set to 55 °C. Since the chassis is based on the combination of conduction and convection, the radiation dissipation method is not considered.

(2) Establish a simplified geometric model of the chassis

There is a lot of information in the real chassis that has little effect on the thermal simulation results. The existence of this information will greatly increase the complexity of the thermal model and prolong the operation time. Therefore, it is necessary to simplify the chassis model according to the actual situation of the thermal design. Since the chassis is sealed, conduction plays a major role in the heat dissipation of the chassis. Therefore the convection and radiation heat transfer modes inside the chassis can be ignored, and only the models of the PCB board, the chip, and the heat conduction board are built when modeling the internal modules. A system-level chassis thermal analysis model is built using the parametric modeling method and model library provided by the software, as shown in Fig. 2.

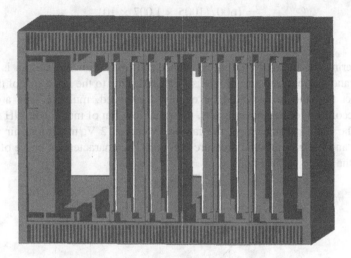

Fig. 2. Server thermal analysis model

3 Fan Selection Design

3.1 Fan Selection

There are 11 modules in the chassis, including 2 power supplies, 4 motherboards, 1 management module, 2 switch modules, 1 data module and 1 debug module. The heat loss of the whole chassis is set to 600 W.

According to the heat balance equation [8], the ventilation of the whole chassis is

$$Q_f = \phi/\rho C_p \Delta t (m^3/s) \tag{4}$$

Where ρ is the density of air, kg/m^3; C_p is the specific heat of air, J/(kg $^\circ$C); φ is the total loss power, W; Δt is the temperature difference between outlet and inlet of the cooling air, $^\circ$C.

The inlet air temperature of the chassis is taken to be the test temperature of 55 $^\circ$C, and the outlet air temperature is taken to be 65 $^\circ$C. The arithmetic mean of the air temperature in the duct is 60 °C, and the characteristic parameters of the cooling airflow at this time: the density of the air is 1.077 kg/m³, the specific heat of the air is 1005 J/(kg °C)

The temperature of the cooling air inlet and the outlet is:

$$\Delta t_f = t_1 - t_2 = 10\,°C \tag{5}$$

In forced convection heat transfer systems, convection accounts for approximately 90% of the total heat exchange; according to the heat balance equation, the air volume required for chassis is

$$
\begin{aligned}
Q_f &= \phi/(C_p \times \rho \times \Delta t) \\
&= (600/(1005 \times 1.007 \times 10) \\
&= 0.059\,m^3/s = 124\,CFM
\end{aligned}
\tag{6}
$$

Considering the internal thermal resistance and loss of air, the design is 1.5 times redundant, and the required air volume is 186 CFM. Due to the large size of the chassis and the fact that the heat should be evenly discharged, multiple fans are used in parallel. According to the above results, the axial flow fan of model 612 NH is initially selected. The main parameters of the fan are: voltage 12 V, maximum air volume is 25.3 CFM, and maximum wind pressure is 80 Pa. The characteristic curve of the fan is shown by the curve ⑤ in Fig. 3.

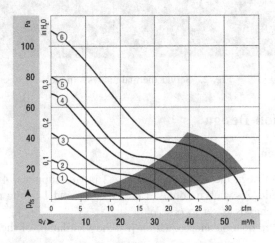

Fig. 3. The characteristic curve of the fan

3.2   Fan Working Point

Refer to the high-temperature test conditions of the Environmental Test Program for Reinforced Computers and External Equipment for Naval Vessels, the inlet air temperature of the chassis is taken to be 55 °C, and the outlet air temperature is 65 °C. The arithmetic mean of the air temperature in the duct is 60 °C, at which time the characteristic parameters of the cooling airflow is [9]: the density of the air $\rho = 1.077$ (kg/m^3), the specific heat of the air $C_p = 1005$ (J/(kg °C), dynamic viscosity $v = 18.97 \times 10^{-6}$ m^2/s, Prandtl number $P_r = 0.697$, Thermal Conductivity $\lambda = 4.56 \times 10^{-3}$ (W/(m °C).

The flow calculation and judgment process of the cooling airflow in the fin area are as follows:

Equivalent diameter of single rectangular heat exchange unit [10]:

$$d = 4A/U = 5.37 \times 10^{-3} \, \text{m} \tag{7}$$

Where A is the cross-sectional area of the pipe, $A = 25.7$ mm $\times$ 3 mm $= 77.1$ mm^2; U is the wet perimeter length, $U = 2 \times (25.7 + 3) = 57.4$ mm;

The entire cross-sectional area of the cooling airflow through the air duct of the chassis is:

$$S = 2 \times 79A = 1.22 \times 10^{-2} \, \text{m}^2 \tag{8}$$

12 models of 612 NH fans are installed symmetrically on the rear of the reinforced chassis. The air volume is 43 (m^3/h). The airflow rate in the air duct of the chassis is:

$$\omega = \frac{Q_f}{S} = \frac{0.059}{1.22 \times 10^{-2}} = 4.84 \, \text{(m/s)} \tag{9}$$

Reynolds number of cooling airflow at the fin position of the chassis:

$$R_e = \frac{\omega \times d}{v} = \frac{4.84 \times 5.37 \times 10^{-3}}{18.97 \times 10^{-6}} = 1370 < 2300 \tag{10}$$

For the cooling airflow in the pipeline, when Reynolds number is less than 2200, the flow is laminar. When Reynolds number is between 2200 and 104, the flow genus is the transition from laminar to turbulent. When Reynolds number is greater than 104, the flow is turbulent. From the above analysis, it can be seen that the air flow state in the air duct belongs to the laminar.

The air duct resistance is:

$$H = \left(\frac{64}{Re} \times \frac{L}{4d} + \xi + 1\right)\frac{\omega^2 \rho}{2g} \tag{11}$$

Where L is the length of the duct; ξ is the local drag coefficient; g is the acceleration of gravity.

The local drag coefficient can be found in Table 9-2 on page 60 of the GJB/Z27-92 Electronic Equipment Reliability Thermal Design Handbook. According to the structural characteristics of the air duct, $\xi = 0.5$ [11].

$$H = (\frac{64}{1370} \times \frac{0.243}{4 \times 5.37 \times 10^{-3}} + 0.5 + 1)\frac{4.84^2 \times 1.077}{2 \times 9.8} = 2.57\,\text{mmH}_2\text{O} = 25\,\text{Pa} \qquad (12)$$

Compared with the characteristic curve of the fan of Fig. 3, it can be seen that when the wind pressure is 25 Pa, the air volume of the fan is 18 CFM, and the total air volume of the 12 fans is 216 CFM, which is larger than the air volume value of 186 CFM calculated by the above system. The fan can meet the cooling requirements of the system forced air cooling.

4   Simulation Result

4.1   Initial Thermal Design Simulation Results

In the initial stage of the solution, in order to verify the degree of influence of the height of the chassis and the structure of the air duct on the heat dissipation of the reinforced server, the heat dissipation of the 6U and 7U high-density servers is compared. For the chassis with better heat dissipation performance, it is compared that the heat dissipation performance of the double-fan air duct and 12 small fan air duct structure to the reinforcement server, and finally obtain the structural form of the chassis. The specific simulation results are as follows.

4.1.1   Simulation Results of Different Height Rugged Servers

A server module that power consumption is 75 W is inserted in the chassis with the height of 6U and 7U respectively. At the same time, there are one power module and three other boards in the chassis. The temperature distribution of the whole server is strengthened in both cases. Figures 4 and 5 are shown.

Comparing Figs. 4 and 5, it can be seen that in the forced air cooling system, the maximum temperature of the processor on the server module with a height of 6U is 87.4 °C, and the maximum temperature of the processor on the server module with a

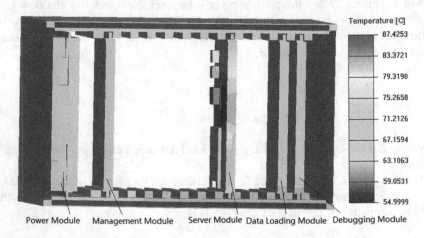

Fig. 4. 6U reinforced server temperature cloud chart

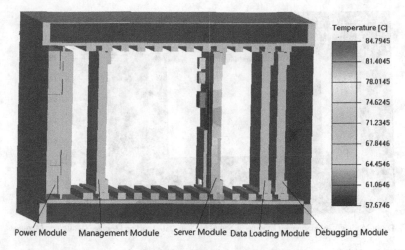

Fig. 5. 7U reinforced server temperature cloud chart

height of 7U is 84.8 °C, which is 2.6 °C lower than the temperature of the processor on the 6U server chassis. It can be seen that the heat dissipation capability of the chassis is improved because the heat sink area increases with 7U height server chassis.

4.1.2 Comparison of Simulation Results of Different Air Duct Servers

Comparing Figs. 6 and 7, it can be seen that the air duct structure has a great influence on the heat dissipation of the chassis. The maximum temperature of the processor on the server module of the reinforcement server is 78.1 °C with the air duct structure of 12 small fans, which is lower 6.8 °C than that of the reinforcement server of air duct structure of double fans °C. It shows that the structural reinforcement server is the one with best heat dissipation performance. Therefore, the reinforcement server of this paper adopts this finally.

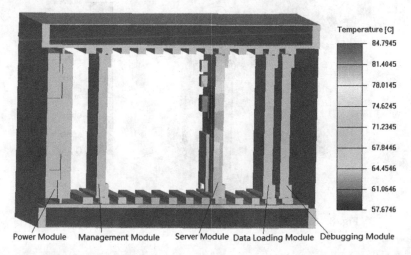

Fig. 6. Reinforcement server temperature cloud chart with the air duct of double fans

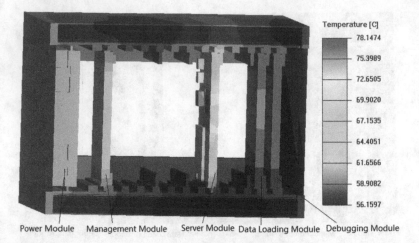

Power Module   Management Module   Server Module   Data Loading Module   Debugging Module

Fig. 7. Reinforcement server temperature cloud chart with the air duct of 12 fans

4.2 Optimized and Improved Simulation Results

According to the simulation results, the final reinforcement server structure is obtained. The whole chassis is thermally simulated according to the structure. There are 11 modules in the chassis, two pieces of power supply, four server modules, one management module, two pieces of switching modules, one data loading module, one debugging module. The power consumption of the chassis is 600 W, and the ambient temperature is 55 °C.

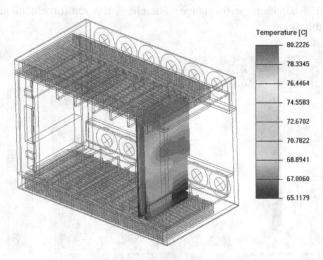

Fig. 8. Server module temperature cloud chart in the first slot

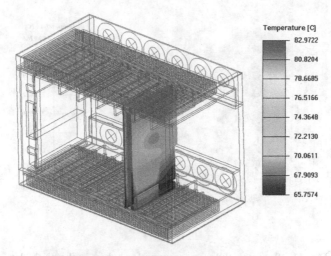

Fig. 9. Server module temperature cloud chart in the third slot

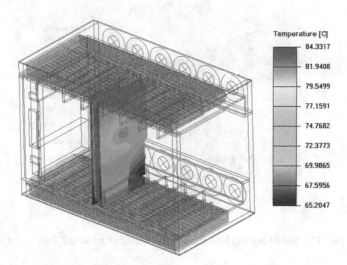

Fig. 10. Server module temperature cloud chart in the seventh slot

Figures 8, 9, 10, 11, 12 and 13 are the temperature distribution clouds of the four server modules and two switching modules in the hardened server. The simulation results show that the maximum temperature of the four main module processors is 80.2 °C, 82.9 °C, 84.3 °C, 80.2 °Cin the ambient temperature 55 °C. And the maximum temperature of the two switching modules is 90.2 °C and 90.8 °C respectively which are lower than the junction temperature. It can achieve long-term stable work and meet the requirements for use.

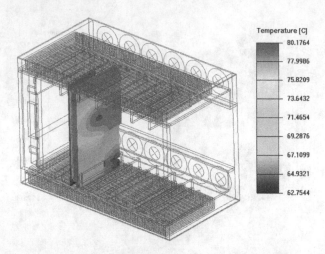

Fig. 11. Server module temperature cloud chart in the ninth slot

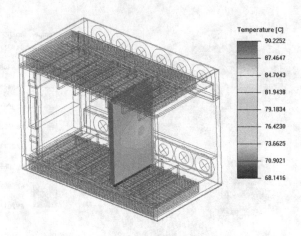

Fig. 12. Switching module temperature cloud chart in the fourth slot

Figure 14 shows the speed vector diagram of the whole machine. It can be seen from the heat flow distribution diagram of the model that the forced air from the fan brings the cold air at the inlet into the air duct, and then the cold air flows through the heat dissipating fins to remove the heat. It can be seen from the figure that in the existing air duct structure of the whole machine, the wind speed of the whole machine is relatively uniform, and the wind speed at the exit of the fan is about 3.6 m/s.

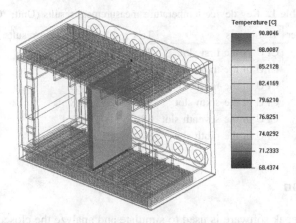

Fig. 13. Switching module temperature cloud chart in the sixth slot

Fig. 14. Cutting speed vector distribution of the chassis

5 High Temperature Test

According to the above thermal design scheme, the reinforcement computer is subjected to high temperature test after assembly and debugging in order to verify the effectiveness of the software analysis. This equipment has been tested at 55 °C and is working properly. In the high temperature test, the test points are set at the key positions of the server module and the switching module inside the reinforcement computer. The comparison between the actual test results and the simulation results is shown in Table 1. It can be seen that the simulation results reflect the actual working conditions of the equipment more realistically. After the equipment is delivered to the user, the actual heat dissipation capability of the equipment is consistent with the thermal analysis after many practical applications. The performance is stable and meets the design requirements.

Table 1. Key device temperature measurement results (Unit: °C)

Serial number	Test points	Test results	Simulation results	Error (%)
1	CPU in the first slot	84.3	80.2	4.9
2	CPU in the third slot	86.2	82.9	3.8
3	CPU in the fourth slot	92.5	90.2	2.5
4	CPU in the sixth slot	93.6	90.8	3.0
5	CPU in the seventh slot	88.1	84.3	4.3
6	CPU in the ninth slot	84	80.2	4.5

6 Conclusion

In this paper, Icepak software is used to simulate and analyze the closed reinforcement server. The internal airflow distribution and the working temperature of each component are predicted. The rationality of the thermal design scheme is analyzed and the optimal design scheme is found. The results show that the improved scheme improves the heat dissipation capability of the electronic device, effectively controls the temperature rise and improves the reliability of the electronic device. The temperature rise of the key components of the optimized reinforcement server is measured by thermocouple sensor. The maximum error between the measurement results and the simulation results is 4.9%, which indicated the accuracy of the simulation results. It effectively demonstrated the Icepak software superiority and reliability of the application in the thermal design of electronic products. Therefore, researching thermal simulation technology to improve the cooling effect is of great significance to improve the computer design success rate and work reliability of the harsh environment.

References

1. Li, L., Lin, J.: Simulation analysis of thermal runaway of sealed chassis based on ANSYS icepak. Electro-optic Technol. Appl. **27**(6), 75–79 (2012)
2. Sun, Y.: Application of icepak in thermal design for rugged computer. Comput. Technol. Dev. **23**(3), 215–222 (2013)
3. Zhou, J.: Study on thermal analysis method of closed electronic systems. Comput. Simul. **29**(11), 416–419 (2012)
4. Song, H., Bin, H.: Application of thermal simulation in the structural design of electronic system. Appl. Sci. Technol. **28**(8), 4–6 (2001)
5. Liu, M., Dong, Q., Chen, S.: Investigation on thermal design for opening cabinet of electronic equipment by numerical simulation. J. Air Force Eng. Univ. (Nat. Sci. Edn.) **6**(4), 62–65 (2005)
6. Wang, F.: Computational Fluid Dynamics Analysis-CFD Software Theory and Applications. Tsinghua University Press, Beijing (2004)
7. Tao, W.: Numerical Heat Transfer, 2nd edn, pp. 1–8, 332–356. Xi'an Jiaotong University Press, Xi'an (2004)
8. Yu, J.: Electronic Equipment Thermal Design and Analysis Techniques, 2nd edn, pp. 50–120. Beijing University of Aeronautics and Astronautics Press, Beijing (2008)

9. Qiu, C., Zhao, D., Jiang, Q., et al.: Electronic Device Structure Design Principles, pp. 127–128. Southeast University Press, Nanjing (2007)
10. Li, F., Zhang, Y., Shen, X., Hao, Y.: Application and research of fan in rugged computer. Comput. Eng. Des. **34**(9), 3307–3326 (2013)
11. GJB/Z 27-92. Reliability of Electronic Equipment Thermal Design Manual[S]

Design of High Performance Server for Shipboard Common Computing Applications

Peng Zhang$^{(\boxtimes)}$

The Computer Department, Jiangsu Automation Research Institute,
Lianyungang 222061, China
Peng.Zhang@126.com, pengpengwenxinwukui@126.com

Abstract. Analyze the advantages of the Shipboard "Common computing" application model, and analyze the server design requirements and design ideas for "common computing" in combination with the vessel application environment. On this basis, introduce the design of the server structure, hardware topology, computing blade and cloud operating system. Finally, performance testing is performed. The physical performance of the server compute blade and the virtual machine performance of the server are tested and compared with the current shipboard computer. The results show that the server has outstanding computing performance, and the performance of virtual machine is better than current shipboard computer. In terms of real-time performance, the virtual machine is equivalent to the current shipboard computer. The virtual machine can realize the function of the physical machine on ships.

Keywords: Common computing and services environment · Blade server · Virtualization · High performance · Shipboard

1 Introduction

Shipboard computers are generally dedicated computers. The display computer and the task computer are usually installed in standard display cabinets. The display computer is used for human-computer interaction, and the task computer is used to complete task processing functions. Each display cabinet handles its own tasks. In this mode, sometimes, it is necessary to design different computers according to the complexity of the task, and the standardization level is low. If one of the computer failed, The tasks it handles are unattended and affect the entire system. To solve the problem the concept of "common computing" has been proposed by drawing on the development route of the US in China [1–4].

The application mode of "common computing" is "server+ terminal" mode, which divides the shipboard computers into servers and display terminals. In this mode, the computers on the traditional display cabinets are only used for display the data provided by servers and send control data to servers, while the task processing is handled by the virtual machines running on the physical servers. In this mode, the display terminal computers can be designed in a unified manner. Virtual machines which

© Springer Nature Singapore Pte Ltd. 2019
W. Xu et al. (Eds.): NCCET 2019, CCIS 1146, pp. 212–222, 2019.
https://doi.org/10.1007/978-981-15-1850-8_19

replace the functions of traditional task computers are created on the servers as needed according to the complexity of the processing task. The virtual machine has the features of migration, upgrade-ability and centralized management, which solves the problems faced by traditional shipboard computers such as lower degree of computer standardization, repetitive design and high replacement cost.

The development of hardware and software basic platform for "common computing" are still in the exploratory stage. The basis hardware of "common computing" is the server and terminal. This paper analyzes the requirements and design ideas of the shipboard server. Based on the above analysis, a high-performance hardened blade server using dual Xeon processor is designed. In order to evaluate whether the virtual machine running on the server meets the ship's needs, the performance of the virtual machine and the traditional physical machine are compared and tested. The results show that the virtual machine running on the server can meet the calculation requirements of the traditional physical computing equipment on ship.

2 Shipboard Server Demand Analysis and Design Ideas

2.1 Functional and Performance Requirements

The shipboard server plays the role of computing resource pool in "common computing" system. Ideally, resources can be allocated on demand. In order to meet the needs of the shipboard "common computing", the server must meet the requirements of multi core and multi-threading, large capacity and low latency memory, hardware virtualization, and multi-node collaborative working.

Multi-core and multi-threading are the foundation for high-performance servers to meet the performance of virtual machines. Usually, virtual machines exist as threads in the operating system. In order to meet the requirements of creating more virtual machines, mainstream server processors aim to achieve more exclusive threads. The main methods are to increase the number of processor cores and Hyper-Threading technology. Hyper-Threading Technology is a technology that simulates a physical core into multiple logical cores through special circuits. It improves the execution unit utilization of the CPU. In this technique, if a hardware resource conflict occurs, a thread wait will occur. In some cases, the virtual machine will be slow to respond, which cannot meet the needs of the ship application. Therefore, increasing the number of physical cores is the most effective way to improve the performance of a shipboard server. In order to increase the number of physical cores, multiprocessor technology can be used. Usually multiple processors are interconnected through a dedicated high-speed interface to implement a NUMA system. This technique effectively increases the number of physical cores of a single node.

Requirements of large capacity and low latency memory. The virtual machine memory is mapped to the physical memory. To meet the needs of creating more virtual machines, the physical machine must have enough physical memory. At the same time, memory access speed is also another factor that affects the performance of virtual machines. All modern processors have multiple levels of caches to reduce the average cost to access data from the main memory. The processors also design multiple memory controllers to access memory in parallel, which provides both higher memory bandwidth and scalability. For multi-processor NUMA systems, the virtual machine allocation and scheduling strategy must be carefully designed and optimized to reduce memory access latency across CPUs and improve memory access efficiency.

Requirement of hardware virtualization. In hardware-assisted virtualization, hardware provides fabric support to create virtual machine monitoring and allow the guest operating system to run independently. Hardware virtualization technologies include CPU virtualization, memory virtualization, and I/O virtualization. Currently mainstream virtualization technologies Xen and KVM [5] need to run on processors that support hardware-assisted virtualization.

Multi-node collaborative working requirements. For the ship computing scale, the performance of the single-node server cannot meet the resource requirements, and the server must work in a multi-node collaborative mode. Multi-node systems also avoid single point of failure for the server. For multi-node system design, the definition of each node role at the software level is generally divided into control and computing nodes. The requirements of virtual machine migration and virtual machine communication among multiple nodes impose high requirements on the communication bandwidth between nodes. Therefore, it is necessary to design high-speed data communication interfaces for the server node and design a reasonable network topology for the server.

2.2 Requirements for "Six Indexes"

In order to be used in a marine environment, the design of the ship's server should take the "six indexes" into account in addition to the functional and performance requirements. "Six indexes" refer to reliability design, environmentally adaptive design, safety design, maintainable design, testable design and guaranteed design [6, 7].

Reliability design requires high reliability of the server. The measure of reliability is mean time between failures (MTBF). For the MTBF of a serial system, the equation is Eq. 1.

$$MTBF = \frac{1}{\sum_{i=1}^{n} \lambda_i} \qquad (1)$$

λ_i indicates the failure rate of the module i in the system. It can be known from Eq. 1 that reducing the failure rate of each module in the server system can improve the MTBF of the server. The MTBF of the module depends on the failure rate of the electronic components, so it is necessary to select electronic components with high quality. Increasing the redundancy of the server is also a way to reduce the failure rate. The redundant design makes the serial system into a parallel system, effectively reducing the overall failure rate. Longer average interval failure times ensure long-term stable operation of the equipment, which means lower maintenance costs.

Environmentally adaptive design means that the server must meet the ship's environment. The ship environment is more harsh than the air conditioning laboratory environment. The shipboard operating environment requires the server to work stably for a long time in a wider operating temperature range, vibration environment, and salt spray corrosive climate [8]. The server design also takes into account the limitations of space, and the server should be as small as possible.

The maintainability design requires the server to be easily disassembled and repaired in the event of a failure, ensuring that the equipment is disassembled and repaired within a certain period of time.

The testability design requires additional test points, fault indicators to be considered in the server design to facilitate testing and faults locating.

Security design requires the server to be self-safe, secure to other devices, and safe for people. In addition to electrical safety, electromagnetic compatibility, sound and light pollution should also be included in safety design considerations. Information security should be considered at the software level.

The supportive design requires the server to have long-term supply and support capabilities. Unlike commercial products, which are frequently updated, ship equipment usually requires service for 10 years or more. Therefore, there is a high demand for long-term production of electronic components.

3   Design of Shipboard High Performance Server

3.1   High-Performance Shipboard Server Structure Design

Rack servers and blade servers are the two most common forms of structure. Rack servers are the main form of commercial servers. They are usually 19-inch wide and 2U (1U is 44.45 mm) high open air-cooled chassis structure. Each rack server is equipped with a dual-processor server motherboard. Several rack servers and network switches are installed in a cabinet (usually 32U or 47U) to form a complete hardware platform. The servers are interconnected with Gigabit or 10 Gigabit Ethernet cables. Blade servers are widely used in industrial control. It has modular features, which makes it better in terms of maintainability and better resistance to vibration. The ATCA architecture server is the most common blade server. The ATCA server is 8U high and 19 inches wide. Each module has a thickness of 6 HP (1 HP is 5.08 mm). It can realize the function of a rack cabinet server in 8U space and is superior in integration. Therefore, the blade server is more suitable for the ship application environment.

Blade servers used for the industrial control are designed with an open case that cannot be used in the sea environment. Therefore, the server should be designed as a fully enclosed one. The fully enclosed case also ensures electromagnetic compatibility of the device. High-power modules in fully enclosed reinforced chassis have no air channels and their thermal design is difficult to achieve. According to the power consumption of the whole machine, the chassis adopts air cooling or liquid cooling. The module uses the "Vapor Chamber" technology [9] to reduce the thermal resistance between the chip and the cold plate. At the same time, increasing the contact area between module cold plate and the chassis improves the efficiency of heat transfer.

3.2 Hardware Topology Design

The blade server system is mainly composed of 8 computing blades, 2 switching blades and 1 management blade. The data plane consists of 40G Ethernet and SRIO interfaces to meet the needs of high-speed communication. The control plane consists of a Gigabit management network, which can meet the system configuration requirements. The management plane consists of the IPMB bus. The 40G network interface and the SRIO interface of each computing blade are respectively connected with two switching blades to form a double-star architecture, and the dual-star architecture ensures redundancy and reliability of the network. The SRIO communication interface is suitable for applications with low latency communication requirement. The Gigabit management network of each compute blade is connected to the management network switch of the management blade to form a star network architecture, which satisfies the remote management requirement of the chassis. The baseboard management controller (BMC) of each computing blade and the chassis management controller (ChMC) of the management blade are connected through the IPMB bus, thereby realizing centralized monitoring and management functions of the field replaceable unit (FRU, i.e. blade, fan, liquid cooling controller, etc.) in the chassis. The chassis management module implements the functions of health monitoring, power on and off control, remote control, and heat dissipation adjustment of the servers. The design of the management blade increases the testability of the server. Figure 1 shows the blade server system architecture.

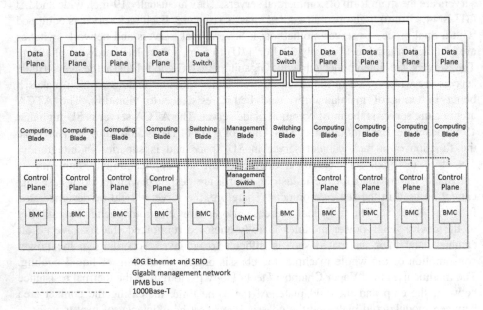

Fig. 1. System architecture of high performance shipborne blade server

3.3 Design of Dual Xeon Processor Computing Blade

As can be seen from Fig. 1, the design of the computing blade is the key of the entire server design.

From the perspective of satisfying the functional performance, the server selected the Intel Xeon E5 2600 V4 series processors as the processing core. The series of processors uses 14 nm lithography, have the features such as multi-core, large cache, dual expansion support, 4-channel memory controller, hardware virtualization, and IO virtualization. They meet the "cloud" computing needs in both performance and software ecology. At the same time, the embedded version of the processors have a supply cycle of at least seven years to meet long-term supply requirements.

The dual Xeon E5 server computing blade function modules include: processor, chipset, DDR4 memory, 40G Ethernet, SRIO, BMC, etc. The block diagram of the computing is shown in Fig. 2.

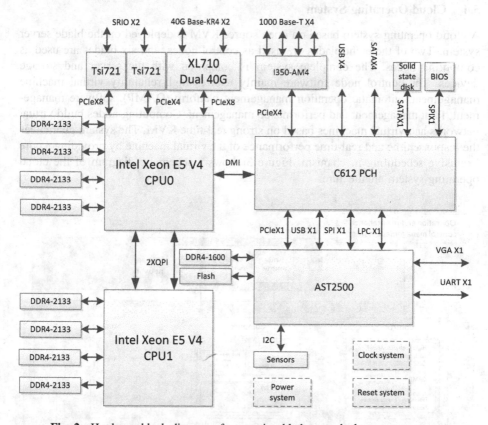

Fig. 2. Hardware block diagram of computing blade uses dual xeon processors

The computing blade is configured with two Intel Xeon E5 2600 V4 series processors, and the two processors communicate via two QPI channels. The computing blade is a NUMA system.

In commercial designs, the server board is configured with memory modules (RDIMM), which maximizes the memory capacity of the motherboard. However, the installation form of the memory module cannot meet the requirements of anti-vibration and three-proof design [10]. In order to improve the environmental adaptability of the module, the computing blade adopts a design method of soldering the memory chip to the PCB. Up to 128 GB of memory can be achieved.

The two 40GBase-KR4 interfaces of the data plane are implemented by the XL710, and the two SRIO × 4 interfaces are implemented by the TSI721. 4 Gigabit Ethernet interfaces for the control plane is implemented by I350. BMC uses AST2500, which implements baseboard management in accordance with the IPMI 2.0 specification [11].

The computing blade draws on the ATCA standard and adopts an 8U board. The reinforced cooling structure design has strong resistance to harsh environments and is suitable for shipborne equipment with high computing power requirements.

3.4   Cloud Operating System

A cloud operating system based on open source KVM is deployed on the blade server system. Two of the eight blades are used as control nodes, and six blades are used as computing nodes. The complete system is composed with the server and storage devices. The control node software mainly realizes high-reliability virtual machine management, automatic operation management platform (OAMP), software management, fault management and performance management. Computing nodes build virtual networks and virtual machines based on strong real-time KVM. The system guarantees the response time and real-time performance of the virtual machine by providing a core exclusive scheduling mechanism. Figure 3 shows a schematic diagram of the cloud operating system architecture.

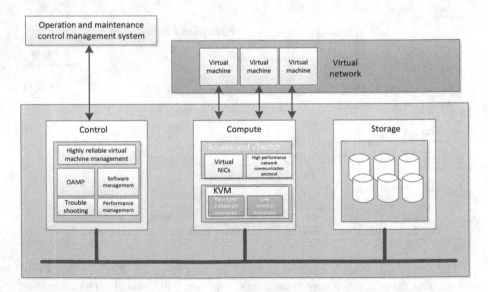

Fig. 3. Sketch of cloud operating system architecture

4   Performance Test

The performance of the server is tested from the aspects of computing and real-time performance.

4.1   Physical Machine Computing Performance Test

At present, the shipboard computer usually uses the Intel core i7-2655LE processor. The performance of the shipboard computer and the computing blade configured with single and daul E5 V4 processors (the processors selected is embedded version) are tested. The testing software is linpack which is widely used [12]. The testing results are shown in Table 1.

Table 1. Computational blade performance with different processors

Processor type	Core number	Base frequency	Single processor peak floating point performance	Daul processor peak floating point performance
E5-2648L V4	14	1.8 GHz	388 Gflops	696 Gflops
E5-2628L V4	12	1.9 GHz	349 Gflops	625 Gflops
E5-2618L V4	10	2.2 GHz	337 Gflops	604 Gflops
E5-2608L V4	8	1.6 GHz	196 Gflops	350 Gflops
i7-2655LE	2	2.2 GHz	30 Gflops	/

From the testing data in Table 1, it can be seen that the computing blade with the dual Xeon E5-2648L V4 processors has a floating-point operation speed of 696 Gflops, and the calculation speed is equivalent to the speed of 20 shipboard computers. The calculation speed of computing blade configured with two processors is about 1.8 times that of the computing blade configured with a single processor, which makes good use of the synergistic work of dual processors.

4.2   Virtual Machine Performance Test

Perform virtual machine performance testing on a server with a cloud operating system. The six compute blades are equipped with dual E5-2648L V4 processors. The virtual machine performance test also uses linpack, and the performance test results are shown in Table 2.

Table 2. Server virtual machine performance

Num.	Number of core	Memory size	Peak floating point performance (virtual machine)	Peak floating point performance (physical machine)
1	4	4 GB	98 GFlops	99 GFlops
2	8	8 GB	190 GFlops	198 GFlops
3	10	10 GB	236 GFlops	248 GFlops

The calculation method of physical machine performance in the table is: physical floating point performance of dual E5-2648L V4 blade * core number/28. The data in Table 2 shows that the performance of the virtual machine is 1%–5% lower than that of the corresponding physical machine, and the performance loss can be neglected.

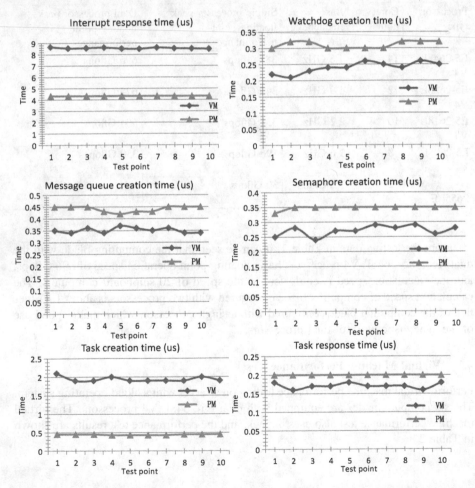

Fig. 4. Real-time contrast diagram of Virtual Machine (VM) and Physical Machine (PM)

Since CPU cores and RAM can be allocated on demand, the performance of virtual machine can exceed the Intel core i7-2655LE processor. So, the virtual machine meets the requirements for the replacement of the shipboard physical machine.

4.3 Virtual Machine Real-Time Performance Test

The biggest difficulty in replacing a physical machine with a virtual machine is to ensure the real-time performance of the virtual machine. To verify the real-time feature of virtual machines, we tested the real-time performance of virtual machines on a cloud operating system with real-time enhanced extensions. The main test items include interrupt response time, watchdog creation time, message queue creation time, semaphore creation time, task creation time, and task response time. The physical machine uses the Intel core i7-2655 processor and is equipped with the Vxworks real-time operating system. The test results are shown in Fig. 4.

As can be seen from Fig. 4, the performance of the physical machine is more stable in various tests. In terms of response time, virtual machines and physical machines have their own advantages and disadvantages. The overall response time of the virtual machine can meet the real-time requirements. In terms of real-time performance, virtual machines can meet the goal of replacing physical machines.

5   Conclusion

This paper presents a high-performance server design approach for shipboard common computing applications. Experiments have shown that virtual machines running on servers can replace physical machines. The server system has been tested in an environmental adaptability test and can be used in a shipboard environment. This design is instructive for the design of future hardware and software platforms for shipboard common computing.

References

1. Pei, X.: Analysis of TSCE design of US navy and its enlightenment to our Army's information system integration model. Comput. Digit. Eng. **2015**(9), 1607–1614 (2015)
2. Ma, Y., Tao, W., Xie, H.: Overview of public computing and service environment. Comput. Digit. Eng. **2016**(7), 1298–1303 (2016)
3. He, Y., Hui, C.: Study on the architecture of intelligent warship's TSCE based on multi-view. In: International Symposium on Distributed Computing & Applications to Business (2015)
4. Zhu, W., Fan, Y., Nie, K.: Formal verification algorithm for computing environment of whole ship. Digit. Technol. Appl. **2017**(6), 140–141 (2017)
5. Peng, T.: Application of KVM virtualization technology in cloud platform. Comput. Knowl. Technol. **2015**(14), 28–30 (2015)
6. Ge, J.: Analysis of "six indexes" in structural design of military electronic equipment. Electromech. Eng. **31**(2), 1–6 (2015)

7. Tao, G., Peng, D., Li, F.: Research on data collection method of ship's "six indexes". Ship Stand. Qual. **2017**(4), 50–54 (2017)
8. Zhu, H., Yin, H.: Environmental adaptability design method of military electronic equipment. Avionics Technol. **2015**(2), 42–46 (2015)
9. Zhao, L., Tian, W., Yang, L.: Experimental research on heat dissipation performance of vapor chamber. Mech. Eng. **2016**(2), 23–25 (2016)
10. Xu, L.: Product electronic component packaging and reinforcement technology. Equip. Environ. Eng. **13**(4), 157–161 (2016)
11. Intel, Hewlett-Packard, NEC, DELL, IPMI-Intelligent Platform Management Interface Specification Second Generation v2.0 [S]. United States: Intel, 2013.10.1
12. Zhang, Y.: Analysis and prospect of China's high performance computer development. Democracy Sci. **2017**(04), 26–27 (2017)

Automated Deadlock Verification for On-Chip Cache Coherence and Interconnects Through Extended Channel Dependency Graph

Kun Zeng[✉]

National University of Defense Technology, Changsha, Hunan Province, China
zengkun07@nudt.edu.cn

Abstract. Cache coherence and On-chip interconnections are of great importance in many-core system. The verification of deadlock freedom is challenging, since modern coherence protocol and communication fabrics are becoming increasingly complex. Formal methods play an important role in the verification of deadlock, which need extraordinary work of modeling and long computation time. Thus, formal methods cannot model the system in a fine-grain way, leading to the failure of discovering deadlocks introduce my certain implementation details, such as two types of messages sharing a common FIFO, two channels sharing a credit counter, etc. This paper proposes a simple but efficient automated methodology for deadlock verification through the extended channel dependency graph, which extends the channel dependency graph to consider not only the interconnection node, but also the coherence processing node. The methodology allows fast and cross-layer verification of both the protocol, the network and the implementation all at once. The methodology is applied in a case study where eight 64-core chips cooperate with multiple direct inter-chip links. It is proved to be generally applicable and shows promising salability.

Keywords: Cache coherence · Deadlock verification · On-chip interconnection

1 Introduction

As the number of cores integrated in a single chip increases, the on-chip interconnections becomes increasingly complex. Efficient, and deadlock-free cache coherence protocol as well as on-chip interconnection become a major challenge.

Often, formal methods [2] are applied to analyze the correctness of the cache coherence protocol. And channel dependency graph base methods [7] are of great importance in the deadlock verification of network design. Some researches show that a correct coherence protocol together with a dead-lock free network may result in a deadlock-prone design [1]. We argue that, even if the combination is deadlock free, some minor improper implementation choices may lead to deadlock.

© Springer Nature Singapore Pte Ltd. 2019
W. Xu et al. (Eds.): NCCET 2019, CCIS 1146, pp. 223–230, 2019.
https://doi.org/10.1007/978-981-15-1850-8_20

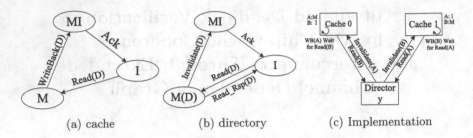

Fig. 1. The simple MI protocol and a error-prone implementation

For example, the directory based MI protocol has been proven deadlock-free for point-to-point communication using UPPAAL [1]. But a minor mistake in the conflict resolving logic in the cache may incur deadlock into the system. Figures 1a and b show the state transitions of the protocol. On a load or store miss, the cache send a Read packet to the directory to access a block of data. It send a WriteBack packet when an invalidate packet from the directory is received or a replacement is triggered by itself. Then it goes to a intermediate state MI to wait for an acknowledgement. The directory change the state from I to M and record the owner of the block when it gets a Read packet. The directory may send an invalidate packet to the owner at any time, and it will return to its initial state whenever a Write-back packets is received. A packet is stalled and moved to the end of the queue when it cannot be consumed.

Figure 1c shows a deadlock in an implementation of the MI protocol. In the design, the invalidate packet and the read packet share a same queue, which means the invalidate packet cannot be consumed if an infighting Read has not been responded. Consider two caches in the system, cache 0 owns data block A, while cache 1 owns data block B. Cache 0 send a Read packet for B to the directory and ant the same time cache 1 send a Read packet for B. The directory then send an invalidate for A to cache 0 and an invalidate for B to L2 cache 1. At the time, both caches cannot consume the invalidate packet and generate a WriteBack packet to the directory, leading to the directory waiting for ever.

This paper focus on the verification of deadlock of the whole memory system. We propose extended channel dependency graph to model the dependency incurred by protocol design, interconnection design, or various implementation decisions. The deadlock verification is simplified to the work of finding circles in the extended channel dependency graph. We didn't consider formal methods because the complexity of formal methods make it expensive to model the system in a fine-grained way. For example, formal methods model the packet transmission in a queue through a state machine, but it is hard to consider the dependency between different types of packets sharing the same queue.

2   Related Work

Deadlock verification is such a critical job that numerous efforts are devoted in this subject. Formal methods [3,6,8,9] have played a major role in the design and verification of cache coherence protocols as well as communication fabrics. Channel Dependency Graph base techniques [3] plays on important role in the deadlock verification of on-chip networks. However, most the work consider cache protocol and network deadlock independently [1,2,4,5,10,11]. Verbeek [8] shows that correct protocol and deadlock free network together may lead to a deadlock prone design. He propposes a formal method to cross-layer formal methods. But the computation time needed by formal method is usually long.

This paper proposes a different thought. We extend the channel dependency graph to offer cross-layer deadlock verification, namely ECDG. ECDG covers not only the protocol layer and the interconnection layer, but also the implementation detail layer. It can effectivly detect deadlock in the system at a high speed compared to the formal methods. On the other hand, however, the extended channel dependency graph approach cannot other attributes of the system. It cannot be used to proof the correctness of the cache coherence protocol.

3   Deadlock Verification Through ECDG

3.1   Extended Channel Dependency Graph

In a typical on-chip memory system, two types of nodes are connected by multiple communication links. Figure 2a shows a typical 2×2 mesh connecting two caches and two directories. The eclipse nodes are routers, which do not generate or consume any packets. The rectangle nodes are end nodes, which may generate new output packets or consuming incoming packets to implement a certain cache

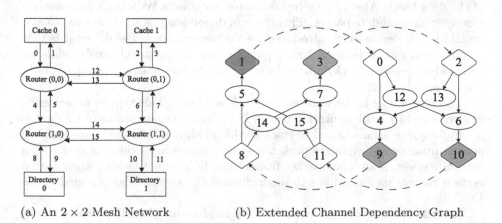

(a) An 2×2 Mesh Network   (b) Extended Channel Dependency Graph

Fig. 2. An 2×2 mesh network and corresponding ECDG

coherence protocol. The links connecting two nodes are abstracted as channels. A channel can be a physical link. Also, multiple channels can share a physical link (virtual channel in this case). Each channel can transfer packets in one direction. If a channel can transfer packets to a certain node, we call it an input channel of the node. On the contrary, if a channel can transfer packets from a certain node, we call it an output channel of the node.

Channel dependency graph (CDG for short) is a technique widely used in deadlock verification of routing algorithms. It considers the dependency between the input channel and the output channel of the routers. A CDG is directed graph the nodes of which denotes the channels in a communication network. And the edges denotes the dependency between the channels. For a router in the network, if a packet from a input channel C_i can be route to a output channel C_o, an edge is added in the CDG from the node C_i to the node C_o. A network is deadlock free if and only if the CDG of the network does not contain a circle. CDG models the behavior of the routers very well, but it cannot model the behavior of the end nodes. It cannot be used to verify the deadlock freedom of the whole cache system.

We extend the CDG to model the behavior of the end nodes, namely the Extended Channel Dependency Graph (ECDG for short). ECDG is a directed graph the nodes of which denotes the channels of the system. The edges of it denotes not only the dependency introduced by the router nodes but also the dependencies between the input channels and output channels of the end nodes, which are designed to implement a certain cache coherence protocol. Two types of dependencies should be considered.

The first one is the request-respond dependency. This type of dependency is introduced by the coherence protocol. In order to implement a certain coherence protocol, the end nodes of the system must generate proper response packet on receiving a request packets. For example, a directory node must generate a response packet to the requester and one or more invalidate packets to the owner of the data block. Also a L2 cache node must generate a WriteBack packet when receiving an invalidate packet. This types of dependency is straight-forward and much like the dependency introduced by the router nodes. The different is that a router can switch packets from input channels to output channels, while an end nodes consumes packets from input channels and generate new packets to the output channels.

The second one is the wait-on-output dependency. This type of dependency is introduced by implementation detail. In many implementations of L2 caches, a inflight queue is maintained to track the life of all the unfinished requests. The consumption of an invalidate packet may be delayed until the completion of a certain request. If an input packet from channel C_i cannot be consumed until a certain packets be flushed out through channel C_o, a extra edge is added to the ECDG.

Assume the memory system in Fig. 2a implements the MI protocol shown earlier and X-Y routing algorithm is implied, the corresponding ECDG is shown in Fig. 2b. The diamond nodes in the graph denotes the channels directly lined to the end nodes. The edges drawn in dotted lines are introduced by the end nodes. The dotted edge from 9 to 8 and the one from 10 to 11 are introduced by the MI protocol, while the dotted edge from 1 to 0 and the one from 3 to 2 are introduced by the implementation of cache node. More than one circles exist in the graph, and the implementation is not deadlock free. According to the ECDG, we can modify the cache implementation to remove the edge from 1 to 0 and the one from 3 to 2, which break all the circles in the graph, to make the design deadlock free.

3.2   The ECDG Analysis Toolset

We develop a group of tools to aid the ECDG modeling process. The tool set consists of two parts: the cache system modeler and the deadlock analyzer.

The cache system modeler is a tool to help model the whole memory system. It provides a simple python interface to describe the topology of the memory system. The cache system modeler make an output of json model file, which describes the nodes in the system and the interconnection relationship.

The deadlock analyzer take the output of the cache system modeler and generate the ECDG. Then it try to find circles in the graph through a wide-first traversing. The deadlock analyzer can map the circle back to the nodes and channels in the cache system model, if any. The re-mapping helps the system designers to identify which node or channel is the key.

3.3   Techiniques to Eliminate Deadlocks

As is hown earlier, ECDG can identify the channels and nodes which are involved in the deadlock circle. Once a deadlock circle is identified, several ways can be employed to eliminate deadlock without re-designing the protocol or routing algorithm.

Firstly, avoid sharing queues when design end nodes, such as caches and directories. Sharing queues in end nodes may incur unnecessary dependency between the input channels and output channels at end nodes.

Secondly, carefully design the conflict resolving logic. Conflict resolving logic is of great importance for the nodes which my process requests from different sources simultaneously. For example, a L2 cache my receive requests from L1 caches and directories at the same time. It must make a request wait for others if they access the same data block or tag bank. This my incur extra dependencies in the ECDG. The strictness must be carefully tuned not to incur un-predicted dependencies. For example, a snoop request from directory should not wait for the completion of a read for the same data block.

Thirdly, enlarge packet buffers. If a router employed unlimited packet buffers, there would be no dependencies between its input channels and output channels. Usually, the number of in-flight packets in the on-chip network is limited. If we put a big enough buffer in certain key node, the deadlock circle can be broke.

4   Case Study

We apply ECDG in a project which aims to design a 64-core processor which support three direct links between chips. As is shown in Fig. 3, the memory system consists of 16 L2 caches and 16 directories. The interconnection fabric is a 2 × 4 mesh network with eight router nodes. Two L2 caches and two directories are connected by a router, which in turn acts as a four-direction router in the on-chip mesh. The direct link bridge manages three physical links to other chips, which is connected to the mesh at the (1,3) router. Eight chips are connected through direct links to form a multi-chip system. The MOESI protocol is implemented to maintain the coherence between the L2 cache nodes across all the chips.

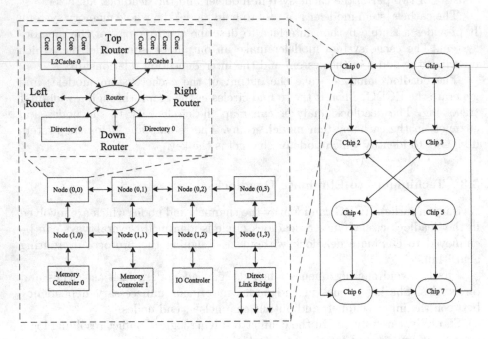

Fig. 3. The test case consisting of eight 64-core chips

The validation of deadlock for such a complex system through formal method is sophisticated and time consuming. It is reported that the formal validation of dead lock for a 5 × 5 mesh network incorporated with the MESI protocol takes 56 min [1] With the help of ECDG toolset, it is done in 1.28 s. During the whole validation process, several deadlock circles are found due to queue-sharing and path sharing in the direct link controller. We will explain one of them in detail here.

The IO controller receives PIO request from L2 cache node. In the meanwhile, it may generate DMA access to the Memory Controllers. All the request in the

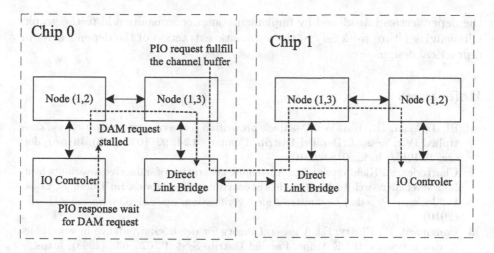

Fig. 4. A deadlock case detected

IO controller are handled in a strong order way, which means a response packet cannot be send until all the prior request complete. Such a design incurs a dependency from the input request channel to the output request channel, which lead to a deadlock circle in the ECDG. Figure 4 shows the case. Firstly, two L2 nodes in different chips keep send PIO requests to each other's IO controllers, fulfilling the request channel buffer of the direct link controller. Secondly, two IO controllers from different chips send DMA requests to the Memory Controller from the other chip, which are stalled at the Direct Link Controller since the request buffers are full. Thirdly, two IO controllers cannot send PIO responses because the prior DMA requests hasn't been responded, which means the PIO request can never complete. The deadlock circle is broke by enlarging the request packet buffer at the Direct Link Controller. A big request packet buffer is employed to make sure the request buffer can never be fulfilled. This breaks the dependency from the input request channel to the output request channel at the Direct Link Controller.

5   Conclusion

This paper focus on cross-layer deadlock verification, by extending the Channel Dependency Graph to model the behavior of the coherence processing nodes in the system. The ECDG can cover three layers of deadlock: the protocol layer, the interconnection layer and detailed implementation layer.

We applied ECDG in a 64-core processor project and the verification of deadlock is proofed to be highly efficient. Several deadlock cases are discovered and effective ways of avoidance of them are directly extracted by ECDG.

The drawback of ECDG is that the dependency of end nodes in the network is a little tricky. We must examine the design carefully to make sure that all the dependencies introduced by implementation decisions are add to the graph. Challenging future work rely in the automatic extraction of the dependencies in a practical design.

References

1. Bi, J., Yuan, H., Tan, W.: Deadlock prevention for service orchestration via controlled Petri nets. J. Parallel Distrib. Comput. **124**, 92–105 (2018). https://doi.org/10.1016/j.jpdc.2018.09.010
2. Chatterjee, S., Kishinevsky, M.: Automatic generation of inductive invariants from high-level microarchitectural models of communication fabrics. In: Touili, T., Cook, B., Jackson, P. (eds.) Computer Aided Verification, pp. 321–338. Springer, Berlin (2010)
3. Fraigniaud, P., Fleury, E.: A general theory for deadlock avoidance in wormhole-routed networks. IEEE Trans. Parallel Distrib. Syst. **9**, 626–638 (1998). https://doi.org/10.1109/71.707539
4. German, S.M.: Formal design of cache memory protocols in IBM. Formal Meth. Syst. Des. **22**(2), 133–141 (2003). https://doi.org/10.1023/A:1022921522163
5. Gotmanov, A., Chatterjee, S., Kishinevsky, M.: Verifying deadlock-freedom of communication fabrics. In: Jhala, R., Schmidt, D. (eds.) VMCAI 2011. LNCS, vol. 6538, pp. 214–231. Springer, Heidelberg (2011). https://doi.org/10.1007/978-3-642-18275-4_16
6. Mejia, A., Palesi, M., Holsmark, R., Kumar, S.: HiRA: a methodology for deadlock free routing in hierarchical networks on chip. In: Networks-on-Chip, International Symposium on(NOCS), pp. 2–11 (2009). https://doi.org/10.1109/NOCS.2009.5071439, doi.ieeecomputersociety.org/10.1109/NOCS.2009.5071439
7. Talupur, M., Tuttle, M.R.: Going with the flow: parameterized verification using message flows. In: Proceedings of the 2008 International Conference on Formal Methods in Computer-Aided Design, pp. 10:1–10:8. FMCAD 2008, IEEE Press, Piscataway, NJ, USA (2008), http://dl.acm.org/citation.cfm?id=1517424.1517434, event-place: Portland, Oregon
8. Verbeek, F., Yaghini, P., Eghbal, A., Bagherzadeh, N.: Deadlock verification of cache coherence protocols and communication fabrics. IEEE Trans. Comput. **66**, 1–1 (2016). https://doi.org/10.1109/TC.2016.2584060
9. Yin, J., et al.: Modular routing design for chiplet-based systems. In: 2018 ACM/IEEE 45th Annual International Symposium on Computer Architecture (ISCA), pp. 726–738 (June 2018). https://doi.org/10.1109/ISCA.2018.00066, http://doi.ieeecomputersociety.org/10.1109/ISCA.2018.00066
10. Yin, J., et al.: Modular Routing Design for Chiplet-Based Systems, pp. 726–738 (2018). https://doi.org/10.1109/ISCA.2018.00066
11. Zhao, M., Hou, Y.: Deadlock Control in Generalized Petri Nets, pp. 343–366 (2013). https://doi.org/10.4018/978-1-4666-4034-4.ch014

Author Index

Printed in the United States
by Bookmasters

Printed in the United States
By Bookmasters